Communicating God's Word in a Complex World

Communicating God's Word in a Complex World

God's Truth or Hocus Pocus?

R. Daniel Shaw
Charles E. Van Engen

ROWMAN & LITTLEFIELD PUBLISHERS, INC.
Lanham • Boulder • New York • Oxford

ROWMAN & LITTLEFIELD PUBLISHERS, INC.

Published in the United States of America
by Rowman & Littlefield Publishers, Inc.
A wholly owned subsidary of The Rowman & Littlefield Publishing Group
4501 Forbes Boulevard, Suite 200, Lanham, Maryland 20706
www.rowmanlittlefield.com

PO Box 317
Oxford
OX2 9RU, UK

British Library Cataloguing in Publication Information Available

Library of Congress Cataloging-in-Publication Data

Shaw, R. Daniel (Robert Daniel), 1943-
  Communicating God's Word in a Complex World: God's Truth or Hocus
Pocus? / R. Daniel Shaw and Charles E. Van Engen.
    p. cm.
Includes bibliographical references and index.
ISBN: 978-0-7425-1447-8
  1. Intercultural communication–Religious aspects–Christianity.   I.
Van Engen, Charles Edward II. Title.
  BV2082.I57 S53 2003
  261–dc21

                                                      2002152170

Printed in the United States of America

⊗™ The paper used in this publication meets the minimum requirements of American
National Standard for Information Sciences—Permanence of Paper for Printed Library
Materials, ANSI/NISO Z39.48-1992.

Dedicated to gospel communicators everywhere.

Contents

Figures

Foreword

$\mathscr{I}$ have been given the honor to write a foreword to this book, and I accept it gladly. The authors present a complex and nuanced picture of communicating the Gospel in what has been described as a "complex world." They pay as close an attention to what is being communicated as to the manner and terms of the communication. This is an important feature of the book. Rather than making the simplistic assumption that commitment to the Gospel is all you need to be an effective communicator, the authors argue that it is the beginning of the challenge. Enthusiasm, or, for that matter, grim resolve, alone will not do the job, certainly not in a world that is now so profoundly shaped by information technology and the related lightening speed involved in the transmission of ideas and values. What is needed instead is a grasp of the subject matter to be communicated and the environment and background in which it is being transmitted and appropriated.

While postmodernity has increased the pressure for a deeper understanding of what is involved in communicating the Gospel, it is the case that even in origin the Gospel was conceived in translation, interpretation, and application. It is not just that Jesus did not write or dictate the gospels, but also that the gospels themselves reflect on what he said, taught, and did. Religious hermeneutics has allowed believers to narrow the gap between the Word of God in the gospel writings and faithful response to that Word, and thus to make possible for each generation the hearing and doing of the Word. It is the particular character of Christianity that it is invested in the idioms and terms already established for purposes other than membership in the church, and that means Christianity must make its home in cultures in which it has been preceded and anticipated. The matter of Gospel and culture is not just a discretionary issue for retired Christians; it is the fountain of dynamic faith.

It requires uncommon sensitivity not to fall into the trap, on the one hand, of easy cultural surrender of the Gospel, and, on the other, of stubborn cultural alienation. In the case of cultural surrender, the Gospel becomes only a flag of convenience, unaware of all the cargo that sails under its name. As cultural alienation, on the other hand, the Gospel remains an outsider, with converts becoming nothing better than stowaways. Faithful communication of the Gospel, in contrast, occurs when the culture has been penetrated in ways that challenge and transform society on the basis of genuine autonomous response. Maintaining this fine balance between challenge and recognition, between the "give" of external input and the "take" of local appropriation, is at the heart of communicating the Gospel. The quality of the appropriation determines whether the Gospel has made a breakthrough and, if so, on what terms. In the final analysis, it is by virtue of the choice signified by local appropriation that the Gospel is implicated in culture and history. The fact that such response takes place at all is testimony to the power of the Gospel to overcome limitations of communication and of first impressions. This pattern of response and appropriation, typically triggered by presence and witness, we might describe as the Christian process in history.

This book is a good example of what it means to serve the cause. The authors take us into the numerous ways and byways of communication theory, deepened often with theological observation and insight, but all of that done with the single intention of serving the purpose of faithful and effective communication of the Word of God. They insist that disciplined reading of writings on communication theory is a requirement for the work of committed Christian witness and discipleship. They are keenly aware of the ecumenical dimensions of the task, and of the opportunities that are still under-utilized. They call attention to fields still untilled, and do so by identifying the tools that would make our labor productive and rewarding. The book is aimed at the church in its engagement with the world on terms the world finds congenial. Yet the church's costly engagement with the world is for the sake of the pearl of great price without which the world's hope is vain and its boast empty. It all comes back to walking that fine line between convenience and alienation, between expedience and hostility. This book should be commended for pointing us in the right direction with practical suggestions and ideas about how we should be equipped for the perennial task of having to account in gentleness and reverence for the hope that is in us.

Professor Lamin Sanneh
D. Willis James Professor of Missions and World Christianity
Yale University Divinity School
Professor of History
Yale University
October 2002

Preface

$\mathcal{I}$n this book we deal with Gospel communication in the broadest sense of presenting a message intended by an original author. Communication of the Gospel message involves presentation that accounts for the original communication as well as the communicators' and the contemporary receptors' circumstances. Combined, these create a new experience with the text, bringing a change in worldview to those who are part of the process: proclaimer and audience alike. These participants enter into dialogue with the source that cannot change and, therefore, serves as the foundation for theological reflection. This process does not add to the text, yet it fosters a deepening and expanding comprehension of the application of the text in the cultural experiences of people in our increasingly complex world. Such a process may provide a response to the relativizing influence of postmodernity.

As we worked on this book, exploring the dynamic tensions shaping the communication process, we began to appreciate the impact that the communicators' understanding of God has on how they read the context in which they work. We also learned to consider the theological expectations of the people who hear the communication and the way they go about conceptualizing the biblical message. Further, we were forced to look at the perspectives of those who originally received God's Word, directly or indirectly. Finally, we were moved to ask: what about God? What was God's intent in communicating with human beings in the first place? And this became our starting point.

The subject of this book has become a much larger enterprise than we initially envisioned. It has taken us on a journey that has clarified our own thinking about God, who we are in relationship with God, and what God has communicated down through the ages since creation. God wanted to ensure that human beings everywhere understood what God had to say. Adapting what God has done and applying the principles missionally is what this book is about.

Despite centuries of modern mission, and the development over two millennia of Christian tradition, there has been little effort to document the impact of the Gospel communicators' assumptions on the way individuals do exegesis and on their subsequent communication of their understanding of the Gospel. Even fewer are the studies that reflect upon the nature of theological development based on a biblical text in a particular context—that is, the impact of culture on the text and what it communicates. Our guiding question has been: how do communicators' perspectives bias their view of Scripture on the one hand and their proclamation of it on the other?[1] A follow-up question might be: what impact do theological perspectives have on the development and growth of the church's understanding of the Gospel in a given context? What is needed is a combination of biblical study, communication theory, anthropology, linguistics, and missiological reflection interacting with contextual theology. All of these fields affect what happens when we communicate biblical concepts. This calls for an interdisciplinary conversation such as we attempt to provide in this book.

As we embark on this journey into understanding how theological assumptions, communication theory, and cultural awareness all intertwine in their impact on Gospel proclamation, we must not ignore the role of the Holy Spirit. It is the Holy Spirit, in each new context, who reveals meaning both generally (to all humankind) and particularly (to the people within a context). Let us not forget that the Holy Spirit was present in the first instance of God's communication with humanity and now operates in and through the faith community and through communicators to bring about a deepening understanding of truth. If we can see God's communication within the richness of the whole—God's interaction with all human beings—it will soften the grip on our theological assumptions and will illumine how we see the issues addressed in the text within the original context. This, in turn, may yield new insight into how the text might be understood by people in new contexts as they become familiar with God's Word to them.

Our focus throughout this book is on communication as mission, a dynamic process of making God known in particular contexts. This involves the entire transference (or translation) process. It constitutes, in fact, missiological proclamation.

The thesis of this book is that contemporary communication of the biblical message can be modeled after the way the writers of Scripture utilized earlier texts and restructured them for their contemporary audience. Communication of the Gospel takes the entire proclamation process (the original communication, the communicators, and the present-day audience) into account. This entire process is impacted by knowing God, which in turn is informed by all of the relevant contextual data. Our objective in writing this book is to apply theological, communicational, and anthropological principles to the hermeneutical process in order to provide appropriate and relevant messages for the people who hear the word of the Lord.

God does not change, but God created a world that constantly changes. God created human beings in God's image with an incredible propensity for adjusting things to their liking. In the midst of such rapid change and an increasingly pluralist world (Newbigin, 1989), people need to know what God stands for and how they can adapt the circumstances in which they live to God's ultimate ideals. We are rooted in what God has communicated to human beings: eternal, unchanging truth applicable to everyone, based on a relationship with all that God created. At the same time we recognize that those truths must be proclaimed in ever-changing, context-specific circumstances. Because human beings live in a wide variety of contexts, their understanding of God (theology) and how they apply that understanding to their lives (hermeneutics) will vary from one society to another. Therefore, the theology they build must be particular to them and their view of God. But that theology, in turn, must be informed by God. They cannot just interpret God or God's Word any way they like. People must bring themselves to Scripture and allow God's intention through that word to shape the way they understand God's message for them.

Ultimately, this is an issue of Gospel communication in the broadest sense of presenting a message intended by an original author so others may understand and make inferences about that message to which the original communicator could agree. In this book we draw from communication theory, which has much to offer those who wish to present the Gospel in relevant and understandable ways. Gospel communication, then, is mission. It involves conveying God's message in such a way that people understand the original intent and are drawn into God's kingdom. In writing this book we seek to encourage a theologically, communicationally, and culturally informed Gospel in the multiplicity of perspectives that proliferate in today's complex world.

This complexity creates a host of challenges for those who would communicate the Gospel in our day. Yet in each particular context, the proclamation has specific theological implications for those who receive it. As missiologists we are concerned that people theologically apply the message to their lives in such a way that they conform to Christ's image. Our intent in this book is to enable an understanding of God's message that is

- faithful to the Scriptures,
- appropriate to the audience, and
- relevant to each context in using applicable modes of communication.

Realizing this intent will encourage communication that will more likely lead people on a path of living out God's truth in their world.

To accomplish our intent, we have structured the book in three parts, each with three chapters. Part I is devoted to a discussion of God's intended meaning as it impacts the textual issues specific to our focus on faithful communication of God's message and the theological implications of applying the resulting text to present-day contexts. This leads to an appreciation of God's intent in communicating with humankind. Understanding the nature of God's presentation through the text is our purpose in part I.

In part II we examine the communicators' task and the theoretical issues that impact appropriate communication. Here we draw from our respective areas of expertise: theological, communicational, and cultural. Recent developments in relevance theory move us beyond the largely surface structure of dynamic equivalence and help to unlock the deeper conceptual text in order to produce an appropriate response. Texts in their many forms always communicate in context. This is the more theoretical section of the book in which we demonstrate the synergy of multidisciplinary input that allows for appropriate communicability. While the communicator is in focus the biblical and receptor audiences are by no means ignored.

In part III we explore what is going on when new audiences come to understand God's intended meaning in their context. Here we draw from an incarnational perspective to establish a model for the relevance of a God who speaks in the midst of particular contexts. We take seriously the complex nature of most communication contexts and the need for developing team approaches that take account of the richness of the local context while at the same time valuing the biblical text. In this section we apply a deep reverence for biblical understanding to an appreciation for life as it is lived by human beings in the contemporary world. We seek to communicate God's Word effectively by remaining faithful to the intent of Scripture and relevant to the audience, using media and styles appropriate to particular contexts.

The three parts of the book roughly reflect the model we develop and apply. By appreciating the multiple contexts in which God's communication occurred, the principles that the Old and New Testament authors used to present God's intent in their context can be applied to the communicators' task of Gospel proclamation among present-day audiences. This process will help people understand and reflect upon God in ways that are sensible to them. For us, the Bible itself is the model for our hermeneutical method, and we have structured the book to reflect that model. In each section, we approach the subject from theological, communicational, and cultural perspectives. We desire that all people everywhere may come to know God by understanding God's Word in their own context, in their own language.

A word on the title (especially the subtitle) is necessary at the outset. We do not wish to be sacrilegious or in any way offensive—just graphic. The primary title expresses our intent: that God's Word may be appropriately and effectively communicated using a myriad of forms relevant to today's complex world. The subtitle graphically expresses our fear, that at times, as people have sought with all good intention to present truth, the product has been perceived as a counterfeit. The *Oxford English Dictionary* traces the term *hocus pocus* from the Eucharist when the priest intoned in Latin *hoc est corpus,* "this is the body," while handing the wafer to a supplicant. When taken up by people speaking Old English, their alliteration of the Latin phrase took this holy imagery and transferred it into an allusion to the mysterious, expressed through some magical formula. Such transfer of meaning from truth to lack of truth illustrates the theme of this book. In order to avoid theological slight of hand, God's intentions must be understood by humans, the crown jewel of God's creation (Ps. 8). Therefore, those who would present God's communication must ensure, to the extent possible, that those who hear will receive truth, God's truth, rather than modified truth, or even untruth—hocus pocus.

Despite our collective experience in crosscultural mission and childhoods as missionary kids, we both remain products of modernity, impacted by North American society while living, teaching, and preaching in that context. Together we are traveling, with the rest of the world, into the urbanized, relativistic, and spiritually inquisitive postmodern reality. By combining our backgrounds with our professional training and experience in theology, communication, and anthropology, we seek to contribute something unique that will assist contemporary proclaimers of the Gospel as they grapple with hermeneutical issues of relevance in today's world. Our objective is to draw from our respective disciplines in order to enable readers to interact with the entire communication context as followers of Christ.

Many have been involved in the development of this book: students, family, and colleagues. Our thanks to each of them as well as to teaching assistants and family members who have patiently listened to our expounding on some theoretical point or other that became part of this book. Special thanks go to James Zo, who brought his engineering mind and computer skills to the design of the figures throughout the book. We deeply appreciate Lamin Sanneh's foreword and recognize the influence on our subtitle of Robbin Burling's well-known article in which he chides cognitive anthropologists on their misuse of semantic analysis (Burling, 1964). In truth, this work is a reflection of our life experience and the academic community in which we both enjoy working. May our Lord be glorified through the process as well as in the final product.

NOTE

1. Our general use of the word *communicator* implies anyone involved in communication of the Gospel: missionaries, pastors, Bible translators and teachers, mission and theological educators, and students dealing with communicational issues in crosscultural and pluralist contexts. We also use *proclaimer* and *translator* almost interchangeably throughout the book.

Introduction

The Communicability of God's Word

> Gospel presentation seeks to facilitate a process whereby people everywhere, belonging to every family, tribe, language and nation, may hear God speak in appropriate and relevant ways that impact the deep-level meaning of their worldview.

In the Toaripi region of Papua New Guinea, a cargo movement was touched off by a much-expanded translation of Matthew 6:4 and John chapter 11.[1] In a vision a man was told to read the entire New Testament, but to focus especially on these passages. Not long after, while sitting in the cemetery, he began to teach the people to keep their villages clean, fence burial grounds, respect the dead, and stop quarreling and stealing. While commendable, this teaching showed little relationship to the passages in focus. When challenged, the prophet for this graveyard cult countered that he was simply following God's bidding, which "merely reinforced and made clear what was already set out in the Bible" (Ryan, 1969:114).

Lengthy is the list of such misunderstandings of Scripture, resulting in inappropriate applications to daily living. This culturally appropriate response was inappropriate to the Scripture upon which it was based. The translation apparently did not communicate enough of the original context to clarify the setting for the Toaripi villagers. They equated the Lazarus story with their own graveyard and Mary and Martha's responses to the Lord as a demonstration of physical cleanliness. To pray in "secret" was manifested by retiring to the solitude of the graveyard. In short, they exegeted Scripture based on their own concerns, not those of the original audience the apostles addressed. How people understand God's Word relates directly to how they perceive and interpret the biblical context: culturally, linguistically, and theologically.

Communicating the Gospel in a complex world in the twenty-first century is no easy task. Despite the predictions of hopeful missionaries and the best guesses of mid–twentieth-century linguists, languages and the people who speak them are multiplying, not dying out, and diversifying, not homogenizing. Many

1

countries around the world are establishing government departments that focus on ethnic populations. These departments specialize in cultural and linguistic preservation, bilingual education, celebrating local customs, and affirming the rights of native peoples. National churches must also deal with this complexity, not ignore it. Stephen Niyang notes that for Northern Nigeria, despite the widespread use of Hausa as a trade language, the true meaning of Christianity is not communicated in Hausa, but around the hearth using local languages and dialects often assisted by the use of vernacular Scriptures (Niyang, 1997).[2]

Similarly, the complexity of rapidly expanding urban centers and increasing globalization impacts the communication of the Gospel. While MTV brings young people around the world into a common youth culture, ethnic diversity and tribalism are rampant. Floods of refugees and immigrants looking for a better life increase pluralism in previously homogeneous communities. People are increasingly open to new ideas but often fall prey to bigotry and narrow-mindedness. The church as a whole and missions in particular have undergone radical change in the years since World War II. Leonard Sweet maintains that the formula for adjusting to postmodernity is to join it through a response similar to that of the hit television show *Who Wants to Be a Millionaire?* The secret to success in a postmodern world is to be experiential, participatory, image-driven, and connected (Sweet, 2000: xxi).

The complexity of our world creates a multiplicity of challenges to those who would communicate the Gospel in our day. That communication has theological implications for those who receive it, whatever the form may be: reading or hearing a translation of Scripture; listening to a sermon; observing a narrative drama; or enjoying a song. As missiologists we are concerned that people theologically apply God's message to their lives in such a way that they are conformed to Christ's image. We want to see their understanding lead them on a path of accepting God's truth, not moving away from their creator and into the open arms of the devil who anxiously waits to ever so slightly twist the truth and lead people into "hocus pocus." In the Genesis story, the serpent asks Eve, "Did God tell you not to eat fruit from any tree in the garden?" Eve knew the answer, but the serpent turned the truth into a lie (Gen. 3:1–4).

Perhaps more than ever in the history of the church, effective communication of the Gospel requires careful theological reflection. A people's response depends upon understanding the truth that will set them free. Theology can help communicators avoid the pitfalls of history, learning how the church has sought to fulfill Christ's commission to communicate with all peoples. There have been many dead ends, but through it all, faithfulness to the Bible's call to focus on a loving God who cares for creation inspires each generation to respond anew and enables others to "hear the word of the Lord," as the Old Testament prophets expressed it.

David Bosch called this approach "critical hermeneutics" (Bosch, 1991: 23, see also Van Engen, 1996b: 39–40). It requires recognition of biblical contexts and languages and their impact on an understanding of the text as it is read again by people centuries later. Bosch said it well: "The challenge . . . [i]s relating the always-relevant Jesus event of twenty centuries ago to the future of God's promised reign by means of meaningful initiatives for the here and now" (24). This tension will influence all of our thinking as we seek a new theoretical construct for relevant and meaningful Gospel communication.

COMMUNICATION AS TRANSLATION

The process of Gospel presentation we seek to describe draws from a broad view of translation (some prefer "re-communication" or even "re-description," Ricoeur, 1991: 177) in all its many forms: preaching, Bible teaching, counseling.[3] Throughout this book we use "communication" in its fullest meaning— presenting eternal truth in human contexts for the transformation of those who hear, respond, and allow the message to impact their lives. This is what Sanneh was emphasizing in *Translating the Message* when he wrote, "Translatability became the characteristic mode of Christian expansion through history" (1989: 214). It goes far beyond the enterprise of Bible translation narrowly understood, as important as that may be, to embrace the development of biblical ideas in general and, more specifically, an appreciation of the source who is ultimately God. "Missionary adoption of the vernacular, therefore, was tantamount to adopting indigenous cultural criteria for the message" (Sanneh, 1989: 3). And those messages conveyed theological information. Communicators of the Gospel must translate those issues into the human contexts in which they personally interact.

Missiologically, we are dealing with a human understanding of relationships. But in addition to horizontal relationships with people, this understanding also includes a vertical relationship with God. And this vertical interaction is crucial to the communication process. It is important to understand that the Bible—and the message based upon it—is not just another book, not just another "life instruction." As we seek to communicate the truth of Scripture we hold a sacred trust. We dare not get it wrong lest we miscommunicate and people misunderstand the intended message. This would be "hocus pocus." Rather, we want people to receive God's truth: to come to know God by understanding God and their relationship with God as well as to all other human beings.

Among the Samo of Papua New Guinea, for example, there may be no word for "love," but every householder demonstrates care and concern for each member of the longhouse community.[4] When that relationship is extended beyond the human realm it points to God who cares about the people God created, collectively and individually. This is a crucial message to the Samo, living in the jungle worrying about the next cannibal raid or where they will find their next meal (Shaw, 1996).

Communication as translation is more than grappling with exegetical issues and their transference into a particular context. Christianity is not about knowing; it is about appropriate living, about being, about each person's relationship to the God who has spoken in Jesus Christ through the revelational activity of the Holy Spirit. It is about incarnation. It is about a life lived today so people can see Jesus in believers—to paraphrase McCluhan (1967), "the communicator is the translation," or to put it another way, the "communicator is the message." Though Christian communicators, like everyone else, are sinners living in a sinful context, they intend to demonstrate how they think Jesus might have lived had he been where his messengers are today. To do that they must know what Jesus, in fact, did and then apply that knowledge. With this understanding, they can then translate it into the present context. This requires theological consideration, communicational understanding, and cultural sensitivity. To this end we use the term *communication* to refer to the entire process of re-communicating God's intended message into the plurality of contemporary human contexts.

This view of communication focuses on the process of presenting truth across the ages. Culture, time, and space impact a pastor preparing and presenting a sermon as much as a translator seeking how best to use a "key term" to ensure that recipients can adequately understand the miracle of God's intentions in communicating with human beings. All communicators of the Gospel deal with this problem. All must go through the process of exegeting the text as well as dealing with the hermeneutical issues.

From the beginning of time, communication has been central to presenting God's Word. At creation, God spoke and what He said was manifest in the creation (Gen. 1, Rom. 1; cf. Shaw, 1988, 9). Throughout the ages, whenever God interacted with human beings God did so using a particular language bound in a particular time and place. In many circumstances a particular language was not satisfactory for adequate communication, and Scripture was translated so it would have maximum impact (see, for example, Ezra, Nehemiah, and Acts 2). In the Greek-speaking world of the intertestamental period it became evident that the Hebrew Torah was not understood by the Jews of the Diaspora or by the Romans or Barbarians. So the Septuagint (LXX), the Greek rendering of the Old Testament, came into being. Furthermore, in their communication with the people of New Testament times, the Apostle Paul and other New Testament writers used the language of the day not only to write to a particular audience, but also to clarify Old Testament passages (Hays, 1989). Thus communication as translation is modeled throughout Scripture.

The early church began when people from many nations heard the Apostles using their "languages to tell the wonderful things God has done" (Acts 2:11). As Sanneh notes, "The flowering of Christian activity in modern Africa has taken place in ground suitably worked by vernacular translation" (Sanneh, 1989: 4). That was because "Language is the intimate, articulate expression of culture" (Sanneh, 1989: 3). God wants people to know what God says and to understand God's Word within their particular circumstances. The preservation of God's intended meaning demands both theological and contextual awareness. And God himself utilized these principles. If they were important for God, and are modeled in Scripture, then surely they are important for those who would respond to God's love and seek to communicate the Gospel to all people while discipling and instructing as the Lord commanded (Matt. 28:19). It is in obedience to this call that we write this book.

THE MISSIOLOGICAL PURPOSE OF COMMUNICATION

The central concern of this book is to pursue a conscious awareness of missiological implications at every step of proclaiming the Gospel: the biblical/ theological, the communicational, and the cultural context are all interwoven.[5] Elsewhere they have been called the "translation context" (Shaw, 1988; 1994). Each aspect reflects a different perspective that impacts each of the others. Our objective is to proclaim God's message to human beings in all contexts in ways that ensure they understand God's intention vis-à-vis creation and in relationship with all peoples.

Theology must not be abstract; rather, it must be "of, in, and on the way" (Van Engen 1996a). It must be centered in Jesus Christ (of the way), take place among real people in time and place (in the way), and move people over time in a faith pilgrimage as they walk in God's way in their context (on the way). All this, in a word, is missiology.

Mission studies should not be confused with actually crossing barriers in missional action among people with a view to their coming to faith in Jesus Christ. In this book, our working definition of mission is as follows:

> God's mission (*missio Dei*) involves primarily the People of God as they intentionally cross barriers from church to nonchurch, faith to nonfaith, to proclaim by word and deed the coming of the Kingdom of God in Jesus Christ; this task is achieved by means of the Church's participation in God's mission of reconciling people to God, to themselves, to each other, and to the world, and gathering them into the Church through repentance and faith in Jesus Christ by the work of the Holy Spirit with a view

to the transformation of the world as a sign of the coming of the Kingdom in Jesus Christ (Van Engen, 1996b: 26–27).

Human interaction is central to modeling Christian principles, and
when the Holy Spirit steps in, it becomes incarnational. This is what Gospel
communication is all about. Hence the *Imago Dei,* the incarnation, and the
expansion of the church are all crucial objects of our examination in this
book—so are the modern/postmodern assumptions of present day exegetes
and missionary communicators who, in turn, seek to present God's Word to
needy people everywhere, including across the back fence, or in the next
apartment. There must be self-examination and understanding in order to
approach the biblical texts that serve as our window on God's intent through
the ages. Similarly, as we interact in an increasingly complex world, we need
to appreciate the issues that impact people, thereby bringing God's Word to
their contexts in ways as unaffected by our own assumptions as possible. We
want to be sure the receptors hear God, not a litany of the communicator's
assumptions.

Communication, rooted in the biblical text, will help Christians avoid
mistranslation—avoid *hocus pocus.* It will ensure the communication of eternal
truth that God has provided for all who follow God. God calls humans to place
their trust in the answer God has provided: Jesus Christ, through whom "God
himself was pleased to live fully . . . and to make peace by sacrificing his blood
on the cross, so that all beings in heaven and on earth would be brought back
to God" (Col. 1:19–20).

Our intent is that this book may contribute to the process of bringing people into relationship with God through recognition of the incarnated Christ in
their midst. As good as the sociological, anthropological, historical, linguistic,
and literary models are, scholars have rarely applied them to the vertical context
of the relationship between God and human beings. As we teach and write in
our respective disciplines we recognize that the Bible, as we have it, reflects the
sociological and theological models and we seek to apply these principles to our
communicative task. Both a vertical understanding and a horizontal application
give us new admiration for what God was doing throughout the canonical time
frame. Furthermore, how might such an understanding assist us when we apply
these models to the entire communication context: biblical authors, communicators, and contemporary audiences? These are the issues we now tackle.

We desire to see God's Word impact real people living in rural, homogeneous communities as well as postmodern cities where congregations are linguistically, culturally, ethnically, and generationally plural. Such diversity increases the complexity of the task, yet remains grounded upon the simplicity
of the biblical message: "God so loved the world that he gave His only Son."
The Toaripi people need not find solitude only in their graveyards and clean
their villages in anticipation of Christ's return. The message is not just exter-

nal but internal, a spiritual solitude born of appreciating God's message to them. God's Word in the midst of God's people will look and feel very different in each human context because each society is distinct. God's intent for all humans is that they may know God and enjoy him forever.

NOTES

Lamin Sanneh's groundbreaking work on the nature of the "translatability" of God's Word into the languages of West Africa (1989) has guided our own reflection on "communicability." We are indebted to Dr. Sanneh for the impact his research and creativity has had on our thinking.

1. These passages, with their emphasis on secrecy and Jesus raising Lazarus, confirm the cargo cult thinking so rampant throughout the island of New Guinea. Bible Translators often unknowingly play into the hands of cult "prophets" who use the Scripture as a means to get people to follow them (Osborne, 1970; Stralen, 1977).

2. Rev. Dr. Stephen Niyang wrote a dissertation on translations and their use in Nigeria (1997). He was the Africa Media Coordinator for the United Bible Society when he was tragically killed in an airplane crash in January 2000.

3. Glenn Rogers has written a dissertation tracing the impact of communication theory and hermeneutics on an understanding of what he calls the "meta-theme" of Scripture. He maintains this meta-theme is a relationship both of God with all human beings and of all people with each other. Communicating this in particular contexts is a process he calls, "re-communication," making God's intent clear to people everywhere.

4. The Samo are seminomadic horticulturists living in the dense rain forest of Western Province, Papua New Guinea. Contacted late in colonial history, and only officially pacified in 1969 (from constant raiding that resulted in frequent cannibalism) they provide a fascinating opportunity for anthropological study (See Shaw, 1990 and 1996). Their response to the Gospel was no less remarkable, the result of anthropologically informed Bible translation (Shaw, 1981). Throughout this book we draw from coauthor Dan Shaw's experiences as a Bible translator among the Samo and coauthor Chuck Van Engen's experiences as a missionary and Bible teacher among the peasant Mayan peoples in Chiapas, Mexico.

5. By using the term *missiological*, we focus on the centrality of redemption and God's interaction with human beings. This goes far beyond mission as "sending" trained personnel to "preach" to people in the "regions beyond." It incorporates the social sciences with the theological and communicational concerns of biblical scholars to bring the passion of the great commission to every human interaction. Van Engen defines missiology as multidisciplinary with a focus on Jesus Christ who provides the integrative center of a theology that serves to "question, clarify, integrate and expand the presuppositions of the various cognate disciplines" (1996: 18ff, 22). Theology, communication, and anthropology as presented in this book are but three of these disciplines, but we use them to assist in presenting our message.

I

FAITHFUL COMMUNICATION

God's Intention in Communicating to Human Beings: Textual Issues

God has spoken in human language. Gospel communication must be faithful to what God intended human beings to understand about God and apply to their lives. Part I explains *why* it is important to examine the theological, and sociolinguistic dynamics that influence faithful communication.

In part I, we introduce the need to understand and appreciate the biblical text in its context. We begin our reflection by recognizing that Gospel communication stems essentially from the fact that God has spoken and God's purpose and intent is the most fundamental issue at hand. With this in mind we establish a rationale for Gospel proclamation that interacts with the theological, communicational, and cultural issues associated with the fact that God has spoken. As God's Word enters the human context, there are factors that must be considered in order to clarify the nature of, and the interaction between, text and context. To do so we call for faithfulness to the intent of God's communication (chapter 1), we recognize the true source of Gospel communication (chapter 2), and we comprehend the message that forms the truth of that communication (chapter 3). Our purpose is to effectively present what God has proclaimed through God's Word in ways that will clearly exhibit God's truth—what God intended human beings to understand and apply to their lives.

The Intent of Faithful Communication

God's purpose or intent of Gospel communication is that women and men come to know God. (Rom. 10:8–15)

Paul and Dorothy Meyerink dedicated a lifetime of missionary service to translating the Bible for the Tzeltal people of southern Mexico. Some years ago coauthor Chuck Van Engen sat in their living room discussing a major translation problem Paul was facing. With obvious frustration, Paul explained his problem. "The Tzeltal have no word for king, and no concept of kingship. They have the concepts of the head of a clan, the president of a municipality, and a large ranch owner. But none of these accurately reflect the biblical idea of the kingdom of God." Paul asked, "How can the Tzeltal people come to know God as their Lord who reigns in heaven and earth, without a concept of a king? What will they understand when they pray the Lord's Prayer? 'Your kingdom come, your will be done on earth as it is in heaven.' (Matt. 6:10)" Chuck discussed this communication problem with Paul for the purpose of ensuring that God's intent be clear to the Tzeltal.

During this discussion, it became increasingly clear that Paul and Chuck were dealing with something much deeper than "dynamic equivalence" communication. Paul's question was fundamentally one of epistemology—that is, about knowing God as the creator, sustainer, provider, and director of the universe over which God rules—and of knowing God in a context that seemingly had no concept of "king." As the discussion continued, it became clear that the problem was ours—the communicators—as well. There were other similar biblical concepts that we could scarcely grasp ourselves. How could westerners whose mathematics teaches that one does not equal three conceive of a trinitarian God? How could North Americans steeped in a materialistic, modern view of the cosmos think about God as "spirit"? How could a couple of highly individualistic missionaries comprehend the "body" image of the Apostle Paul's ecclesiology?[1]

Paul and Chuck were at the bedrock of the problem of contextualized Gospel communication—a problem much deeper than communicating the

11

Gospel by Christians to non-Christians. Contextualized Gospel communication is most fundamentally a matter of knowing God within the limitations of (and sometimes enriched by new wisdom from) culturally specific human contexts. God's self-disclosure in the midst of human cultures is like a square peg in a round hole, the dialectical mystery, at once revelatory and hidden, whereby we come to know God and understand that we do not fully know God. The first question, then, in proclaiming God's Word is not the communication of the Gospel so much as the understanding of the Gospel, the knowledge of God in context.

KNOWING GOD IN CONTEXT

The misfit of the Gospel with human cultures has been a perennial problem faced by the church in its mission. The apostle Paul referred to God's hidden self-disclosure both in terms of the created order and in relation to God's special revelation in Jesus Christ (Rom. 1:20; 11:33–34). Revealed hiddenness—this is the paradox of divine self-disclosure in human consciousness and the most difficult part of communicating the Gospel.[2] The very fact that we know God only through faith should tell us that we do not know all there is to know about God. In fact, we see only through a mirror, darkly (I Cor. 13:12). Texts like Job 36:26; Psalm 139:6; Acts 14:16–17; Romans 11:25, 33–336; I Cor. 2:7; Eph. 3:3; Col. 1:15, 26; I Tim. 1:17; 3:16; and Rev. 10:7 emphasize the mystery and unknowability of God. Many theologians have affirmed this basic characteristic of God's revelation.[3] Gospel communication then, involves the mystery of God's self-revelation in human cultures (Van Engen, 1996: 71–72).

In the midst of the dialectical tensions of knowing God only in God's hiddenness, the Bible also affirms that God is a self-disclosing God who wants to speak to humans in understandable speech forms that reflect a covenantal relationship between humans and God.[4] Based on their reading of the Bible, Christians proclaim the Gospel because they believe God has spoken to humans created by God. Communicating the Gospel originates, therefore, from God's Word—divine word in human words. The Bible is a unique book. It purports to give us a record of God's speaking and acting. Thus the Bible is not a book about religion, nor is it a human product of religious reflection. Rather, it presents itself as recording and revealing God's self-disclosure to humans. Here is the heart of the matter. How can human beings worship a God they cannot see? How does an unknowable God become known by the persons whom God has created?

This is our starting point. We begin with an appreciation of the infinitude of God and the finite nature of God's creation, including human beings. In creation lies the structure of the relationship (Walsh and Middleton, 1984) God created in order to have fellowship with human beings who were to care for the whole earth-bound context. That relationship was clearly characterized in the Garden of Eden when God came to talk with humans. This "chat mode" characterizes nearly all God-human encounters throughout the Bible. God wants to interact intimately with human beings who, because of the way they were created, always live in a social context of their own making. Humans were created to be creative and express that creativity in a multiplicity of cultural perspectives. Therefore, whenever God decides to connect with human beings God does so in their particularity, on human terms, rarely on God's turf (Enoch and Elijah being the most notable exceptions).

God Revealed Himself in Biblical Contexts

Notice the way the Bible uses a phrase like the root metaphor: "I will be your God and you will be my people and I will dwell in your midst."[5] This standard formula flows throughout the whole Bible, from Genesis to Revelation. Throughout the canon we see God revealing God's self in different circumstances. In each context, while God is fundamentally the same, God reveals something new about himself and his relationship with people because each human context is different. Figure 1.1 shows each element of revelation contributing to the next

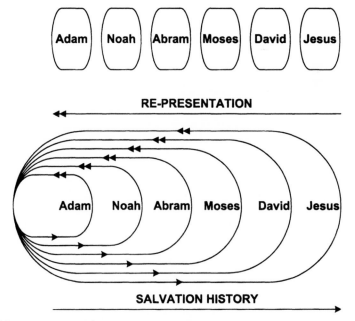

Adapted from Van Engen, 1996b: 80.

Figure 1.1.   The Re-presentation of God in Different Contexts[6]

and enabling people to experience God in new and vigorous ways culminating with Jesus in the incarnation. So we begin with the need to know God who, in turn, needs to be known in order for relationship to take place. Knowing God in a particular context is knowing God in God's hiddenness. Across time and space, we gain a broader understanding that extends from the biblical context in its broad spectrum and projects itself down through the ages to us. Mortals can never fully know God. In this book we are trying to encourage the presentation of God's Word revealed in a particular context that will, in turn, shed new light on God's hiddenness in other contexts. Thus Gospel proclaimers discover new truths about God because of what they learn from their receptors.

In figure 1.1 we see that God expressed himself in terms of a relationship with Adam, Noah, Abraham, Moses, David, Jesus, and, obviously, many others. These patriarchs represent totally different cultural, linguistic, and epistemic contexts. They were shaped in totally different types of societies. Yet the exact same root metaphor ("I will be your God . . .") appears and continues throughout the Gospels and Revelation. It continues on down to our day and to the people to whom we seek to communicate the good news of the possibility of a grace-filled relationship with God. Each context is radically different in each type of society, in the rituals and the ways the symbols take shape in each context. They range from people in kinship and peasant societies such as the Samo and Mayans both Shaw and Van Engen have worked with, as well as the burgeoning urban contexts of today's world. Yet we are dealing with the same root metaphor. This is what Martin Noth had in mind when he used the term "re-presentation"—the past is made to be present again. We understand the present by working back through the various contexts that re-present the past (Noth, 1960).[7] Walk your way backward through the tapestry of time and space and no matter where you end up you will find the relationship concept. It is central to humanity, as anthropologists have long known. God programmed it into creation itself.

This series of differing revelations of the same covenant formula demonstrates the same relationship in radically different contexts. Followed through to a relationship with Jesus Christ, this suggests that the Old Testament is foundational to the New Testament. It provides the conceptual and contextual background for the Messianic covenant. Together the Old and New Testaments become God's revealed hiddenness not only to the people of biblical contexts but ultimately to all human beings everywhere. This is theologically essential for what we are saying in this book. The root metaphor reflects the theological, communicational, and cultural circumstances that enable all people to understand God in relationship.

God Revealed Himself "Anew" through Incarnation

Jesus' incarnation can be seen as another manifestation of the root metaphor, "I will be your God . . ." Jesus came to fulfill the Old Testament, but Jesus was unique. His uniqueness is a fulfillment of that which went before. What did Jesus mean, for example, when he said, "A new commandment I give to you"? In this regard the Greek New Testament uses two different words for "new": *neos* and *kainos*. How these words are used is important to furthering our argument here. "New" as *neos* is totally discontinuous. It only appears two or three times in the New Testament with reference to revelatory continuity. "New" as *kainos,* on the other hand, is much more common and reflects continuity in the midst of change. It is not addition but rather completion-plus: it is completion-and-then-more. The uniqueness of Jesus Christ is a *kainos* kind of deepening from the Old Testament. It is never discontinuous, but always adding something new. It is the same well, but we draw water from ever-deeper places in the well. This understanding and its application to meaningful communication are crucial for our development of the four horizons in chapter 4; communication builds, progressively applying "old" understanding to "new" contexts. Note that we are not making a value judgment here; just because there is progress toward the future does not necessarily imply that there is something better or wiser. Rather, it is simply different, with the meaning derived by going back to the root metaphor. Ultimately we reach the root of all root metaphors related to knowing God—Jesus the Christ who was at the creation and is the "living word" presented throughout the whole of Scripture (cf. Van Engen, 1996: 81–83).

God Reveals Himself through Illumination

Believers today are in historical continuity with Abraham and Moses. As the Old Testament personages looked forward to the coming of Jesus, so we look back. Christians are in continuity with the Old Testament (Gal. 3:29). But care must be taken to distinguish the uniqueness of Scripture as revelation from what takes place on this side of the cross: resurrection and ascension. Understanding the historical contexts that are part of the biblical story is crucial for our understanding of how a particular community receives the Gospel. This, in turn, influences how a faith community in a particular context understands God's communication through the hermeneutical perspective drawn from that context.

Around the world today, especially in the majority world, and in part due to the work of translator-missionaries, Christians now see things in Scripture that westerners did not previously understand.[8] Take, for example, the reading of the beatitudes that appear in both Matthew chapter 5 and Luke chapter 6. People in upper-middle-class American churches almost always read the beatitudes in Matthew while peasants in Latin America prefer to read the passage in Luke. Liberation theology helped us understand why this is so. It is because of the impact of the respective contexts. In Luke's narrative Jesus sees the misery around him and responds with deeds: assisting the poor, feeding the hungry, encouraging the sorrowful, and healing the sick. Matthew, on the other hand presents the message in a more abstracted fashion as a speech on the mountain—in a context of serenity. In our day the wealthy and powerful members of state and institutionalized churches are not very sympathetic with the action focus of Luke, preferring to read Matthew's verbal propositions.

As the church's theology continues to take shape, we find that we have another series of contexts that further impact the missionary activity of the church. The western church does not yet know how to deal with all of the input from the majority world, since it finds itself in a relatively new postcolonial era. Following the concepts of modernity, seen as an expression of the Enlightenment (Newbigin, 1979; 1989; Middleton and Walsh, 1995), westerners tend to assume that if something is "true," it is true everywhere and always. And if it is "always" true it is unchangeable. This reasoning leads to the idea that meaning established in one context must apply to all contexts. Unfortunately this idea has prevailed since the Reformation and has gained momentum in evangelical churches during the last century. If the "old old story" is true and unchangeable then it must be presented the same way to all peoples everywhere. Such "truth," however, has been bound largely to a western context and makes little sense when presented as "unchangeable truth" elsewhere. In fact, it is often considered irrelevant to the life issues of people in nonwestern contexts. This implies the need for a multiplicity of theologies. But how far can such contextual theologies be allowed to multiply? How long will it be before the Gospel is fragmented to such a degree that truth becomes everyone's religious opinion (McCallum, 1996)? In order to avoid such fragmentation, there must be a truth that can be presented as such in multiple contexts. It is the context that varies, not the truth.

Here is where the root metaphor concept is so helpful. Root metaphors "gather to themselves metaphors borrowed from diverse fields into realms of associated meaning. On the other hand, they maintain the ability to give birth to a wide array of new (potential) interpretations" (Bailey, 2002: 41). Time and place, history and context, are intimately connected to the meaning of truth. That is what Scripture is about. And communication is about ensuring that people in their context understand what God said. And what God said always took place (and still does) in time and space. In other words, Scripture gives us a clear model for our discussion: God, above all else, is a God of context. The people God created expressed their creativity by developing new cultural environments, and God in his sovereignty chose to interact with people in their respective circumstances. God desires to reveal himself, and in so doing, through the Holy Spirit, illuminates people's understanding about God.

This is participation in illumination with an understanding of the importance of context that impacts a people's understanding of God in their midst. This relationship between revelation and illumination is something we return to time and again because it establishes the identity of the communicator, and that identity is bound to the nature of relationship with God who is revealed in hiddenness.

THEOLOGICAL DEVELOPMENT
OF COMMUNICATION

Theology can be defined, perhaps too simplistically, as "thinking about God." By this definition every human being is a theologian because everyone thinks about God in one way or another. Today we continue the story into a post-modern era. But in so doing, we dare not add to the canon of Scripture. Theological concerns must interface with hermeneutical appropriateness. There is a sequence here: exegesis, hermeneutic, and then theology.[9] An understanding of the text (exegesis) must then be processed hermeneutically within a community, which in turn develops its theology as it applies God's Word to its reality. This provides a new understanding that gives greater appreciation to the text in new contexts. The Korean New Testament scholar, Seyoon Kim, looks at the apostle Paul's Damascus Road experience as determinant of almost all of the aspects of Paul's radical reinterpretation of the Old Testament text (Kim, 1982). Paul is apparently moved to reinterpret the Old Testament on the basis of his conversion experience. The Holy Spirit thus enables Paul to understand his experience as a contemporary application of what went before.[10] Paul was a rabbinic theologian. He knew the Scriptures. Based on his Damascus Road experience, Paul reinterpreted the Old Testament. If this process was true for Paul and other New Testament authors as a hermeneutical community interpreting the Old, doesn't this provide an insightful model as to how God's Spirit frees us to look at both Old and New Testaments today?

Theology, then, involves looking at the biblical text and interpreting it or making it relevant to a particular time and place. Each time and place provides a cultural adaptation or a kind of contextual lens through which people view God. When God's people are informed by what God has said through the text (exegesis), and that in turn is brought to bear upon their time and place (hermeneutics), theological reflection is the result. Culture provides the context for thinking about God. It is a lens, a worldview that impacts biblical understanding (Kraft, 1996: 19).

How much are cultural issues involved in the creation of the text itself, first in the source text and then in its transfer into a new context? The Bible itself often raises this question. Arthur Glasser notes this when he discusses terms used for God:

> The basic word for deity in the ancient Semitic world of the Near East was *El*. This was also the proper name for the supreme god of the Canaanite pantheon. . . . The Israelites appropriated it and gave it new meaning, in much the same way that the Jewish translators of the Old Testament into Greek appropriated the word *Theos* and transformed it . . . to conform to God's unique revelation of himself. (1989: 36)

Clearly the greater the overlap between text, faith community, and context that we can structure into the process, the better the chance people have of understanding what God is doing from a perspective that makes sense to them. If we can adequately present the source content in a new context, people have a better chance of building a relationship with God who, through God's Word, will interact with people in their circumstances.

Westerners have much to learn about God and the supernatural from Christians in the majority world. Often nonwesterners understand spiritual issues through natural revelation and religious systems that are far closer to the contexts in which God originally communicated. Therefore they appreciate the biblical contexts better than most westerners. Western thought draws heavily from Greek and Roman philosophy and from the assumptions of the Enlightenment as it pertains to scientific development.[11] While the west has become increasingly compartmentalized and specialized, the rest of the world is more holistic and able to see God in an integrative and cohesive fashion (cf. chapter 6 for a discussion of these basic values). For most people in the majority world, God is far more understandable than to most westerners. Thus many majority-world peoples seem able to understand God's revelation in ways that the people of biblical times would probably recognize and applaud.

SOCIOCULTURAL DEVELOPMENT
OF COMMUNICATION

The dynamic tension of text, context, and faith community over time must be brought to the communication process spanning multiple contexts in which divine relationship with human beings took place. As soon as we say "text" we are forced to deal with both exegesis and hermeneutics. This raises theological issues that trace their way through the entire time-space continuum. When we say "context," we are talking about anthropological concerns and issues of language and worldview: the cultural perspectives that pertain to understanding the meaning of text in a particular community. All of this happens simultaneously. Exegesis and hermeneutics inform communication in particular faith communities. The bottom line has to do with God's relationship with people.

To use strictly literary and linguistic methods and principles as if the Bible were like any other book presents a theological problem. While the principles of communication God used were the same as any horizontal communication between those who share a language and culture, there is something unique about the Bible that makes it infinitely translatable like no other literature. The Bible itself affirms its own uniqueness and upon God's Word people have staked their faith commitments with life and death consequences. Humans will either understand truth as God intended it, or they will follow their religious traditions that lead to pursuing the angel of light who twists truth and leads human beings away from a relationship with God. Since Adam and Eve, human beings have continually looked for ways to return to Eden. More than the idyllic lifestyle that was lost, the relationship with a God who desires to communicate was broken. Returning to that state is the longing of every human soul, and enabling that to happen is the missional challenge faced by God's messengers of truth in every age. Their intent in communication should be to ensure that what God has said is clear and that it is clearly understood within particular communities where people so desperately desire to know the truth that will set them free.

Missiologists working in the realm of social concerns that reflect both cultural and theological issues have used secular disciplines like anthropology and linguistics to analyze and understand their audiences in an attempt to more effectively proclaim the Gospel. The models they have developed help them approach the theological task of communicating God's truth in ways that make sense to those who listen. Traditionally, theologians have not done well in relating the social science models to the biblical text itself. Missiologists have talked about meaning in terms of God as the ultimate source, and in another vein they have considered the audience. But they have often held these two far apart, considering each in its turn with little association between them. They have been slow to see the dynamic relationship between these two. The role of the text and the assumptions of communicators have also been studied independent of their relationship to God as the ultimate source and to receptors as the object of God's love and Gospel presentation.

As we discuss in chapter 2, the issue is fidelity to the message: we seek faithfulness to God's communication so that his intent is understood. We want to ensure relevance using Sperber and Wilson's (1986; 1995) development of a broader communication theory (cf. chapter 5). Throughout this process, however, biblical scholars too often assume a horizontal (within this world) perspective: communication from human to human—"from below." They assume that human social sciences are an acceptable tool to see this process in its movement from source to receptor. They assume that the Bible is like any other human book, written by humans in the midst of human contexts. It is too easy to assume that the principles of grammatical-historical interpretation are sufficient for establishing the original intent of the author of the biblical text. While we agree that careful literary analysis, exegesis, and hermeneutics of any given biblical passage is necessary to arrive at the original content that can then be stated in meaningful ways for new receptors, we also desire to ensure that we recognize God as the true source of the text and treat the text as "from above." We also assume that if we do our job well, the end product will be exegetically cohesive and hermeneutically appropriate in terms of the receptors' understanding. In short, we think that the product of our effort will by itself communicate in ways that are coherent and relevant for new receptors in their contexts.[12] However, analysis must apply to both sides equally: both to the text as the carrier of God's Word and to the receptors' understanding of the text. In other words, God's original message was cast in such a way that we assume effective communication took place: people responded (either positively or negatively). A new Gospel communication needs to do the same. It should precipitate a response to God.

This was the issue facing Paul Meyerink and the Tzeltal church, and it impacts every missional communication the world over. The faithful communicator of God's message wants to ensure that people are able to discover God's hiddenness and apply it to their circumstances. To accomplish this mission requires that we examine both the person and the nature of the source—God's Word.

NOTES

1. Adapted from Charles Van Engen, "The New Covenant," (1989: 74–75).

2. See, for example, Karl Barth, *Church Dogmatics* (1958, 2.1: 184). Barth devotes an entire section (27: 179–254) of volume 2.1 to discussion of the knowledge of God, which he divides into two parts: the *terminus a quo* (the point from which our knowledge proceeds by the grace of God's self-revelation to us) and the *terminus ad quem* (the point to which our knowledge conduces—faith in the hidden God). It is important to compare this section of Barth's *Dogmatics* with 1.2, section 17: 280–361, 4.1: 478–501, and 4.3: 135–165.

3. See, for example, Louis Berkhof, 1932: 1:17–19; G. C. Berkouwer, 1955: 285–332; Emil Brunner, 1949: 117–136; and Hendrikus Berkhof, 1979: 41–56, 61–65.

4. See, for example, H. Berkhof, 1979: 105–111.

5. Recent writings about metaphor (cf. Lakoff and Johnson, 1979, 1999; Nishioka, 1997; and Addai, 1999) make an important contribution to missiology. Metaphor enables people to conceptualize the unknown via their experience with the known. Visible and touchable experience enables people to understand the invisible and intangible. Metaphoric more than propositional approaches provide an analog for reality—people cannot see God but they experience him in many ways often expressed through the modes of creation. The Psalmist sings, "The heavens declare the glory of God!" "This analogical mode in the cognitive process, provides new insight for understanding the intersubjective nature of constructing knowledge" (Nishioka, 1997: 171).

6. Adapted from Charles Van Engen, "The New Covenant," (1989).

7. Noth notes that re-presentation does not only look back but enables an interpreter of Scripture to look to future events so long as they are informed by what has already transpired under the impact of God's presence: "Re-presentation" is founded on the premise that "God and his action are always present, while man in his inevitable temporality cannot grasp this present-ness except by "re-presenting" the action of God

over and over again in his worship" (Noth, 1960: 85). It is this that we seek to demonstrate in figure 1.1. Communicators can learn much by working backward, beginning with what they know and learning how they are informed by what went before. Similarly, when working with Scripture, communicators may start with the author's point of view and then work back to the initiation of an argument or story that can provide a broad perspective of the whole discourse.

8. We use the term *majority world* to highlight the fact that the western perspective emanating from the Enlightenment is a minority position in the world at large. This term also highlights the respective numbers of people who hold to assumptions impacted by a worldview that more clearly reflects biblical truth and God's perspective of human beings. We desire to reduce the pejorative use of economically based terms like *third world* and more accurately reflect the changing structures of the "postmodern" world of the twenty-first century.

9. This order is significant. Any other order reopens the canon, as it were, and keeps extending it as new experience impacts truth rather than vice versa. Theology must be built on interpretation of truth. Theology, then, comes from the source, thereby avoiding the heresy that results when the reverse takes place.

10. Dr. Kim has recently published a revision of this important work (Kim, 2001) in which he argues that Paul's Gospel comes from both his radical conversion experience and his use of Jesus' teachings in light of the Damascus Road. This, he notes, provides the foundation of the Gospel that Paul presented in his first-century context.

11. For example, scientifically astute theologians have difficulty understanding creation, the Noaic flood, or the parting of the Red Sea, to name but a few biblical issues that do not appear to square with scientific evidence. To accommodate a scientific explanation and not to appear naive, scientifically oriented theologians have come up with explanations that juxtapose science and theology. These often result in explanations that impose concerns upon the text that were in no way intended in the original context but serve to keep those from a particular, western, worldview happy. These issues, however, never occur to the more holistic peoples who populate much of the world. They are happy to read the text and accept it as truth because their worldview says that supernatural influence pervades the world and impacts much of human endeavor.

12. We deal with these factors of communication theory and text analysis at some length in chapter 5 and appendix 2. We introduce them here as elements that are crucial to the communicability of the text and the true nature of exegesis—to ensure that the original, intended message is understood by those who receive it, both historically in the biblical context as well as in the contemporary world in which we seek to proclaim God's Word.

• 2 •

The Source of Faithful Communication

The ultimate source of Gospel communication is God. The biblical text is important because it informs, contributes to, and determines human relationship with the God who is the source of Gospel presentation. (cf. Isa. 1:2; Jer. 1:2, 4; Ezek. 1:3; Hos. 1:1; Joel 1:1; Amos 1:3; Obadiah 1:1; Jon. 1:1; John 1:1; Heb. 1:1–2)

When the Lord began to speak through Hosea, the Lord said to him, "Go, take to yourself an adulterous wife and children of unfaithfulness, because the land is guilty of the vilest adultery in departing from the Lord." So he married Gomer, daughter of Diblaim, and she conceived and bore him a son. Then the Lord said to Hosea, "Call him Jezreel, because I will soon punish the house of Jehu for the massacre of Jezreel, and I will put an end to the kingdom of Israel. In that day I will break Israel's bow in the Valley of Jezreel." Gomer conceived again and gave birth to a daughter. Then the Lord said to Hosea, "Call her Lo-Ruhamah, for I will no longer show love to the house of Israel, that I should at all forgive them. Yet I will show love to the house of Judah; and I will save them—not by bow, sword or battle, or by horses and horsemen, but by the Lord their God." After she had weaned Lo-Ruhamah, Gomer had another son. The Lord said, "Call him Lo-Ammi, for you are not my people, and I am not your God." The Lord said to [Hosea], "Go, show your love to your wife again, though she is loved by another and is an adulteress. Love her as the Lord loves the Israelites, though they turn to other gods and love the sacred raisin cakes" (Hosea 1:2–9; 3:1:1; cf. I. Peter 2:10).[1]

This passage from Hosea is most unusual and amazing. The prophet is told to marry an adulterous woman (most probably a local prostitute). Here is a real-life narrative metaphor that God uses to communicate God's deep sadness over the way the people of Israel (the northern kingdom) have been unfaithful to God's covenantal relationship with them. The metaphor seems especially powerful because it involves Hosea's own personal life: his marriage to Gomer, the naming of their children, Hosea's pain over Gomer's unfaithfulness, and

23

Hosea's willingness to receive Gomer after she has been unfaithful. God's message of love is conveyed through the emotional and personal pain of broken relationships. Hosea conveys a picture of the God of Israel that is "a merciful God; he will not abandon or destroy you or forget the covenant with your forefathers" (Deut 4:31).[2] The propositional affirmations found in the Old Testament regarding God's graciousness and mercy are given narrative form in Hosea's family life as a conduit for the communication of God's intent with regard to Israel.

IN SEARCH OF THE ULTIMATE SOURCE

God's narrative approach to communicating with Israel through Hosea gives us a clue to the relationship of God as the ultimate source, the text as the conduit of proclaiming God's intent, and the receptors whose context and worldview influence the means God uses to convey his intent. And in Hosea we can see that God's final objective was not the meaning to be found in Hosea's relationship to Gomer, but rather the renewed relationship of Israel in covenant with God. The issue at hand was God's call to Israel to return to God. And God communicated that call by means of the lived-out metaphor of Hosea's family. God's final objective was a renewed relationship with Israel—not merely the creation of a new real-life drama full of pathos. Yet that pathos led people to give serious consideration to the identity of the One who desired such a close relationship. Who was the source behind this message of hope in a seemingly hopeless context?

We know in our heads, and maybe also in our hearts, that the ultimate source is God. The Bible itself repeatedly makes this affirmation. "Thus says the Lord" and "The word of the Lord came to" are phrases that appear hundreds of times throughout Scripture. In fact, that is the whole point of enscripturating God's message. We give assent to the fact that God has communicated with humankind. But human beings are culture-bound creatures. And because we are culture-bound, we are forced to deal with what we have, which means we operate on the horizontal plane. At the same time we must recognize that it is God who is in focus, not the text. Yet the text is representative of God.

How does God, then, relate to human beings? He relates to human beings always in their context. This is the message of the whole Bible. An unknowable God, who is wholly other, makes himself known. How? Where? Always in a human context. This side of heaven, human beings have never known God outside of a human context. God then is forced to use our human context-specific linguistic and sociocultural settings to communicate. God often does this in the form of metaphors or figures of speech, such as in the passage from Hosea. God also does this in human cultural contexts as he conforms to particular cultural principles through incarnation.

The Bible is full of stories where God, knowing that he cannot interact with human beings outside of the human realm, enters that context. We call these theophanies, as, for example, when the angels came to talk with Abraham. Remember how the visitors arrived walking along the dusty road? Abraham as a good host went out to meet them. He stopped them on their way saying, "Come into my house." He went through an entire culturally appropriate scene: they sat under the tree, he implored them to stay for dinner. They refused, saying, "No, we have business. We cannot stay for dinner." He continued to urge them. "Just wait. Just stay." It seems so very different from our hustle and bustle, hurry-up-and-get-on-with-life kind of approach. But their behavior was culturally appropriate. Finally the angels agree to stop. The servants go out and kill a calf. Sarah cooks the meat.

At this point Abraham and the angels talk about the year to come and the fact that Sarah is going to have a baby. Sarah overhears the conversation and thinks this is the funniest thing she has ever heard. After all she is by now over ninety years old. She, the barren one, is going to have a baby? Yes, she heard right. Then when the angels leave, Abraham as a good host sees them on their way and walks the road with them. This is God in a human and cultural context. And it is wonderful! Then the angels leave for Sodom, where they are treated quite differently. That was an entirely different context. The process we are describing here is the way God has chosen to communicate God's intention. An infinite, supernatural, and supracultural being communicates with finite, human culture bearers.

If we use the word "source" and ask where the texts came from we begin to expand our view of both the Scripture and the source behind it. Is the source, the author who is God, knowable? And what was the author's communicational intent? How did God convey intent through the lives and speech of human authors and human faith communities?

This matter is very important because ultimately at issue is the quest for the self-revelation of God. What is the relationship of the source to the context? In answering this question, some theologians used only horizontal criteria that accounted for a scientific view of religious belief in human history. In doing so, they discovered they could not find Jesus. They could not discover the source. They could find people who talked about Jesus, but they could not find Jesus the Christ. Because the concept of incarnation is not historically valid, they took that out. Since the concept of virgin birth is not historically or scientifically supportable, out it went. In fact, when their horizontal list of social and scientific facts based on purely horizontal definitions was pressed rationally upon the data, they could not find Jesus because Jesus the Messiah does not allow himself to be objectified or quantified. It is this fact that allows for less rationalistic people around the world to find God, while supposedly more enlightened ones may think that God is not really there. Once again we are dealing with context, for the mind of the receptor becomes part of the ground into which the seed falls, to paraphrase Jesus' well-known parable (Matt. 13:3–10).

When we look at the biblical worlds, the major concern is one of relationship: "I will be your God, you will be my people and I will dwell in your midst." The nature of this relationship keeps changing throughout Scripture so as to interact with different sociolinguistic contexts. A whole range of semantic constellations is introduced to help human beings caught in their horizontal dimensions, begin to appreciate in a small way the vertical implications of their existence. These contextual differences are not problematic to the Bible because Scripture assumes that God has existence apart from the universe God created. What humans say about God does not determine God's nature.

As cultural and theological specialists we have been trained to think phenomenologically, so it is a very different thing to start by positing One who exists. We affirm the existence of One who has a nature apart from the language used about that One. This One is not the extrapolation of human desires or of human cultural values. The essence of the biblical message calls for us to interact with the One who exists, the God who is. This viewpoint changes our experience of reading as well as interpreting Scripture.

For example, have you ever taken off your shoes with Moses? He was just taking care of his sheep on the mountainside and suddenly he saw the burning bush (Ex. 3:1–6). There Moses met the One who is. In fact, he asked him his name. And God answered, "I am who I am." And Moses responded, "The Israelites won't believe me. How do I tell them who you are?" Thomas Cahill captures the scene and discusses the concept.

> We can take comfort in the certain knowledge that God is a verb, not a noun or adjective. His self-description is not static but active, appropriate to the God of Journeys. YHWH is an archaic form of the verb *to be;* and when all the commentaries are taken into account, there remain but three outstanding possibilities of interpretation, none of them mutually exclusive. First, *I am who am:* this is the interpretation of the Septuagint, the ancient Greek translation of the Hebrew Bible, which, because of its age and its links to the ancients, bears great authority. It was this translation that Thomas Aquinas used in the thirteenth century to build his theology of God as the only being whose essence is Existence, all other beings being contingent on God, who is Being (or Is-ness) itself. A more precise translation of this idea could be: "I am he who causes (things) to be"—that is, "I am the Creator." Second, *I am who I am*—in other words, "None of your business" or "You cannot control me by invoking my name (and therefore my essence) as if I were one of your household gods." Third, *I will be there with you:* this is Fox's translation, following Martin Buber and Franz Rosen-

zweig, which emphasizes God's continuing presence in his creation, his be-ing—there with us. (Cahill, 1998: 109)

All the way through Scripture there is a positing of the nature of God that is apart from the language we use, whether that be Hebrew or Greek or English or any other human language. Neither the human author of the biblical text nor the receptor determines the nature of God who is above and beyond the human condition but at the same time part of it. Again, Cahill captures this awareness of God and God's name as the source of all that is.

> How should we pronounce the Name when we come upon it? One may, of course, substitute "the Lord" for the tetragrammaton YHWH. Others will boldly attempt a pronunciation, *"Yahweh"* (as English speakers usually say it) or *"Yahvé"* (after the French and Germans) or even "Jehovah" (a mis-pronunciation, much in evidence in Protestant hymnody and based on an inadequate understanding of the conventions of medieval manuscripts). But for me, when I attempt to say the consonants without resort to vowels, I find myself just breathing in, then out, with emphasis, in which case God becomes the breath of life. (Cahill, 1998: 109–110)

In the biblical world, then, God is crucial to understanding both the local context and the broader God-human perspective. So when Jesus talked with the woman of Sychar, mentioned in John chapter 4, her question was, "Where do you worship this God? To which mountain do you go?" Jesus replied that she did not need to go to any mountain. God is not in an altar or a mountain. Rather he must be worshiped in spirit and truth. Now stop and think about this. In some ways, from the viewpoint of the woman, Jesus' answer was non-sense. Yet from another standpoint Jesus' answer strikes at the very heart of the issues she was facing. What were the deep issues in her life? She was concerned about family. She was concerned about sexuality, or more accurately, reproductivity, because she was probably barren. She was concerned about men, because she had probably been used by them—passed around. She was concerned about society. She was concerned about feeding herself and getting a drink of water—she was at Jacob's well. In the immediate context of the question, however, she was concerned about Samaritan Judaism. She was a wonderful theologian. She asked all of the right questions. She was, as far as we know from the Gospels, the only one, other than the disciples, to whom Jesus said clearly, "I am the Messiah." And she was not even Jewish. She was not a leader of the Jews. And she was not a man. She was a woman, a Samaritan, a socially, and perhaps physically, dysfunctional outcast. Yet in this conversation Jesus clearly reveals to her the source of all worship, and even his own true identity. God was there and could be worshiped in spirit and in truth (John 4:23).

As the conversation unfolded Jesus asked her if she was ready to worship him. Look again at the way John told the story. There are a number of "worlds" or horizons colliding here. There is the woman's world. We can call her the receptor. There is a biblical world. The woman knew all of the Old Testament history, all about Jacob, his physical and spiritual journey, his search for water, his need for sustenance. She also understood Rachel's pain. Then there was Jesus' world, the world of the proclaimer. Notice what Jesus did as he "translated" the grace of God and told the woman that God is broader than the ethnicity of the Jews. In communicating his Gospel message, Jesus was approaching heresy in terms of his own theological context. He violated several established theological categories. But in so doing he gave her a new understanding of the biblical world, a new hermeneutic that was directly opposed to that of the Pharisees who wanted to capitalize on the popular religious viewpoint. The Pharisees, because of their traditions, had lost touch with the original source and had replaced it with the Targums, expanding the law. Their focus was on their own interpretation and their expansive development of God's original communications. By keeping the focus on Jerusalem and the temple, they benefited because everyone had to come to them. In contrast, the Samaritans said, "No, you must come over to us—don't go to Zion, come to our mountain." Do you see all of the nationalistic issues floating around there? For the Pharisees, their relevance was wrapped up in their identity and the Jerusalem temple that established for them who God was. But Jesus offered a new "translation" by removing the rationalistic, ethnic barriers and presenting a new way to understand the situation.

Now, if Jesus was the presenter, who is the source? The text might be considered the source. Or is God the source? What Jesus did in this encounter is amazing. He cut through the hermeneutical issues of the text to a hermeneutics of being, of spiritual reality. He creatively exegeted Old Testament revelation in order to generate a new understanding of God's being rather than a new understanding of the text. He helped the woman and her friends look at their identity in relationship to God—not to the mountain, but to the spirit and truth of God rather than the place of worship.

Similarly, we must shift from a rote, horizontalist viewpoint that presents a mere book to a vertical, deeper perspective that asks more basic questions about the nature of the source. Who is God? Are we interpreting the text as a purely human product? Or, do we see the text itself as so holy that it is untouchable and untranslatable as the Muslims view the Qur'an? Do we encounter the text as a communication from One who is the source? The Bible is not a mere book. The Scriptures represent a new relationship with the source. The text is not itself holy. The text is a communication, a link that enables the development of a new relationship between the source and the receptor. On the surface, what Jesus said to the Samaritan woman appears to be nonsense if it is related only to a horizontal, human context. For the Bible, then, Ricoeur's dictum that "the author is dead to the text" is not true (Ricoeur, 1981: 147). As the author of the "living text" God builds vertical relationships with human beings into the communication event—it extends through all time to all people. It began in the Garden of Eden and extends to the destruction of the earth as we know it. God is in control of all that was made. At the same time this vertical relationship extends to people who are assigned to care for the earth and all that is in it (Gen. 2:28), including all of us. Thus God's vertical relationship impacts the horizontal context and ultimately extends to all people, as Jesus demonstrated in the story about the Good Samaritan (Lk. 10:25–37). Clearly God is not dead to the text. On the contrary, God intends to reveal God's self in the text.

How, for example, should we present the concept of "spirit"? How do we communicate the idea of a supracultural, uncreated being? If we only hold to cultural and horizontalist categories, communicating about "spirit" would appear to be nonsense. But when Jesus said, "You must worship in spirit and in truth," the woman of Sychar understood that he was talking about a spiritual journey (a metaphorical reference to the "living water" that began the conversation) that combined the vertical and horizontal dimensions of reality. Indeed, Jesus himself incarnated that spirit for her and lifted the veil from her eyes so she could see the God of the Old Testament in the very location where Jacob had come to a new understanding of God hundreds of years earlier. The place was clearly not the issue; it was spiritual insight. How can we communicate in such a way as to create that same sense of awe, of wonder, of inspiration? We must move beyond the horizontal principles, important as they are.

Scripture, then, is a completely different, special, unique collection of material emanating from the same source. The Bible is not the final source—God is. The Bible itself affirms this over and over again. The Bible is such a unique book that it is, in fact, impossible to truly translate. Though this affirmation may seem to overstate the case, we want the reader to feel its impact. Gospel proclaimers are not really communicating the content of Scripture. Rather they are presenting God in God's loving covenantal relationship with God's People who are called to respond and let the Creator of the universe transform them—to conform them to the image in which they were originally created.

HISTORICAL THREADS
IN MULTIPLE CULTURES

The Bible is not merely the record of religious experiences, nor the dictates or guidelines for spiritual exercise. Rather, the Bible, in the sense of truth communicated from a spiritual source, is a narrative of God's self-revelation through history, in the midst of a multiplicity of persons and cultures. It is a revelation of God's being in the context of life's reality. It is not primarily a history. You can find better histories of ancient civilizations. Much of the Old Testament is a repetition of the same story structured to answer the questions posed by people in a particular time and place. For example, I and II Samuel deals with pre-exilic Judah and emphasizes the people's reliance on God rather than on the kings of Israel. I and II Kings encourages the people in exile, enabling them to remember who they are. I and II Chronicles analyzes the same story from the perspective of those who have returned from the exile and helps them recall why their fathers and mothers were in the exilic predicament and how they could avoid the same fate. The text encourages them not to make the same mistakes as their forbearers. Hence, the focus is not on history as such, but on remembering God and God's dealings with God's people.

Nor is the Bible a psychology manual any more than a five-step course on spirituality. Taken as a collection of horizontal, human texts, it is a little of many things, but it is not really good at any of them. For instance, take a standard library catalog and try to figure out where to put the Bible. Either you have to put it on every shelf or you cannot put it anywhere. Furthermore, this rather motley collection of texts talks about history and persons and cultures and events, none of which are the essential matter of its fundamental message. The real issue is: "I will be your God, you will be my people and I will dwell in your midst." The Bible is really about relationship, about covenant, about connection between the Creator and that which is created. All of the horizontal, linguistic categories cannot fully communicate God's intent. Only as we experience the vertical dimension through God's love, as we stand in God's presence, when we are illuminated by the presence of God's Spirit, and as we experience God's grace do we find new life. By the same token, that relationship with the Source is informed, guided, circumscribed, and shaped by the textual narrative that God has given us as a way of hearing God's proclamation, the "good news." Now the text used to convey all of this finally has meaning.

John plays this out with the concept of *Logos*. The *Logos* is the Creator, the one who was at the beginning (John 1:2). And the *Logos* is Jesus Christ, the one who lived among us and revealed the glory of the Father (John 1:14). The *Logos* is also the written word about Jesus the Christ, written so that people might put their faith in the Messiah and in so doing discover true life (John 20:30). This analogy makes little sense unless you meet Jesus who came as light in darkness, as John explains throughout his entire Gospel. Christ came to his own and his own refused to accept him. It is a logical impossibility for the divine word to be incarnated in human form, speaking human words: and yet it happened. However, it happened because of the source. "Whoever has seen me, has seen the Father" (John 14:9).

John Calvin, in his theological reflection on the inspiration of scripture, does not begin with the words of the text as such, or with the history of its creation, or with the events it records. He starts with the Holy Spirit witnessing to human spirits that this is God's Word. Thus Calvin states that the Bible is "self-authenticating" (Calvin, 1960: 78–81). As people read and understand the Bible, they get to know the source better. As they get to know the source, the better they communicate. This leads us to the matter of fidelity in light of the importance of understanding the biblical worlds (what we call "horizons" in chapter 4).

THE FIDELITY ISSUE

Based on our view of the source and the way the source is connected with the original receptors, the significance of the text takes on a new importance. No longer is the focus upon whether a translated book or story says the same thing as what the original book or story said. Rather, fidelity will result as the receiver of the communication gets to know the source through a new and personal covenant relationship. Here, then, is the demonstration of fidelity. It is no longer simply understanding a book (which only reflects the surface structure of the communication—the horizontal issues). Rather, fidelity, at its root involves changing a life through a restoration of relationship with the One who gives life (a deep structure application of the content of a book to appropriate living—accounting for the vertical dimension). Remember that merely receiving the Bible at times also led to heresy. Simply reading a text does not guarantee communicability. Merely reading the text of Scripture is not the most fundamental point. Getting to know the source is the point, as the book of James makes clear, "Don't fool yourselves by just 'reading' God's Word, you must also obey it" (James 1:22–25).

This fidelity issue is the reason why the Pharisees had such trouble with Jesus. They wanted to consider only the letter of the law (the text). When the source showed up, it was a different matter altogether. Just imagine that we send you an e-mail message and you receive it. There you are, sitting at your computer, trying to understand what we said. As you work through the text, suddenly we come walking in the door and greet you. How will you respond? Will you say, "I do not know you. I'm reading e-mail from Dan and Chuck. Don't bother me. I want to read your e-mail." Will you prefer to read the text like the Pharisees did? Will you say, "Wow the source is

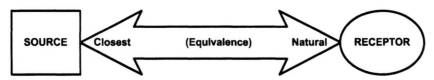

Figure 2.1. Nida's Concept of Dynamic Equivalence

here, let's talk"? The point is this: We cannot really communicate the message faithfully except within the bounds of a relationship with the source (Rogers, 2002: 282).

Communicating God's Word is a deeply spiritual event involving the Holy Spirit. Gospel presentation is a missionary act. Communicators of the Gospel are intimately and personally involved as participants in this process. And the best communicators do it in deep, deep prayer and listening to the Holy Spirit. There is something mysterious about the infinite communicability of the Bible. There is nothing else like it in the world that is proclaimed and then transforms people. True, the Bible by itself does not do this either. The hermeneutical community, the church, works through the text and brings their understanding to what they receive. But we are getting ahead of the story. We start with the source. What did God communicate? What does the text say regarding God's communication?

Eugene Nida was dealing with the concept of fidelity when he generated the idea of dynamic equivalence. His definition of fidelity was "the closest natural equivalence" (see figure 2.1). Nida's concept of "closest" attaches to the source (the meaning must match what the author intended), and "natural" attaches to the receptor (reflecting their native forms of appropriate and effective communication). These two terms are then connected by the whole idea of equivalence. In order for the communication to be natural, it is dependent upon communicating what the author originally intended to communicate in ways that make sense to new audiences. In other words, Nida was focusing on transferring a message in the most communicative way. The source must be faithfully understood in order to be appropriately interpreted and effectively communicated in a new context. And throughout this transfer process he intended that the communication be as "dynamic" as possible (Nida and Taber, 1981: 12–14, 24).

What, then, do we mean by "fidelity"? Our response is "faithfulness to God's communication as given in the text that draws persons to a relationship with God." The focus is not on the words of the text as such but on the nature of God as reflected in the text. This is what makes the Bible a unique enterprise and makes communicating it a missionary activity. The presentation of all other texts is merely horizontal communication. Defined this way, fidelity leads to a greater appreciation of the canon.

CANONICITY

What is the difference between the apostle Paul and believers today? How is what happened to Paul considered revelation, but for us it is illumination? The Scriptures themselves provide the pattern. It is the same Holy Spirit and the same faith community. So there is continuity. Yet if we place ourselves at the same revelatory level as Paul we start a process that leads down a very slippery slope.

Wayne Grudem (1994) presents a helpful set of criteria that provides an answer to the question of canonicity.[3] Normally when we talk about the canon the focus is on the list of the books of the Bible—the writings or autographs. However, in the early church that was not the intent. Instead the meaning of "canon," at least for the New Testament church, was to provide a measuring rod, a yardstick, a set of criteria by which the church recognized those books that were authoritative and considered revelatory. There was a historical process covering about a hundred and fifty years whereby the church decided which books were authoritative because they met certain criteria. Together, the result was the "canon." Let us briefly examine Grudem's criteria.

Apostolic Authorship

The first of the criteria that Grudem notes is apostolic authorship. In order to be considered authoritative the books had to be written by disciples, those who were ocular witnesses of the life and ministry of Jesus Christ. Because of this criterion, Paul also had to demonstrate that he was an apostle. His writings were included because he did, in fact, meet Jesus. Thus Paul was considered an ocular witness. Meeting this criterion is why Hebrews and James were questionable. The Gospel of Mark was included because Mark wrote the memoirs of Peter. And the Luke-Acts corpus was included because Paul could validate its authenticity. This criterion was quite intentional and clear on the part of the early church.

Witness to Jesus Christ

Second, all of the New Testament canonical books had to be directly related to issues flowing from Christ's ministry. More to the point, they had to be focused on Jesus. Centuries later, Martin Luther, John Calvin, and the Wesleys, among others, would ground their acceptance of the text of Scripture on the fact that the text pointed them to Jesus Christ.

This christological foundation of Scripture places the emphasis on Jesus as the One to whom the text points. Rather than overemphasizing the validity of the text itself, the focus for the early church was on the content. In the twentieth century there was a change on this point. In many cases, people did not accept the text as text because of its christological foundation, and then proceeded to subject it to various forms of criticism (textual, historical, form, source, and redaction, among others), focusing on the nature of the text itself rather than the One to whom it points. Downplaying the faith dimension, however, violates the intent of the Scriptures themselves.

If Gospel writers and early church thinkers considered the christological connection important, should it also be a concern to communicators of the Gospel message in the twenty-first century? The foundational issue here is the extent to which receptors come to know Jesus Christ through the conduit of the communicators' presentation of the message. The Gospel writers were con-

II Peter	Bible References		
2:1 2:5; 3:6 2:6,7 2:10	Deuteronomy 13:1-3 Genesis 7 Genesis 19 Exodus 22:28	Pentateuch	OLD TESTAMENT
1:21 2:15	II Samuel 23:2 Numbers 22:4-20	Historical Books	
1:19 2:15 3:8	Psalms 119:105 Proverbs 26:11 Psalm 90:4	Poetic Books	
1:19 1:21 2:1 2:21 3:2 3:10 3:13	"Prophets" Jeremiah 23:26 Jeremiah 6:13 Ezekiel 18:24 "Prophets" Isaiah 34:4 Isaiah 65:17; 66:22	Major Prophets	
2:3	Habakkuk 3:9	Minor Prophets	
Intertestamental Period			
1:16-18 2:20 3:2 3:10 3:10	"Witnesses" Matt 17:15 Matthew 12:45 "Apostles" Luke 12:39 Matthew 24:43	Synoptic Gospels	NEW TESTAMENT
1:18 2:10	John 17:3 John 8:34	John	
2:2 3:15	Acts 16:17; 22:4; 24:14 Acts 9:17; 15:25	Historical Books	
1:7 2:1 3:15-16 3:9 3:10	Romans 12:10 Galatians 2:4 "Letters of Paul" and "Other Scriptures" I Timothy 2:4 I Corinthians 1:8	Pauline Epistles	
1:19 2:1 3:1 3:1 3:14	I John 2:11; Hebrews 2:2 Jude 4 "Second Letter of Peter" I Peter 1:1 I Peter 1:7	Pastoral Epistles	
1:19 2:4 2:9 2:15 3:9 3:10	Revelation 22:16 Revelation 20:15 Revelation 3:10 Revelation 2:14 Revelation 2:21 Revelation 21:1	Prophetic Books	

Figure 2.2. The Bible as Referenced in II Peter

cerned that their receptors know the living Jesus. So, for example, in John's words, "Now Jesus did many other signs in the presence of his disciples, which are not written in this book. But these are written so that you may come to believe that Jesus is the Messiah, the Son of God, and that through believing you may have life in his name" (John 20:30–31). Should this perspective be any less true today? Seen in this light, we begin to understand that Gospel proclamation is an inherently missiological endeavor.

The Power of the Holy Spirit

The third criterion Grudem presents is that, through the text, the Holy Spirit witnesses to the human spirit that this is, in fact, the word of the Lord. John Calvin stressed this pneumatological foundation (Calvin, 1960: 74–81). The Holy Spirit points to Christ and in response people recognize that they become children of God through faith in Jesus (John 1:12). In the text we meet Jesus and, therefore, we know that it is authoritative. In the midst of reading the Scriptures, "The (Holy) Spirit testifies with our spirit that we are God's children." (Rom. 8:16) This crucial element was missing in the inerrancy debate of the mid-twentieth century, involving the "battle for the Bible." Because some inerrantists were trying to prove the validity and truthfulness of the Bible based on certain scientific, historical, grammatical, demonstrable, and rationalist categories, a different set of criteria emphasizing purely horizontal perspectives was imposed. This is quite different from how (prior to the twentieth century) the Bible had been perceived as a vertical communication transmitted by the power of the Holy Spirit.

Scripture Quotes Itself

The fourth and final criterion imposed by the early church theologians dealt with the way the various authors of the Bible quoted one another. If a book was quoted by another biblical author and met the other three tests of authenticity, it was considered a candidate for inclusion in the list of authoritative books of the New Testament.

Grudem points out that in the postcanonical period the church accepted none of the writings after the New Testament and questioned none of the accepted books (Grudem, 1994: 66). Other options (for example, the Epistle to Barnabas) were not accepted because they were not written directly by the apostles, they did not point specifically enough to Jesus Christ, and no other New Testament writer quoted them. The church had specific, clear, intentional, and testable criteria, and the books in the Bible are those that measured up to that canonical yardstick.

The book of II Peter is an example of how these criteria work in a specific book. As can be seen in figure 2.2, every part of the Bible is mentioned in II Peter. A careful reading of II Peter shows citations from the Pentateuch, the Poetical books, the Historical books, and the Prophetic books (both major and minor) from the Old Testament. II Peter also quotes from the Gospels, from Acts, from Paul's epistolary corpus, and even the book of Revelation.[4] II Peter is part of the New Testament because it meets the canonical criteria: it is written by an apostle, specifically points to Jesus, it is witnessed to by the Holy Spirit, and it is both quoted by other New Testament writers and quotes other portions of the Bible.[5]

Canonicity, then, involves the criteria for measurement, not the product. There is a big difference here. Canonicity is the criteria on which the church accepted (or did not accept) each book as authoritative. The product of that canonicity ends up to be a collection of books. The reason this distinction is so important is the way it structures the discussion. The determining factor involves setting the basis for including or excluding a book from the list rather than asking which books are in and which are out. The argument surrounding inclusion goes back to the uniqueness of Jesus Christ, which in turn forces an examination of our understanding of the Old Testament and how the material there pointed toward Christ. This is the heart of the criteria. Jesus the Christ (the Messiah) is pivotal because that was what God seems to have intended all the way through the canon. The early church emphasized this and it is what we must continue to communicate. Based on divine revelation, we gain a new appreciation of Jesus Christ: who he is and why he came. Faithful communication of the incarnation calls us to examine the transfer process from source to the receptors.

THE VALUE OF METAPHOR
IN BIBLICAL COMMUNICATION

Because the vertical dimension is so important and is prior to the horizontal dimension, it is essential to take seriously the way God communicates and examine this as a model for us to follow. As human beings we are accustomed to anthropomorphisms that ascribe human characteristics to God. For example, consider the texts that speak of God's "mighty hand and outstretched arm" (Deut. 7:19; cf. Num. 11:23; Deut. 4:34; Ps. 44:3; Ps. 98:1; Jer. 27:5). Does this mean God really has an arm? No. The focus is not God's arm, or any other anatomical analogy, but on relating God's being to human experience, to what we can know. God becomes enculturated through the language of metaphor. The Bible says that God wants to be known even as he knows us. God knit us in our mother's womb. God numbers our hairs. God knows the number of our days (Ps. 139). But God is also aware that such knowing can only happen in a particular cultural and linguistic context. And so God must use a range of communication styles in order to be known by humans. One of these is imagery via word pictures, metaphors that proliferate in all languages. Because the human mind produces many more ideas than words to express them, we have to expand the meanings of the words we have "beyond their ordinary use" (Ricoeur, 1976: 48). Metaphors reflect both literal and figurative meaning, and the extended usage of the latter creates new understanding as words are placed in new relationships within a text.

Biblical Metaphors

Psalm 27:1 says, "The Lord is my light and my salvation." Again the psalmist says, "God wraps himself in light as with a garment" (Ps. 104:2), and "The night will shine like the day because even the darkness is as light to you" (Ps. 139:12). Isaiah picks up on this and notes, "The Lord will be your everlasting light" (Is. 60:19-20). Wherever we find this juxtaposition of God and light we gain new perspectives of perceiving God through this metaphor. This is a semantic constellation with several thousand stars. The concept expands meaningfully because of its association with the ultimate source about whom it speaks. So in the New Jerusalem of Revelation 21 there will no longer be any sun there because the Son, Jesus Christ, is the light. Paul tells us we will stand face to face with God and there will be no more need for metaphor or any other "re-description," to use Ricoeur's term, because we will then "know fully, even as [we are] fully known" (I Cor. 13: 12).

An example taken from the human use of mythology may be helpful. In many ways Israel's mythology was the same as that of the Babylonians and others around them. Israel's stories were borrowed stories (Cross, 1973). However, the people of Israel reinterpreted those stories in light of knowing the true God, the Creator of heaven and earth. It is not all that significant that they borrowed from the Babylonians. What is critical is that Israel's portrait of God (using images borrowed from surrounding cultures) reflected the nature of the God of Abraham, Isaac, and Jacob as the God who revealed himself to them. This brings us back to our definition of fidelity. The images and metaphors Israel borrowed from its neighbors underwent a radical transformation. Israel took the stories and metaphors and filtered them through the lens of God's revelation, using them as vehicles to understand the source to which the images pointed. And the source was God, whose activity included the dispersion of languages at Babel. While almost all of the neighboring peoples had variations of the same story, the Jews understood the stories in a way others did not. As God's special people, they believed they had received a special revelation concerning that God—a revelation that they expressed in the text. Thus the receiving of the text became a spiritual event. Passing it on in an understandable manner was an issue of fidelity, and the myth became ultimate truth about their heritage, not from Abraham or even Moses, but from God.

It is easy for people to begin focusing attention on the image, or the textual exposition of the image, rather than on the source of the text. The problem is expressed well in Exodus with the episode of the golden calf. When Moses stayed up on the mountain too long, the Tabernacle not yet having been built, the group of former slaves rescued from Egypt began asking how they could worship a God they could not see. So with Aaron's help, they created a visible focus for their worship. In doing so, however, they substituted the image for the real thing, as Paul pointed out (Rom. 1:23). God designed the Tabernacle as a visual symbol to help Israel know the source. It was not intended to be a substitute for the source. It was a pictorial representation of the covenantal relationship God was establishing with God's People. "I will be your God, you will be my People and I will dwell in your midst." The physical picture and the covenantal relationship became so closely associated that later the Gospel writer, John, would speak of God "tabernacling" with us in Jesus Christ (John 1:14; Rev. 21:3).

Narrowing the tabernacle to christological typology misrepresents the original intent and produces deep-level confusion for contemporary receptors. Through the metaphor of the tabernacle, God was seeking to communicate visually to the Israelites who fled from Egypt. It was a pictorial representation of the relationship of God with God's people. The question was: Did the metaphor, the visual image, help them to know God? And, on the other side of the communication equation: What perspective does it bring to people who desire to know God in our day? The Bible is full of such imagery. Try writing the twenty-third Psalm, "The Lord is my shepherd. I shall not want," without metaphor. The entire meaning is lost without the poetic language.

Now herein lies the amazing quality of Scripture. If one image, or set of metaphors or myths does not work, there are others that may. The Bible's images are always different, driven by the context. And there is a progressive movement in the images of Scripture. The metaphors build on each other throughout Scripture. Take the example of the Babylonian king, Nebuchadnezzar in Daniel chapter 3. He built a large furnace into which he threw the three Jewish men who would not bow down to the king's statue. When Nebuchadnezzar looked into the furnace he saw four people walking inside. As a result, he came to know the Most High God. All he saw was the fourth person. Yet in some way God used those three people (together with the fourth) to communicate (we could say "translate") in such a way that Nebuchadnezzar could come to know God. We do not worship the images or metaphors. The words or the experience are neither the object nor the deep-level content of our worship. They are only referential pointers that symbolize meaning and direct our attention toward knowing God.

In this sense the words of the text are secondary for communicators of the Gospel. They represent surface-level symbols rather than deep-level understanding. Together the discourse-level flow of the words serves as a medium for the deeper significance of the text, often symbolized in metaphor. What is primary is the deep-level communication conveyed in the way that receptors may receive the text, the actual words. Both the text of Scripture and the audience that receives it are in tension. Both are integral dimensions of the contexts that influence the deep-level conceptual frameworks represented by the words and grammatical structures.

Words convey analogies, metaphors, images. For example, when Jesus talked with Nicodemus (John 3), part of the misunderstanding came about because Nicodemus chose to take Jesus' words literally: "You must be born again." Nicodemus chose to analyze the words on a propositional level. "How can one be born after having grown old?" Nicodemus asked. "Can one enter a second time into the mother's womb and be born?" (John 3:4) What was Jesus talking about? Nicodemus fixated on the words rather than looking to the source. Therefore, what Jesus said was nonsensical to him. Jesus, however, was communicating deep-level truth that had to do with the radical, total, personal transformation that Nicodemus needed to experience in order to know God and at the same time to know Jesus the Christ through the ministry of the Holy Spirit.

When talking with the disciples, Jesus spoke of *agape* love through the descriptive medium of self-givingness. "By this (everyone) will know that you are my disciples, if you love one another" (John 13:35). Following Jesus' missiological injunction, in contexts where self-sacrifice for the sake of others is missing, the church should demonstrate the nature of God by being a hermeneutical community that lives out God's self-giving love. Then people outside of the church may be able to understand that God is love. Such modeling was precisely what the disciples did in Jerusalem (Acts 2:42–47).

In chapter 1, we mentioned that we know God only in God's revealed hiddennesss (cf. Van Engen, 1996c: 75). We do not know all of God. We only see through a glass darkly. But the point is that we do see, and we can know. And our knowing and our seeing does not determine the nature of the One we know. If God's nature is defined by the words used to represent God, then God is imprisoned and reduced within the confines of the semantic constructs. We end up in a position similar to that of animistic societies where the power of the objects and the power of the magic is created by the shaman's words. He must know and use the right words in the right way. Most of the world's religions have some sort of verbal formulae: words, incantations, sacred sayings, mantras. Mystery religions keep their formulas secret due to the spiritual power ascribed to them. Such sayings are never to be translated or publicly unveiled. The Bible, on the other hand, calls for proclaiming from the rooftops (another figurative expression) the truth about the living God (Mt. 10:27). Jesus comes as the *Logos* and proclaims that it is not the formulae or words or incantations that matter. People do not need to repeat the same words over and over again.

The One with whom we speak and worship exists and hears us. Prayer does not determine the nature of God, nor does it predetermine God's response to a believer's prayers. But prayer builds a relationship of trust, acceptance, faith, and anticipation between the disciple and the Lord.

Contemporary Metaphors

In our world it is essential to use contemporary issues to convey God's intent in communicating with human beings. We may be able to use a people's mythology or body of metaphors and images to convey truth about God. For example, Samo myths all begin with *omu kogwa*, "long before the ancestors." When coauthor Dan Shaw translated the opening lines of Genesis using that mythical introduction, the Samo response was to pay close attention. They wanted to enter into relationship with the One who created the ancestors. They wanted to know who that really was. The focus of communication was not on the mythical opening line, but on the source of the myth with whom they desired to be in relationship. We in the west need to learn this from the ancient cultures of the world.

The feminist movement provides another contemporary example of metaphor usage. Some women choose to avoid using the word "father" for God because of potentially negative images that may have been the product of an abusive father or other dysfunctional male relationship. These negative inferences within a particular audience must be taken seriously. But in calling for avoiding the word "father," feminists have also lost God's intent. To speak of God as "father" is to emphasize God's personal, loving, caring, providing, and upholding relationship with God's people whom God considers to be "children." In the Bible, relational language about God assumes a referent to which the language refers. When we use the word "father" for God, we are not creating God in our image of fatherhood. By using the word "father," we do not intend to project upon God all of the baggage of our experiences with earthly fathers. Rather, there is a reality, a referent, God who is the "father" of our Lord Jesus Christ whose nature is separate from all of the words we use about him. We intend to speak truth about God, but the only way we know the truth about God is to come to know God as the One who relates to us in the fashion described by the concept "father."

Ultimately, we can communicate the Gospel only insofar as the receptors know the One of whom we are speaking. And until they know God, the truth we speak will not yet be understandable in their context. This requires the work of the Holy Spirit as the one who affirms truth, who draws people to God. The Holy Spirit works through the hermeneutical community, the church. One aspect of the Holy Spirit's work is to use all of the cultural and linguistic tools available to convey God's relevance. But the social sciences will not be enough for the receptor to come to know the source. That illumination takes the power of the Holy Spirit.

There are two sides to the communication of God's Word: being overwhelmed by the awesome responsibility on the one hand, and treating the text like it was merely a human book on the other. We have wrestled with both of these aspects when preparing sermons. This involves a theology of homiletics. Preaching is a form of communicating God's Word in human words. Ultimately, it is not a matter of presenting an error-free sermon. What really matters is whether the preaching enables people to know God.

Most of us in western evangelicalism like propositions. We lightly say, "God is love," but find it difficult to communicate what that really means. In fact, "God is love" cannot be understood apart from reference to God's Son. It is actually the sacrifice on the cross that gives content (historical, experiential, and relational) to the phrase "God is love." So how can those who do not have a concept of "sacrifice" understand that God is love? This was Don Richardson's well-known dilemma while trying to communicate God's love to the Sawi of Papua. Only when he stumbled upon the concept of a "peace child" was he able to communicate redemption. He would later develop this idea into what he came to call a "redemptive analogy" (Richardson, 1974).

These examples raise an epistemological issue. Gospel communication must be examined with respect to people coming to know God. Effective communication today needs to replicate God's intent in the way God communicated in the biblical worlds. As we seek to help people know God, whether through a written text, audio or videotapes, the Internet, or other media, it is crucial to include an invitation for them to know God. The presentation is the means of introducing people to the source who draws all people to God's self through the work of the Holy Spirit.

A THEOLOGICAL
UNDERSTANDING OF REVELATION

How does all of this impact the way pastors, missionaries, Christian business people, or teachers communicate information about God? It does not mean they rely solely on the Holy Spirit and, therefore, do not use theological, historical, cultural, or social tools. It does mean, however, that as they apply those tools to the task of communication, they are prepared to be flexible, open to surprises, and willing to adapt the communication to make it appropriate to the context in order to enable people to know God.

The presentation of truth, broadly understood, is not an end in itself. Neither is it only a methodology used to get people to think about God. Rather, it is a process through which people may come to know God. Gospel communication, then, is the beginning of a relationship. As Paul notes in II Corinthians chapter 5, we are ambassadors of Christ calling for people to be reconciled with God. That makes communication a theological and missiological process—a process of proclaiming the truth about God. We could say, then, that though we do not actually bring God to people, we bring a series of contextually appropriate images through which the Holy Spirit is able to reveal God. Communicating the Gospel is about establishing relationships between culturally conditioned human beings and the culture-free God who created all things. We communicate using all of the facts and knowledge about the culture we can muster. We utilize all of the words, sentences, discourses, and semantic constellations available in the context. Through all of this as well as through building relationships with people, we are communicating a relationship with the source, not just exegeting a text. Meanwhile, the Holy Spirit convinces people of sin, righteousness, and judgment (John 16:8). He is the one who works in the world before communication ever happens. In a given context, the Holy Spirit may be working to help a communicator figure out what anthropomorphisms, metaphors, symbols, and communicative styles are the best to use. The Holy Spirit touches the souls of the receptors to allow those images to lead them to a personal relationship with God in Jesus Christ.

The text of Scripture is part of a process through which the triune God speaks to human beings. They hear God's intent in their context. This is not a matter of form over against meaning. It is a matter of a deep-level understanding of a new relationship with God who is the source. On the basis of God's communication in their context, the hearers make inferences about God's intent for them. Fidelity is defined as the receptors coming to "know God in context" rather than as semantic faithfulness to a text—or "natural equivalence" to the text. The text is a secondary source, the conduit, the instrument, through which God speaks to each new group of receptors.

God used Hosea's deeply moving personal experience to present a picture of his concern for Israel in particular and generally with people everywhere. People identify with Hosea's pain and in so doing recognize the pain they have caused God. The God who knew them before they were conceived knows the intimate details of their lives. This Creator God wants to be in relationship with them, for only then will they fulfill the rationale of their existence (cf. Hubbard, 1990).

This brings us to the subject of the next chapter. How do communicators of the Gospel take seriously the cultural glasses that color their reading of Scripture, yet allow what they read to illumine their relationship with God? If the text is to point people to God, how do we take into account the influence of our own worldviews when we receive the text? In chapter 1 we reflected on the source. In chapter 2 we considered the text as a conduit for communicating a Gospel that points people to the source. In chapter 3 we consider the matter of culture: To what extent do the context, the faith community, and the communicator's personal pilgrimage impact an understanding of Scripture?

NOTES

1. We don't have space here to explore whether the episode in Hosea chapter 3 is a restatement of Hosea's calling in chapter 1, or whether Gomer was unfaithful to Hosea after he had first married her. It is also beyond the bounds of this book to delve into whether this metaphor is purely symbolic and allegorical or was actually lived out by Hosea. The semantic flow of the text itself gives the impression that this was Hosea's actual family life, and that his own life became the acted-out metaphor of the message God wanted to convey through Hosea to Israel.

2. Also see the following relating to God's covenantal relationship with Israel: Ex. 34:6; Neh. 9:17, 31; Dt. 31:6, 8; Jos. 1:5; I Kings 8:57; I Chron. 28:9, 20; Ps. 9:10; 27:9; 71:9; 86:5; 103:8; 111:4; 145:8; Isa. 42:16; Joel 2:13; Jon. 4:2; Heb. 13:5.

3. There is a vast literature discussing canonicity—too much for our purposes here. In this section we depended on Wayne Grudem's excellent summary of the issues (1994: 54–72). These criteria are specifically oriented to the canonicity of the New Testament. The matter of Old Testament canonicity involves a rather different set of criteria that ranges over a much wider historical development. We deal with canonicity here only within the bounds of its implications for our understanding the theological issues facing those who deal with the text of Scripture in order to communicate the Gospel in new contexts. See also Otto Weber 1981: 248–268.

4. Peter notes that Paul writes so that no one can understand him—a wonderful testimony to the humanity of biblical authors while at the same time recognition of God as the ultimate source.

5. The Intertestamental Apocryphal books pose a problem. For instance the Bible Societies in Latin America have often printed translations, including the Apocryphal books, because of their cooperative effort with the Roman Catholic Church. The context in which the Apocryphal books were written and a consideration of what was happening in the Jewish community during that period is important. The most critical issue, however, is that when Grudem's criteria are applied we find no citation of the Apocryphal books in any of the accepted New Testament writings. Furthermore, they became prominent three hundred years after the canonical era (Grudem, 1994: 59–60).

• 3 •

The Message of Faithful Communication

People read the biblical text through their own cultural glasses. This colors the way they understand God's intent as that is communicated through the cultural background of the biblical text.

One of the earliest prophets, Nathan, was given the task of communicating God's Word to David after he committed adultery with Bathsheba. Upon discovering that she was pregnant by him, he arranged for the death of her husband, Uriah the Hittite.[1] In II Samuel 11 we are informed of the many details of the case. The stage was set for God's Word to be communicated to David. How could Nathan bring David to understand the depth of the sin he had committed against God, against Bathsheba, against Uriah, and against all of Israel?

The Lord sent Nathan the prophet to David, and when he entered his presence, he told this story: "A rich man and a poor man lived in the same town. The rich man owned a lot of sheep and cattle, but the poor man had only one little lamb that he had bought and raised. The lamb became a pet for him and his children. He even let it eat from his plate and drink from his cup and sleep in his lap. The lamb was like one of his own children.

One day someone came to visit the rich man, but the rich man didn't want to kill any of his own sheep or cattle and serve it to the visitor. So he stole the poor man's little lamb and served it instead."

David was furious with the rich man and said to Nathan, "I swear by the living Lord that the man who did this deserves to die! And because he didn't have any pity on the poor man, he will have to pay four times what the lamb was worth."

Then Nathan told David: "You are the rich man. Now listen to what the Lord God of Israel says to you" (II Samuel 12:1–7).

Nathan's choice of a conduit to communicate God's message is amazing. David's cultural background was that of a shepherd. What more natural way to get to David's heart (along with communicating to his mind) than to tell a story

45

about how a rich man unnecessarily and cruelly oppressed a poor man, taking away the only sheep the poor man had, the beloved lamb for which he cared so deeply? The narrative builds on the pathos of the situation: The poor man loved that little ewe lamb, Nathan said. "He reared it himself, and it grew up in his home with his own sons. It ate from his dish, drank from his cup and nestled in his arms; it was like a daughter to him."

David's reaction clearly indicates that Nathan's story hit the mark. "David was very angry, and burst out, 'As the Lord lives, the man who did this deserves to die! He shall pay for the lamb four times over, because he has done this and shown no pity.'"

This is marvelous narrative theology! In the story itself God conveyed his intent—to be subsequently explained propositionally and applied personally. But there is another more profound element here. The story has such power because Nathan used David's cultural perspective as the vehicle for the message. Only a shepherd would react so strongly, so passionately, so immediately to the story. We know that David himself had cared for sheep; he had himself carried the ewe lambs in his arms. David's deepest faith relationship with God was entwined in the metaphor of sheep and shepherd. He had written, "The Lord is my shepherd, I will not want."

However, Nathan was not simply finding a handy metaphorical device to gain David's attention. Rather, Nathan conveyed God's intention as a constellation of profound concepts by way of a cultural metaphor that David would immediately grasp. The cultural background of Nathan's story is not extraneous to the message; neither is it a barrier to the message or a distraction from the message. Rather, it is the essential instrument that carries the message to David's heart and mind. This intimate relationship of message and culture in Gospel proclamation is the subject of this chapter. And for western missionaries, pastors, and evangelists, this step in the process of communicating the Gospel is especially important.

Since the Fundamentalist/Modernist debates of the 1920s, North American evangelicals have tended to assume that theology is not affected by culture. Truth was to be found in the Bible. The Bible was propositionally understood; it said what it said, meant what it said, and was to be taken at face value. Within this perspective, few people asked: Who is reading the text? On what basis is the text being read? What do people see in it? What cultural assumptions influence our reading of the text? Evangelicals tended to perpetuate a myth that theology is somehow separated from culture as if it were a set of universal truths with no cultural attachment.

We open this chapter emphasizing the cultural context of enscripturation because of a crucial theological point that has to do with the way culture impacts the reading of Scripture. Not only does Scripture come wrapped in culture, but the worldview of that original context influences the way the text interacts with all subsequent contexts. This has significant theological ramifications, for not only is revelation contextualized, but human understanding of a message is also, at all times, culture-bound. People view what God has said from a perspective strongly influenced by the worldview in which it was initially proclaimed and their own cultural perspective. Due in part to worldview, or cultural biases, all people are predisposed to read their perspective into a text and ignore other aspects of a text that do not make sense from that perspective. These natural biases impact how people read the Bible and how they apply the Bible to their life. We must be conscious of this hermeneutical issue because it has profound implications on the entire process of theological development that emerges from appropriate communication of the Gospel.

THEOLOGY IS IMPACTED
BY CULTURAL DYNAMICS

The myth that theology is somehow pure, devoid of cultural contamination, is a direct reflection of a modernist, dichotomist worldview that creates a split between what people think and how they act in a given cultural context. If we held to the hypothesis that truth, theology, and knowing God are somehow independent of culture, then examining the cultural background that colors the narrative of Scripture would make little sense. However, culture always provided the context in which the events of the Bible took place and should be accounted for whenever God's truth encounters a new context today.

There is no such thing as pure theology; all theologies are local theologies. Seen this way, western theology is probably one of the most culture-bound of all theological systems. Impacted by Aristotelian logic and the Enlightenment, westerners tend to read the biblical text with a set of glasses quite different from those of people in Africa, Asia, Latin America, or Oceania. The real problem over the last 150 years of theological education around the world is that well-meaning missionaries too often gave the impression that theology had to be systematized in a western, propositionally dependent way, therefore not tied to any particular time, place, or culture. Theological education was considered unchangeable and was to be exported to the ends of the earth. Few questioned the logic of the system. In seminaries around the world, students continue to learn "systematic" theology, often taught to merely repeat what others (mostly westerners) said about God in the past. Rarely are they encouraged to inquire about the perspective at hand when a particular theologian developed certain ideas, or ask what impact those ideas had on the people of that context.

In other words, students are seldom challenged to consider the culture out of which particular theological ideas emerged—the sociological and anthropological issues of the moment. Typically, theology students the world over have been taught to repeat the final product of theological thinking—reflection that, despite its initial relevance to the moment, becomes increasingly irrelevant when passed on to other contexts with different prevailing assumptions. Sadly, students in nonwestern cultures are seldom encouraged to analyze their own cultural context or develop thoughts about the local implications of Scripture. Jean-Marc Elà's book, *My Faith as an African*, for example, is a sad commentary on the damage done to people who are not allowed to examine their traditional theology, taught instead to impose the theological reflections of outsiders on their own cultural contexts (Elà, 1988).

Revelation does not happen in a vacuum. It always takes place within a particular worldview, in a particular cultural setting: contexts like Abraham under the trees at Mamre, Moses on the top of Mount Sinai with the people clamoring to have a God they could see, or Nathan helping David understand the depth of his sin. God always comes to humans in the midst of life, often surprising those who experience him. Scripture always enters culture; it is "Christianity in culture" (Kraft, 1979). The Bible comes "wrapped," so to speak, in culture, and the communication of God's intent is always a cultural event. Naked, unwrapped revelation is an impossibility!

Many western Christians support anthropologically sound translations for Bibleless peoples, but insist on using literal translations for themselves. This is ironic and raises some interesting questions about the efficacy of how to communicate the Gospel at home. Those translations, so near and dear to many Christians, are full of language the average Christian today (let alone unbelievers on the street) does not understand; words like "grace," "propitiation," "sacrifice," and "sanctification." G. C. Berkouwer notes, "The conviction has gradually become stronger that the human character of Scripture is not an accidental or peripheral condition of the Word of God. . . . [We have] a tendency to minimize the human in order to emphasize fully its divine character and yet these two [do not contradict each other] at all" (Berkouwer, 1975:18, 19). Berkouwer continues, "The historical relatedness of the Christian faith makes it impossible for us to take refuge in a timeless *kerygma*" (Berkouwer, 1975:28). "Just hearing or reading it does not necessarily entail a clear understanding of it. Chasms may open when Scripture is handled in a way that does not do justice to its words. It is even possible to stand within the bounds of Scripture itself and yet to twist it" (Berkouwer, 1975:109). If we are to communicate effectively, we must use words in a context that conveys the intent of the original message. If people are to understand the words, they must appreciate what the words mean—we need to present the message in a manner that reveals God's hiddenness, not hide God in the technicality of the language. God speaks all languages spoken by all the peoples of the globe. Therefore we must grasp the communicational and anthropological issues as well as the theological concerns of Gospel communication.

APPROACHES TO SCRIPTURE

In chapter 2 we emphasized the need for a closed canon as a fundamental theological presupposition. Without reopening the vast literature pertaining to the development of the canon, we simply want to state that as a corpus of what God has said the canon serves as the starting point for theologizing. Inasmuch as the hermeneutical process should begin with Scripture in order to allow for Gospel proclamation, so it stands to reason that a theology based on that proclamation must have a closed canon as its starting point.

The New Testament ends either with those who themselves walked with Jesus or with those who received the reports of those who did. Thus it is a christological issue of the uniqueness of Jesus that serves as a key criterion for inclusion in the canon. An important hermeneutical question is: How can we work within the canon and yet relate that information to present-day people without changing the original intent of the author who is ultimately God? For the answer we can look to how the New Testament writers handled the Old Testament text, for they had a similar problem.

A Biblical Model for Theological Development

As we work with the New Testament when seeking to communicate truth to others, we are amazed at what the New Testament writers did with the Old Testament. Remember, the Old Testament for them was comparable to what the entire Bible is for us today. The way the New Testament writers (including a learned scholar and exegete like the apostle Paul) approached the Old Testament might help us understand how the Holy Spirit enabled them to bridge between the Old Testament cultures and the New Testament world. Knowing how the New Testament handles the Old Testament may suggest a model for our reading of the Bible today. It could help us appreciate the biblical text, apply meaning to our present circumstances, and hint at the amazing communicability of Scripture. Also, New Testament authors may suggest ways in which we can use the whole of Scripture to apply it to circumstances in our day.

For example, an examination of Acts chapter 2 and Acts chapter 15 can help us see how Luke used the Old Testament Scriptures available to him. The event recorded in Acts chapter 2 followed a particular sequence. The Holy Spirit came. Those who had been timid and afraid then burst out onto the street, and the people who heard them thought they were drunk. Then in verse fourteen Peter addressed the crowd and clearly demonstrated a contextual, culturally appropriate approach. He began by reminding the gathered crowd (who were all hearing in their own languages the wonderful things that God had done, 2:11) that these communicators were not drunk, as it was only nine o'clock in the morning. Then he explained the meaning of what they were seeing at that moment.

In the context of recent events in Jerusalem, they were experiencing, Peter affirmed, the completion of what had been foretold by the prophet Joel. Peter then jumped back several centuries to recall the dreams and visions that Joel had promised as future events that would demonstrate the pouring out of the Holy Spirit. He provided an explanation (a hermeneutic) that enabled the crowd to make the connection between Joel's prophecy and the activities of Jesus of Nazareth. As a man accredited by God through miracles, wonders, and signs, Jesus had walked among them over the past several years. Peter then applied this understanding to what the crowd had just experienced in Jerusalem. He described Jesus as the one whom God had allowed to be handed over to the Jewish authorities in order to accomplish his own purpose.

Now Peter did some masterful hermeneutic of the Old Testament. He quoted David as saying, "I saw the Lord always before me. Because he is at my right hand . . . my heart is glad and my tongue rejoices . . . because you will not abandon me to the grave nor will you let your holy one see decay" (Acts 2:25, 26). Peter (as reported by Luke) then used these words to prove that Jesus was this same Lord, since he had been resurrected and his body did not see decay. Then he went on to proclaim himself and the others to be witnesses of Jesus' resurrection. Therefore, the gathered crowd was seeing what God had promised long ago. Incarnation and redemption were manifested in the life, death, and resurrection of Jesus of Nazareth, and these communicators, through the power of the Holy Spirit, were simply ensuring that those gathered did not miss the message. Peter used Scripture to validate what was happening. It had been predicted and now they were seeing it fulfilled through those whom they had heard speaking these wonderful things in their own languages.

The manifestation of multilingual hearing served as further evidence. To ensure they understood God's intent, the Holy Spirit communicated the message in the language and cultural mode the people knew best. For his part, Peter provided the meaning of Joel's text by interpreting the prophecy in such a way that people responded appropriately. The hearers considered the message relevant and demonstrated their understanding by believing and responding through baptism. The little band of 120 believers immediately grew to over 3,000, a wonderful example of church growth as well as the appropriate contextualization of hermeneutical principles.

Luke narrates how the Gospel was proclaimed through Peter's use of the Old Testament to impact the receptors in his context and enable the people to understand God's message. The passage concludes with Luke narrating that the people of Jerusalem were "amazed by the many miracles and wonders that the apostles worked" (Acts 2:43). He presents the Joel passage (signs, wonders, and prophecy) through Peter's account of Jesus' miracles, wonders, and signs, and then provides his own commentary, noting that on that day the people had experienced further miracles and wonders. The repetition demonstrates the theologizing process—exegete the text, understand the context, and apply a new hermeneutical interpretation of its meaning for the present circumstances. Luke's presentation provides an ideal summary of the technical dimension of communication we present later in chapter 5.

The account of the first Jerusalem council found in Acts 15:12–21 provides another example of this exegetical/hermeneutical process that leads to the development of theology. In Acts chapter 10, the Holy Spirit came to Cornelius and his household. Through this event, the apostles discovered that God loves the Gentiles and wants to covenant with them just as much as with Jewish believers. This was a revolutionary idea for first-century Jews who believed in Jesus as the Messiah of the Old Testament. Then in Acts chapter 15 James is the one doing the theological reflection. That is, he communicates their Scriptures into the current context. He quotes from the prophets, beginning by noting that God had promised to rebuild David's fallen house, so "that the remnant may seek the Lord and all the Gentiles who bear my name" (Acts 15:17). He applied this to his context by saying that it was his judgment, based on the prophecy, that they should not make it difficult for the Gentiles to turn to God. He then proceeded to suggest the four most basic laws the Gentiles ought to respect, being free to disregard the rest of the laws of Jewish ritual. The Council of Jerusalem then accepted James' position. The viewpoint was written up in the form of a letter and sent to Gentile believers in Antioch, Syria, and Cilicia as authoritative. The Jerusalem Council affirmed that, "It seemed good to the Holy Spirit and to us" (v. 28). Again, we see the model: exegete Scripture within its own historical grammatical and cultural context, provide a transitional hermeneutic to the circumstances, and draw out the theological principle that relates the two. For James this was an example of illumination that God saw fit to reveal to Luke and the first-century church leaders.

Avoid Additions and Subtractions to the Bible

Throughout this book, we are suggesting that the methodology we use today for understanding Scripture should be similar to what the New Testament writers followed when they adapted the Old Testament to their first-century context. We understand that the New Testament writers were working under the special revelation of the Holy Spirit. That was the point of the canonical criteria we noted in chapter 2. Our own hermeneutic of the Scripture is clearly not of the same kind. We do not theologize under direct revelatory inspiration of the Holy Spirit, nor do our writings qualify for the canon. Yet the same Holy Spirit illumines our understanding, just as it illumined the disciples. The Holy Spirit reminds us and helps us to understand Jesus' words, just as the Holy Spirit did for the New Testament writers (John 14:26). Thus we believe we can borrow for our day the hermeneutical method used by the New Testament authors in order to communicate the same message of God's intent in contemporary contexts.

We believe there is inherent in God's revelation a quality of "communicability" of the message and an openness of hermeneutic that is made possible through the illumination of the Holy Spirit. This allows for theological development. As Lamin Sanneh (1989) rightly notes, the Bible is not a static, cut-in-stone text like the Qur'an in Islam. The Bible gives us a dynamic, "infinitely translatable" Gospel message. It does not require countless layers of added information, as if the text itself could not be touched.

For the Pharisees of Jesus' day the Torah had become a static, unchanging, petrified text. To make it applicable for their day, they had to add the Targums to explain every jot and tittle of the law. The New Testament breaks this static pattern and does something wonderfully dynamic, living, and developmental. This dynamic model is the one we want to apply as effective communicators of this same "word" today. This dynamic model enables us to see Scripture not as a static, unchanging book, but rather as a letter from God to us. It is a love letter that enables God to interact with the creatures God created and, through that interaction, impact human lives and call people to contemplate God, to reflect theologically in the midst of Gospel proclamation.

While we must not add to the New Testament, neither should we subtract from it. By "subtracting" we mean not understanding its fullest scope and depth and thereby not adequately communicating God's true message. The church has decided that there is something unique about the revelation of God as expressed in the Bible through the historical development of the Old and New Testaments, concluding with the apostles. However, this closed canon must be dynamically interpreted in its application to every age. Its deep meanings must be understood as wide and profound as necessary to encompass each new context encountered today, including the new postmodern era.

Here Gospel communicators need to walk a fine line. We must understand God's message as communicated in Scripture, yet we need to avoid two extremes: on the one hand an open canon to which we add our own self-styled revelation, and on the other a closed text that is static, untouchable, and without meaning for today. We seek to proclaim God's message to the people of the twenty-first century. If we stretch too far and open the canon, we move toward universalism, relativism, and in fact violate the heart of Scripture as truth. If we do not go far enough, the Bible becomes a closed box, an untouchable text that cannot be applied to contexts other than those to which it was originally addressed. If we follow the New Testament writers, we can allow their model for theological development to guide us today. We must leave room for expanding our understanding as and whenever the text enters a new context that provides a different perspective. Hermeneutics, with its focus on context, attempts to get inside the author's head in order to understand the content. Taking account of the context of the initial communication and its manner of presentation enables us to infer an author's intent. To do that we need exegesis, which is the analysis of the grammar and structure of the source text. Once understood we can take what was said and connect it, recommunicate it through translation into a contemporary language and culture with all its particularity. In short, both hermeneutics and exegesis are necessary. It is a matter of both-and, not either/or. The Bible, then, must be the source of always-new hermeneutical understanding that provides the way for theological development in new contexts. David Bosch calls this way of thinking "critical hermeneutics" (Bosch 1991: 23).

CRITICAL HERMENEUTICS
THROUGH MISSION PARADIGMS[2]

Before his untimely death in 1992, Bosch was able to finish what will be considered his magnum opus—*Transforming Mission*. One of the most helpful parts of this monumental work is the hermeneutical methodology he illustrates. Bosch begins by affirming:

> We cannot, with integrity, reflect on what mission might mean today unless we turn to the Jesus of the New Testament, since our mission is [tied to Jesus' person and ministry]. . . . To affirm this is not to say that all we have to do is to establish what mission meant for Jesus and the early church and then define our missionary practice in the same terms, as though the whole problem can be solved by way of a direct application of Scripture. . . . [Because of both historical and sociological gaps between then and now], a historico-critical study may help us to comprehend what mission was for Paul and Mark and John but it will not immediately tell us what we must think about mission in our own concrete situation. (1991: 22–23)

Bosch then offers a new approach to the problem by drawing from the theory of paradigm construction that Hans Küng and David Tracy (1989) adapted from the philosophy of science.[3] Bosch suggests that we recognize that self-definitions are offered in the biblical text as well as in our modern contexts. Thus "the approach called for requires an interaction between the self-definition of early Christian authors and actors and the self-definition of today's believers who wish to be inspired and guided by those early witnesses"

(1991: 23). This in turn would move us to reread the biblical text, incorporating the newer sociological analysis of the Bible in its various contexts. With this as background we can then go forward to a series of self-definitions of mission for today's contexts.

> The critical hermeneutic approach goes beyond the (historically-interesting) quest of making explicit the early Christian self-definitions. . . . It desires to encourage dialogue between those self-definitions and all subsequent ones, including those of ourselves and our contemporaries. . . . The challenge to the study of mission may be described . . . as relating the always-relevant Jesus event of twenty centuries ago to the future of God's promised reign by means of meaningful initiatives for the here and now. . . .
>
> The point is that there are no simplistic or obvious moves from the New Testament to our contemporary missionary practice. The Bible does not function in such a direct way. There may be, rather, a range of alternative moves which remain in deep tension with each other but may nevertheless all be valid (Bosch, 1991: 23–24).

Following this method, Bosch examines what he calls the "missionary paradigms" of Matthew, Luke, and Paul. He does not try to reconcile the distinct paradigms of mission he finds in the New Testament. Although he demonstrates the internal coherence and consistency of each paradigm, he shows no compulsion to demonstrate coherence or consistency among them. In fact, he seems to feel that the breadth of their differences may offer new linkages between the New Testament paradigms and the five other paradigms of mission that he traces throughout the mission history of the church.[4]

One way to build on Bosch's hermeneutical method is to approach Scripture from the perspective of a number of themes and subthemes (or motifs) of God's action in the world. We find it useful to think of the Bible as a tapestry of interwoven themes in the midst of multiple contexts. In figure 3.1 the Bible is presented as a tapestry, which yields a perspective simultaneously involving a view "from above" and "from below." The themes may be approached from above because they are the action of God in history. They are from below because they occur in the midst of human history in the context of the lives of men and women. By viewing the Scriptures as an interwoven tapestry, we can affirm the Bible as a unified whole and also deal intentionally with the diversity of the history and cultures of the Bible (Glasser, 1992: 9; Van Engen, 1991: 160–166). This is not an allegorical approach, nor is it purely literalist. We are not advocating a simple, one-to-one correspondence of biblical response to our perceived needs, nor is it strictly a matter of discovering "dynamic equivalence" as Kraft (1979), following the lead of Nida and Taber (1981), suggested. Rather, we see an intimate interrelationship of text and new contexts through the vehicle of

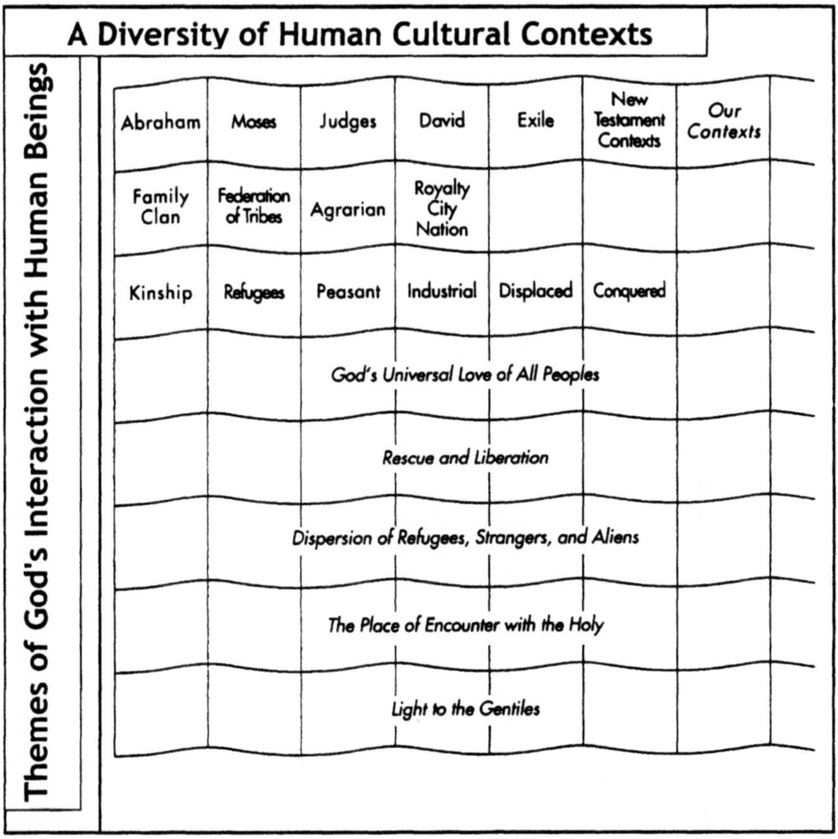

A Diversity of Human Cultural Contexts

	Abraham	Moses	Judges	David	Exile	New Testament Contexts	Our Contexts
	Family Clan	Federation of Tribes	Agrarian	Royalty City Nation			
	Kinship	Refugees	Peasant	Industrial	Displaced	Conquered	
			God's Universal Love of All Peoples				
			Rescue and Liberation				
		Dispersion of Refugees, Strangers, and Aliens					
			The Place of Encounter with the Holy				
			Light to the Gentiles				

Themes of God's Interaction with Human Beings

Figure 3.1. The Bible as Tapestry: The Warp and Woof of God's Missional Intent

particular themes or motifs that bridge the text's initial context with today's contexts of mission.

This, then, provides creative interaction of word and deed throughout the history of God's missional activity. Such a critical hermeneutic helps us get away from finding a few proof-texts or isolated nuggets in the Bible to buttress our mission agendas. It goes beyond the search for a few key words of the Gospel that might lend themselves to missiological reflection (Berkhof and Potter 1964). It is broader and deeper than a set of commands that may be external to the people of God and to their contexts, both old and new.

Approaching the Bible as a tapestry calls us to take seriously the uniqueness of each biblical context in terms of its historical, sociological, anthropological, and linguistic peculiarities. We must be able, therefore, to use all that we have learned so far from source, redaction, historical, rhetorical, and canonical criticism (Muller, 1991: 194–196). But we must also go beyond all of that to ask the missiological question of God's intention in terms of the *missio Dei* as it occurs in word and deed in each particular context (Bosch, 1991: 21). This method involves a critical hermeneutic that attempts to discover the particular self-definition of God's people in a particular time and place—and then challenges all subsequent self-definitions, including our own.

HERMENEUTICAL THEMES
WEAVE A BIBLICAL TAPESTRY

Let us consider this tapestry approach in more detail. A tapestry is composed of a warp (vertical threads) and woof (horizontal threads) that together produce an encompassing pattern as the tapestry is woven. The vertical and horizontal threads represent various historical periods and biblical themes respectively. (See figure 3.1.) Each historical period is in interaction with biblical themes that take different shapes. This combination results in an exquisite tapestry that presents a whole pattern or picture. By viewing the Scriptures as such an interwoven tapestry, we can affirm the Bible as a unified whole, and at the same time deal with the diversity of the history and cultures of the Bible (Glasser, 1992: 9). We can take note of the ongoing development of theology as the various themes or metaphors take shape in new contexts. If we were to trace a thread from one end of the tapestry to the other, we would see how that thread is woven into always-new vertical contexts (the warp). Moving horizontally, each thread continually adds to the tapestry, yet is connected to previous patterns of which it forms a part. The weaver does not change the design in the middle of the tapestry. Each thread must follow through from beginning to end.

When we apply this analogy to Scripture, we can see how a particular idea may be the same concept, but appear differently as it courses its way through the Bible. As it makes its way, it is both informing and being informed by the ongoing process of self-disclosure by the Master Weaver. Seeing Scripture as a tapestry, then, is in contrast to a word-study or word-usage approach that does not show how ideas may be interwoven with other concepts, metaphors, analogies, discourses, and actions in each context of revelation history.

Cultural Themes Influence Theological Development

Let us consider this process of following the development of a theme by tracing the concept of knowing God in context as illustrated by the importance of great trees in the Bible. Trees are a frequent subject throughout the Bible, from Genesis to Revelation. At the start of Genesis we find the tree of "knowledge" and the tree of "life" (Gen. 2:9; 3:2–3). Later, as Abraham embarks upon his physical and spiritual journey, he sets up an altar and worships under the trees of Mamre (Cf. Gen. 12:6; 13:18; 14:13; 18:1). Apparently, the trees were a special place of revelation for him. Continuing through Scripture, we recall the cedars of Lebanon mentioned in the wisdom literature that are also shown as forming the structure of Solomon's temple (I Kings 5). Remember that the righteous person in Psalm 1 is likened to a tree planted by a stream. We are told that trees will sing the praises of their creator in Psalm 96:12 and Isaiah 55:12.

Moving into the New Testament, we see trees appear in Jesus' parables. For example, Jesus rebukes the tree that does not bear fruit (Mark 11:12–24; Matt. 21:18–22; cf. Isa. 34:4; Jer. 8:13). Jesus affirms that one way people may be known to us is by their fruit (Matt. 3:10; 12:33). Similarly, we can learn a lesson from the mustard seed: It is small and insignificant but grows to support a whole world of teaming life (Matt. 13:31). In John 14, the church is represented as the branches of a vine. At the end of his life on earth, Jesus hangs on the cross, sometimes described as a "tree" (Acts 5:30). In Romans, Paul speaks of the Gentiles as being grafted into the "tree of salvation" (Rom. 11:24). And in Revelation 22, we are shown a picture of the tree of life "whose leaves are for the healing of the nations" (Rev. 22:2). The Bible comes full circle, with the tree of life providing an important but very different picture at the extremes, yet integrating the importance of life as a metaphor of God's intent for his creation. What Adam lost, Christ regained, and we find the true tree, not on earth but in heaven.[5]

The importance of trees continues to the present. Many traditional religions include among their symbols some form of a fertility tree. In southwestern Mexico along the Pacific coast, the Olmec civilization flourished centuries before Christ. The Olmecs believed that the Ceiba tree (a very large tree with an umbrella-shaped canopy) was a fertility tree. If a woman was barren she had only to be tied to the Ceiba overnight and she would conceive. Even today cattle ranchers in the area insist that a Ceiba needs to be a part of their ranch so the cows will have many healthy calves.

Continuing the thread, one only has to stand for a few minutes under the great redwoods of central California to feel a deep sense of the age, beauty, greatness, and mystery that emanates from such trees. Here, within our contemporary world, we have a connection to the trees under which Abraham sat. Yet the trees under which Abraham met God point us forward through time in such a way as to help us appreciate more deeply what the cross was all about. Here we combine the past text with a contemporary context that understands the significance of "tree" as a semantic image of discourse used to communicate new meaning in a new context never envisioned by the biblical author, but known to God.

The woven tapestry offers a deeper appreciation for the whole of Scripture: God's infinite connectability with human beings. The depth of God's love for human beings brings God into their midst (incarnation) and provides salvation (redemption). These two great themes weave their way through the entire

Bible. In many contexts, themes like these provide us with an understanding of God's intent and enable theological development as people in different contexts apply these themes to their lives. What we see here is the historical development of theology amidst the infinite communicability of the Gospel message whenever and wherever it may be found.

A tapestry approach to Scripture enables us to see a progression of development in the symbols God utilized to communicate God's intent for humanity. In an increasingly relativistic, postmodern context, the message must be seen as constant (referring to God's being and intent), yet always changing in the manner it is communicated in a variety of contexts. This involves an effort to present a deep-level understanding of the Gospel in ways that are appropriate to a particular people who hold a specific set of assumptions about the world. Divine revelation flows through the conduit of human contexts, illumined by the Holy Spirit in the lives of those who come to know God in context.

Revelation as a Demonstration of Hermeneutics

Arthur Glasser points out that revelation itself has a history—a rather lengthy one, in fact. There is considerable movement throughout the Bible as God deals with the human condition, first through creation, then through a people, and finally through a God-man who influenced a group of people who turned their world upside down (Acts 17:7). Glasser says it well:

> Even revelation itself has a history for history means movement and revelation in history must be regarded as something linear, moving toward a consummation worthy of the God of history. Hence, the Old Testament is not a collection of ethical generalizations, theological affirmations, orderly analyses of doctrines, or formal prescriptions of personal duty—all detached from the dimensions of time, culture and situation. (1989: 34)

The Gospel message is conveyed through particular cultural means in specific contexts to a particular people. Though it is always the same message, it comes to people in forms particular to them. The word becomes flesh and dwells among people everywhere (John 1:14).

An example of God's unexpected means of self-disclosure can be seen in the exilic Psalms. In Psalm 137:1–4, the exiled people of Israel moan, "By the rivers of Babylon—there we sat down and there we wept when we remembered Zion.... How can we sing the Lord's songs in a foreign land?" The text implies, of course, that as exiles forcibly taken to Babylon from Palestine, far from their homeland, from Jerusalem and the Temple, they could not sing the Lord's song in this distant place.

But these people did not read their Scriptures. If they had read more carefully or had listened more attentively, they would have realized that in Babylon they were in fact closer geographically to where God originally called Abraham than they had been when they were in Jerusalem. They were a people not because of Jerusalem but because of their collective experience in Egypt—another place of exile. They should have seen that their existence as a people was tied to their relationship with God, not to a place. Their attitude questions the infinite translatability of God's truth. The right answer to their question might have been, "The Lord's praises were designed to be sung everywhere, including foreign lands. You are in fact a pilgrim people. Wandering Arameans were their ancestors and so they too are aliens and strangers" (Deut. 26:5).

Throughout Scripture, and particularly in texts like Romans chapter 1, natural revelation is assumed. The apostle Paul claims that all people have a way of knowing God so they have no excuse.[6] Paul points out that when people are left to their natural inclinations concerning what they can see from natural revelation, they invariably end up worshipping that which has been created rather than the Creator. What Paul affirms in Romans 1 and 2 is modeled throughout the Old and New Testaments. There are certain things people know about God. It may be insufficient, but it is clear to all humans. As the Psalmist says, "The heavens declare God's glory and the earth demonstrates what He has done in creation" (Ps. 19:1). Romans 2 goes on to tell us that people chose against God's plan in creating them. They rebelled against that which they knew to be true, which was revealed to some extent in their mythology and lived out in various ways in their cultural ideals.

At this point, Paul shifts his focus to talk about the law and about special revelation. This was given specifically to that motley group of escapees from Egypt during the Exodus. But God called them "God's People." He had set them apart and wanted to ensure they knew who God was and relate to them in a covenantal fashion that built upon that special relationship with Abraham, Isaac, and Jacob. Throughout the book of Romans, Paul weaves an argument that shows that even with special revelation, people chose to misinterpret and deny God's reality, despite what they knew. In fact, general and special revelation weave their way together throughout the Scriptures.

God's general revelation provides a link to God, while the specifics of what God reveals to particular people emerge from the particularity of their time and place. God wants people to discover what God's covenantal love means to them in their circumstances. This interplay between general and special revelation is a recurring idea that weaves its way through the tapestry of Scripture as a source of encouragement to those who hear "the word of God" for the first time. It is also a note of chastisement to those who should know better. In other words, God uses all of creation as a stage for his self-revelation—and God will communicate his intent always in new and relevant ways. God's surface-level methods of conveying deep-level significance are varied, surprising, and unexpected. So much so that Paul exclaims, "Who has known the mind of the Lord? Or who has given him advice? . . . Oh the depth of the riches and wisdom and knowledge of God! How unsearchable are his judgments and his paths beyond tracing out!" (Rom. 11:34, 33).

The Bible is full of illustrations that show how human beings are able to explore the depths of God's self-revelation in constantly new ways. In John chapter 3, Jesus met with Nicodemus and talked about wind and about being born again. Nicodemus was mystified, but what Jesus was really telling him was encapsulated in the theme of God's relationship with God's People. God surrounds people like the wind or like a mother's womb. He knows them, he forms them, and he desires to be in relationship with them. Evangelical Christians often quote John 3:16 and think they know what they are talking about: the Gospel in a nutshell. Yet too often they forget that Jesus's message was said (as John redacts his Gospel) in the context of the arrogant self-righteousness of Nicodemus.

Read the whole story of Nicodemus's encounter with Jesus (as already presented in chapter 2). Watch what Jesus did with the Old Testament. He reinterpreted it for Nicodemus to understand. He expressed Old Testament truths in a way that called for Nicodemus's conversion and transformation: "You must be born again!" (John 3:7). That nutshell Gospel takes on different colors when we see it lived out by Christ's disciples in different cultures around the world. Scripture brings God's love to bear upon the very existence of human beings created in God's image—everywhere in the world. Gospel proclamation calls people to relationships that are always new: first vertically with God and then horizontally with other human beings. The good news is that we do not need to seek after God, for he has already found us and desires fellowship with us: "While we were still sinners, Christ died for us" (Rom. 5:8). This brings us back to our calling; we seek a Gospel presentation upon which others can build a theology that enables them, in their context, to know God.

THE HISTORICAL
DEVELOPMENT OF DOGMA

Throughout the foregoing discussion, we have assumed that a Christian understanding of God (theologically known as dogma) can undergo historical development. We now approach this issue that stands between an appraisal of the Bible in its textual form only and hermeneutics as an appreciation of God's intent—the message both generally and specifically.

The New Catholicity

One of the most helpful and fruitful discussions of the concept of the historical development of dogma occurred in the early 1960s at the Second Vatican Council of the Roman Catholic Church. The question as to whether theological doctrines (dogma) can develop over time has been a topic of discussion and theological reflection on the part of Roman Catholic theologians more so than Protestants. One of the most prominent Protestant theologians to consider this problem was G. C. Berkouwer, working with reference to his Roman Catholic counterpart, Hans Küng. Berkouwer was one of only a handful of Protestant theologians officially invited to observe the proceedings at the Second Vatican Council. Based on what he observed, Berkouwer wrote *The Second Vatican Council and the New Catholicism,* which contains a helpful chapter discussing the historical development of dogma (Berkouwer, 1965: 57–88).[7]

After Vatican I in 1870, with its emphasis on the infallibility of the Pope, certain pronouncements made by the Pope when speaking *ex cathedra* (from the cathedral, or from St. Peter's holy chair) came to be viewed as unchangeable and unchanging dogma. Not only were the Scriptures considered unchanging, but so were the *ex cathedra* theological pronouncements made by the Pope concerning Scripture.[8] Unchangeable and unchanging—that is how Vatican I saw the church's Gospel proclamation. Truth was never to be changed again. The words used to express the supposedly unchangeable truths became the equivalent of what linguists and anthropologists would consider "dead metaphors." It was no longer symbolic; the words themselves contained the meaning.[9]

The Second Vatican Council (1962–1965) called for rethinking the matter of the historical development of dogma (Flannery, 1975). The operative concept was "the new Catholicism" and the catchword was *aggiornamento.* This council maintained that there is movement through history by the Holy Spirit in the midst of the church. As the church moves through history, it deepens its understanding of the Gospel. It does not rewrite or change the Scriptures, but it does deepen its understanding and interpretation of them. That means that what is true is not unchangeable. It can be true at that moment, in that historical context, yet be understood differently later. Without this kind of critical thinking about historical development, there can be no multicultural evangelism. Without the development of theology through history, there can be little communication from one era to another or from one culture to another.

A Perspective on Change

Evangelical Protestant missions place a high value on translation, contextualization, and the local church. They support linguists like those in the United

Bible Societies, Wycliffe Bible Translators, and other translation agencies. They have been enamored with the product: Bibles in the hands of the people. But Evangelicals tend to become uncomfortable when considering the possibility of movement, change, and development over time of the initial meaning of Gospel proclamation in a new context of communication. They show uncertainty about transposing that same intent in the text to new cultural frameworks around the world. It seems that even Eugene Nida tends to view faithfulness predominantly as involving faithful transcription of the text, rather than a faithful relationship as God's intention conveyed by the text. For Nida, it is important to make sure that the right words have been used in a particular language and culture—that is, "the closest natural equivalent" (Nida and Taber, 1982: 12, 13). This is why translation checking and the process of testing key terms is so important. However, if we follow this approach to its logical conclusion, it becomes text-bound and focuses on the words as the objects of study. Once the right key term has been established, it must be used because it is a "functional equivalent" (de Waard and Nida, 1986).

By way of contrast, we wish to emphasize the importance of focusing on the relational aspects of God's intent rather than the propositional structure alone. The New Testament does not affirm "Truth equals Jesus Christ." Rather, the resurrected, living Jesus Christ says, "I am the Truth" (John 14:6). Therefore, just as we have discussed Paul's approach in Romans, so the message can be radically contextualized and adapted to lead people to Christ, to new understandings in new contexts. The unchangeability of dogma in Roman Catholic circles was the unchangeability of propositions. Similarly in the evangelical world, the text itself has too often been seen as sacred in itself. It is held up as holy, and not to be changed.

When communicators take such a position, they tend to work with the text in a horizontal fashion like any other literary text. They merely present (often through translation) the propositional words considered to be the truth with little concern for the contexts in which the message was originally shaped. Similarly, they sometimes remove the contexts into which the propositions will be communicated from the message of the text. Lost is a concern for whether the receptors will come to know God's intention for them. Based on such assumptions, translators and preachers will seek to come up with other apparently equivalent words that they believe will communicate the concepts to the new audience.[10] By this, standard communicators themselves become the judges of truth (or faithfulness) governed by their conception of the meaning of the original words. Lost is the question of whether the new receptors, in fact, can come to know the intent of the Source. Their own theological assumptions and biases may blind Gospel communicators from understanding God's intent in the passage. In such a case, proclaimers need to reexamine the theological assumptions they bring to the task, a topic we develop at some length in chapter 6.

A typical approach involves propositionalizing the text and finding the nearest equivalent in the language of the receptor audience. Ultimately, the accumulation of similar decisions results in communication that is a propositional reflection of a particular theology that may or may not reflect the original intent. Rather than gaining an understanding of God's intent, the members of the emerging church may receive a distilled text that reflects mostly the perspective of the intermediate communicator. How might a new audience understand and be able to respond to God's love for them and their world with this as the process by which they receive "the word of the Lord"? By posing such a question, communicators are drawn to examine a constellation of understandings more profound than finding an equivalent word or proposition in a receiver's language. This is an issue of faith, of theology, of knowing God in context.

SUMMARY

Faithful communication is a hermeneutical task. It is Gospel communication. It is mission. Such proclamation needs to reflect the concerns of the local church. At times, receptors who come to know Jesus Christ can help develop theologically equivalent concepts that transmit God's intent in the new circumstances. We see, then, that communicating the Gospel involves the church as a hermeneutical community, a community of disciples of Jesus.

If faithful communication is not based on propositions, but rather seeks to present the intent of God's message to human beings, then the question becomes: does this new audience know God better? This is an epistemological question. God's desire is that the receptors may come to know God in ways that may be deeper than even the communicator may have known before. At this point, Gospel communicators may come to understand something about God's intent that they did not previously know. The contemporary context in which they now communicate sheds a different light on the human understanding and apprehension of God.

Could this have happened to Nathan the prophet in telling the story about a little ewe lamb and the love its owner had for it? Did Nathan also get a glimpse of God's mercy that he had not known before? And in the way the story came crashing into David's heart, did he come to know God better? We have some indication that he did, when we read his moving words of profound repentance in Psalm 51. We would like to think that in telling and applying the story, both Nathan as the communicator and David as the receptor came to know God's message more fully. This leads us to part II where we more closely examine the communicator's task in seeking ways to foster appropriate communication.

NOTES

1. Notice the cross-cultural issue built into this story. Uriah the Hittite represents a people who had lived for many years in Canaan and were ethnically and culturally distinct from the Israelites. Uriah's name suggests that he had become a proselyte to the Israelite faith, and in II Samuel chapter 11 he is portrayed as a righteous man loyal to David.

2. The following section is adapted from Van Engen, 1996b: 39–42.

3. For examples see Barbour, 1974; Kuhn, 1962; 1977; Lakatos, 1978; and Murphy, 1990.

4. David Bosch's approach seems to closely parallel Paul Hiebert's approach to the issue from an anthropological perspective, a methodology Hiebert has called "critical contextualization" (cf. P. Hiebert, 1987; 1989a; also Hiebert and Shaw, 1995).

5. These references to trees may reflect another root metaphor. Trace the relationship between trees and what happens spiritually in the presence of those trees and you will have a powerful illustration of the connectedness of Scripture to people who, in turn, reflect God's desire to reestablish on the Golgotha tree what Adam and Eve lost at the tree of knowledge in the Garden of Eden.

6. Cf. C. Van Engen, 1996: 159–187 for a detailed discussion.

7. At the heart of Vatican II is ecclesiology, which is really about the historical development of dogma. See also Schreiter's *The New Catholicity* (1997, esp. ch. 2, 28–45).

8. At the end of the nineteenth century the modernist movement that the Pope eventually declared a heresy caused a major problem in the Roman Catholic Church. It advocated historical development of dogma. Some of it was based on an evolutionary paradigm and optimism about progress commensurate with the day. Such concepts were seen to support the creation of new discoveries and new dogma.

9. We are also describing Evangelical rationalism here. Evangelical rationalism is almost as Catholic as the Pope. As long as the right words are used, and given that the right words contain the "truth," they must, in themselves, communicate God's intent. In other words, they are not metaphoric; they are the "root." The implication for communication is profound; it becomes frozen and static.

10. Recall our argument in chapter 2 concerning Scripture being more than just another human text. We must place re-communication of biblical text into a perspective that is both vertical and horizontal so it can impact the relationships of human beings with God and with each other.

II

APPROPRIATE COMMUNICATION

The Communicators' Presentation of God's Intended Message: Theoretical Issues

> Gospel proclaimers must be aware of the hermeneutical, communicational, and cultural assumptions they bring to their task. The communicator's methodology needs to be appropriate to God's intent as developed in the text. Part II describes the Gospel communicator's task and how and where it takes place.

*I*n part II we examine the communicator's task to faithfully and appropriately present God's intended message. Here we present some key theoretical approaches for developing theological, communicational, and cultural models that provide a means of understanding how to facilitate the communication of the textual principles presented in part I. These concepts are developed in order to help communicators appreciate what they must know if they are to be engaged in appropriate proclamation. The biblical horizons into which God originally spoke can be understood better because of an awareness of communicational and cultural issues extant when God spoke (chapter 4). Applying models of communication to what God said (chapter 5) in the cultural context of communicators and their audiences alike (chapter 6) enhances communicability. This section of the book lays out the key constructs that inform our understanding of both the text (part I) and the context (part III).

• 4 •

Theologically Appropriate Communication

Theological assumptions about the text of Scripture and hermeneutical approaches to the text influence the communicator's reading of the Bible and understanding of God's intent. A constructive way to interrelate the various perspectives about God's intention is to envision a simultaneous encounter of four "horizons."

Sam and Helen Hofman spent forty years in southern Mexico, immersing themselves in the culture and worldview of the Tzeltal Mayan peoples of the highlands of the state of Chiapas. Toward the end of their time among the Tzeltal people, they were asked to lead a team of Tzeltal pastors to do a revision of the Tzeltal Bible translation. In the middle of this project, Sam wrote:

> *Yesterday I spent all day working on the translation of the word "wisdom" in Proverbs. It had previously been translated* sbijil o'tanil, *"wisdom-heart." But the translation committee changed most [of the occurrences of the word "wisdom"] to* sbijil c'op, *"wisdom-word." That fits better when it refers to a spoken proverb and good advice, but it does not cover the deeper meaning of the word "wisdom" in Proverbs where it includes faith in God, obedience to God's commands, and making discerning decisions—which is wisdom-heart. Then there is a third Tzeltal word,* sbijil jol, *"wisdom-head," which means intelligence and learning. So yesterday I went through Proverbs and decided which of the three Tzeltal words fit each verse best. It now goes back to the committee for their OK.*

Wisdom is one of the key theological concepts in Proverbs having to do with a person's relationship with God—both in terms of knowing God and in the way that knowledge is lived out in life. By way of example, Brown (2000) identifies (among other uses throughout the Old Testament) the following range of meanings for "wisdom" in the book of Proverbs (with verses that provide key examples noted immediately after):

67

- *Wise in the administration of affairs (20:26)*
- *Shrewd, crafty, cunning (30:25)*
- *Wise in one's own eyes (3:7; 26:5, 12, 16; 28:11)*
- *Prudent (16:14; 11:29; 29:8, 9, 11)*
- *Wise, ethically and religiously (10:8; 16:21; 10:1; 15:20; 13:1; 23:24; 25:12)*
- *Wise learner (14:15; 17:28; 12:15; 1:5; 18:15; 21:11; 10:14; 15:31; 9:8, 9)*
- *Wise teacher, a sage (15:7; 12:18; 15:2; 16:23; 13:14; 13:20)*
- *The wise are prosperous (21:20; 14:3; 3:35; 14:24; 24:5)*
- *The wise one is a blessing to others (11:30; 21:22; 15:12)*

Notice that almost all of these varied "meanings" of "wisdom" in Proverbs are derived from an interpretation of the author's intent within the semantic flow of the text. In English, however, it takes whole phrases instead of single Hebrew words to communicate the concept.

On the other hand, Sam Hofman discovered that the Tzeltal language was more precise than Sam's English. And the receptors (the Tzeltals) noticed that the semantic flow of the concepts influenced the intended meaning of the word "wisdom" in Proverbs. "How did you decide which Tzeltal term to use?" I asked.[1] Sam responded, "I found that I had to use all three terms. Following a contextual reading of the text, I found I had to select the most appropriate reading of the text—whatever fit best. What kind of wisdom was the text trying to talk about? I had to give this careful thought, because the Tzeltal was linguistically more precise than my own English worldview and language."

Clearly, "wisdom" also varies greatly within the New Testament and in comparison with the Old Testament. Thus, in relation to this concept, Sam discovered that he had to work with all four "horizons" that we describe in this chapter.

A HERMENEUTICAL
APPROACH TO THE BIBLE

Grant Osborne defined hermeneutics as "that science which delineates principles or methods for interpreting an individual author's meaning" (1991: 5). In his work *New Testament Exegesis*, Gordon Fee describes how he sees the difference between exegesis and hermeneutics.

> The term "exegesis" is used . . . in a consciously limited sense to refer to the historical investigation into the meaning of the biblical text. Exegesis, therefore, answers the question, What did the biblical author *mean?* It has to do with *what* he said (the content itself) and why he said it at any given point

(the literary context). Furthermore, exegesis is primarily concerned with intentionality: What did the author *intend* his original readers to understand?

Historically, the broader term for the science of interpretation which included exegesis, was hermeneutics. . . . Hermeneutics has come to focus
more on meaning as an existential reality, that is, what these ancient sacred
texts mean for us. (Fee, 1993: 27)

In terms of a hermeneutical approach to the Bible, some scholars feel that
because the text is buried in an ancient context of which we know very little
today, we cannot elucidate the original meaning and so are confined to establishing only what the text means today in our present, varied contexts. On the
other hand, Osborne, among many others, argues, as we would, "that the original meaning is a legitimate, even necessary, concern and that hermeneutics encompasses both what it meant (then) and what it means (now)" (1991: 5).

Kaiser and Silva build on this to explain that in examining a passage of
the Bible, "The question about the meaning of (a) passage can be considered
at various levels" (1994: 20). They mention the following eight levels:

1. The linguistic level: a translation from the original languages of
   Scripture.
2. The historical setting (culture, geography, etc.).
3. The teaching of the passage for today's reader.
4. The historicity of the narrative.
5. The literary setting in which the narrative takes place.
6. The broader canonical context: how does the passage relate to the
   whole canon?
7. The history of interpretation: how has this passage been understood
   throughout the history of the church?
8. The present significance of the passage (Kaiser and Silva, 1994:
   20–22).

To this we would add two more:

9. The cultural worldview of the text as compared to the worldview of
   the communicator.
10. The meaning and significance of the text for the hearers of the com-
    municator's message in the hearers' worldview.

Traditionally, hermeneutics involves the examination of, and reflection upon,
the dynamic interrelationship of at least three elements as shown in figure 4.1.

**Figure 4.1. The Three Traditional Elements of the Hermeneutical Question: Author,
Text, Communicator**

In chapter 1 we made a case for the fact that the Bible has a divine Source as well as human authors. Similarly, Kaiser and Silva affirm that, "Because the Bible purports to be a word from God, the task of locating meaning is not finished until one apprehends the purpose, scope, or reason (indeed, the theology) for which that text was written" (1994: 34). With specific reference to the Old Testament, Robert Hubbard states:

> A method that takes the text at face value, transcendent claims and all, may be the more truly objective one since it leaves all options open, even the possibility of supernatural activity in history. In actual fact, read straightforwardly, the Bible does present God as very much involved directly in the day-to-day world. Only a method that reckons with the OT's "faith" dimensions can be truly "historical exegesis"—that is, one that does full justice to all levels of meaning present in the text. (R. Hubbard et al., 1992: 35).

Thus, our hermeneutical task must include awareness of God's intention. We need to add a component to our diagram, as shown in figure 4.2.

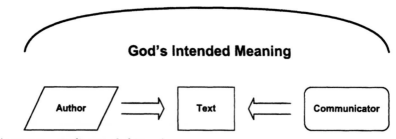

Figure 4.2.   God's Intended Meaning

Kaiser and Silva emphasize the need to include the receptor in the communication mix.

> There is no doubt that the great contribution of our [twentieth] century to the hermeneutical debate will be our concern for the reader and for the contemporary application and significance that a past meaning has for today. One must be careful, however, to follow the lead of authorial intention and to make clear any connection seen between a principle in a text and modern-day circumstances. Focusing on the significance of a text should never lead to proposing a new meaning of the text that is not actually taught in Scripture. To do otherwise is to risk the loss of authority, for such inferences would have no part in the written nature of the text and thus would not be authoritative for us today. . . . As Hirsh has pointed out, the basis for validating the meaning of any passage can only be located in the meaning (i.e., the sense) that the author intended. (1994: 44–45)

From a missiological and communicational perspective, an additional component is crucial for our hermeneutical universe—the receptor. As shown in figure 4.3, we must account for an awareness of the meaning that receptors ascribe to the communication based on their context, community, and worldview.

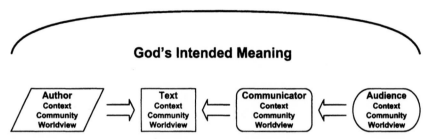

Figure 4.3. Four Elements of Gospel Communication: Author, Text, Communicator, and Receptor

BRIEF OVERVIEW OF MODERN HERMENEUTICS

Beginning with Friedrich Schleiermacher (1768–1834), whom Osborne calls "the father of modern hermeneutics" (Osborne, 1991: 368), and followed by Wilhelm Dilthey (1833–1911), the crux of the discussion has dealt with what part of the hermeneutical continuum (author, or text, or interpreter) should be emphasized. While Schleiermacher and Dilthey emphasized an author-centered hermeneutic (broadly speaking), Hans-Georg Gadamer led others in emphasizing the text, speaking of a "fusion of horizons" between that of the text and that of the interpreter. "Thus both language and text are autonomous entities with a life of their own" (Osborne, 1991: 369).[2]

Around the middle of the last century there was a convergence of interest in hermeneutics in bringing attention to the receptor rather than just the author. This convergence included the French structuralists, a growing interest in semiotics, and the works of the poststructuralists, followed by the advocates of reader-response hermeneutics moving toward deconstruction. Together, all of this pushed the conversation toward the receptor's end of the continuum, advocating a near eclipsing of the text via the subjectivity of the reader. Osborne concludes,

> On the basis first of phenomenology and then of structuralism, the emphasis has shifted further and further from any [possibility of affirming authorial intent] to stress first on pre-understanding and then on an ontological displacement of original meaning by the reader's encounter with the text. This has culminated in reader-response criticism, in which the reader recreates his own text, and in deconstruction, in which reader and text are [both] deconstructed" (Osborne, 1991: 385–386).

Fortunately, some moderating voices also call for a reexamination of the importance of both authorial intent and the autonomy of the text. While there have been a plethora of voices discussing the implications of the hermeneutical process, we find Grant Osborne and Anthony Thiselton most helpful for our purposes.[3] Both are interested in preserving authorial intent while at the same time affirming the impact that the reader's cultural horizon has on the reader's comprehension of the text. This led Thiselton to develop the concept of *The Two Horizons* (1980) and Osborne to offer the idea of *The Hermeneutical Spiral* (1991). We build on both of these contemporary theoreticians in this book.

So then, what does it mean for us to investigate the meaning of a particular passage in the Bible? Kaiser and Silva suggest, "Before continuing directly our search for the Bible's meaning, we need to look more carefully at the very word *meaning* itself. . . . Different senses of this word are intimately connected with several other key concepts of hermeneutics, including those of referent, sense, intention, and significance" (1994: 34).

For the authors of this book, exegesis relates to working with what the author said—the actual words, phrases, paragraphs, and on through to the entire semantic discourse. Hermeneutics is an examination of the presuppositions (cultural, methodological, communicational, and theological) that influence the interpretation of the meaning however it may be applied, irrespective of the forms it may take. The word "hermeneutics" is now used in several different ways, so we need to briefly present the different approaches to "hermeneutics" in order to establish what we intend by using the word.

DIFFERENT KINDS OF HERMENEUTICS

For the purpose of clarification we briefly describe five different kinds of "hermeneutics." At the outset let us be clear: hermeneutics is always a contextual issue, but there are major differences in the way hermeneutical questions have been associated with matters of contextualization.

Reading the Signs of the Times

One way the word *hermeneutics* has been used in the recent past is with reference to reading the present historical moment, seeking to understand the significance and meaning of various elements in that context as they apply to God's work in the world—and subsequently drawing out conclusions as to how the churches may participate in what God is doing in the world.

Within the World Council of Churches, from the 1950s on, hermeneutics came to mean a reading of the signs of the times throughout history. This approach involved both a historical process and analysis of the present context.

It meant discerning what God was doing in history and joining that. Deeply impacted by J. C. Hoekendijk's profound post–World War II pessimism about the church, this perspective brought about a change in the mission order, from God-church-world to God-world-church. What mattered, according to Hoekendijk, was the presence of shalom.

> World and kingdom correlate with each other. The world is conceived of as a unity, the scene of God's great acts; it is the *world* that has been reconciled (2 Cor. 5:19), the *world* that God loves (John 3:16) and that God has overcome in his love (John 16:33); the *world* is the field in which the seeds of the kingdom are sown (Matt. 13:38); the *world* is consequently the scene for the proclamation of the kingdom (Hoekendijk, 1952: 333).

Hoekendijk wanted the Kingdom of God, shalom, and service in the world to replace the church as the central locus of mission and evangelization. Hoekendijk's emphasis also gave strength to a growing awareness of the possible role the churches might play in socioeconomic and political liberation. Once the church became aware of what God was doing in the world (through a hermeneutic of the present historical, economic, and sociopolitical situation), the church was called to begin to act in ways that would support this "mission" of God. In other words, if there was any role for the church at all, it was to be a utilitarian one. The church could be accepted if it was willing to become an appropriate instrument, a useful tool, in bringing about revolutionary change. This utilitarian ecclesiology was particularly strong in Latin American theologies of liberation (Van Engen, 1996b: 155).

This perspective has strongly influenced the missiological directions of the World Council of Churches from the gathering of the International Missionary Council in Willingen in 1952, to the Canberra gathering of the Seventh Assembly of the WCC in 1991. The centerpiece of this viewpoint is a specific approach to carrying out a "hermeneutic" of the present historical moment. This approach is problematic for evangelical missiology. Such a perspective seeks to equate biblical contexts with present-day contexts—what God is doing in the world in the here and now is superimposed upon what God has already done in the biblical context—liberating people from oppression. Following this approach, the Bible ends up taking a back seat to contemporary sociopolitical issues, and the church is devalued as merely one of several possible agents of social change. This "hermeneutic" lays heavy stress on the contemporary readers of the text, downplaying the matter of God's intention.

The Hermeneutical Circle

For the past forty years, Latin Americans have been at the forefront of a second type of hermeneutics. This has to do with the "hermeneutical circle" as it was rearticulated and reinterpreted by people like Juan Luis Segundo (1976), among others.[4] The hermeneutical circle of Latin American Liberation Theology spearheaded an intentional process whereby one's contextual hermeneutic moved toward a commitment to the preferential option for the poor, which in turn opened one's eyes to reread the meaning of Scripture for today's situation (a hermeneutics of significance). This provides new lenses through which one can again reread the context of ministry.

Segundo began with the present context of a people's reality and developed four decisive steps: (1) a people's worldview or plausibility structure (to use Peter Berger's term) leads to a particular agenda or question; (2) a people's agenda, question, or existential concern provides an approach to the text; (3) understanding the text from the point of view of the people's agenda provides a particular application back to the context; and (4) that application leads to a new agenda or question that can be implemented in the context, which starts the cycle over again. This process leads to a circular structure in which present context informs the meaning of the text and maintains the entire circular flow—hence the term "hermeneutical circle."

In Segundo's methodology, certain ideas (Segundo calls them "ideologies") emerge out of a particular context examined by an interpreter with eyes that involve a "hermeneutics of suspicion."[5] These concepts are, then, a reflection of the interpreters' perspective, a hermeneutic of that situation that forces questions about the metaphors used by the people in those circumstances. Based on the new insights into the context gained in such a reexamination, the interpreters should then reread the Scriptures. As the interpreters reread the Scriptures, they see things they did not see before because they are now asking new questions that reflect a new understanding derived from the new context. Drawing from the insights the interpreters have gained from Scripture, they encounter their context anew. Figure 4.4 presents a diagram of this process.

Following this structure, some theologians have used the term "exegeting the context" to signify a paradigm of the perception of reality (which is not quite the same thing as was meant by the World Council of Churches). This process is extremely important for mission in the city. What the city looks like, its symbols and metaphors, must be interpreted. What are the root metaphors for urban peoples? If the root metaphor of city is "chaos," for example, it reflects lack of structure, and ultimately loneliness in a crowd—meaninglessness. In contrast, if the root metaphor is "order," the emphasis shifts to issues of power, law and order, and supporting and defending the powerful. If, on the other hand, the root metaphor is "harmony," the approach to the city radically changes once again.[6] Each of these metaphors has implications for missiology—transforming chaos into meaning, order into interaction—and harmony with the Creator God. The hermeneutical circle seeks to build dynamic interactivity between the contemporary context and the text of Scripture.[7]

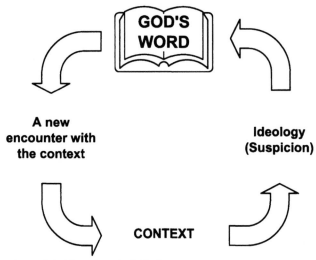

Figure 4.4.   Segundo's Hermeneutical Circle

The Local Congregation as a Hermeneutic of the Gospel

Lesslie Newbigin used the word "hermeneutic" in a completely different way that placed the congregation in the center as the interpreter of the Gospel for the world (Newbigin, 1989). This ecclesiological approach provides a model for the world to read the Gospel through the instrumentality of a congregation. In John chapter 14 Jesus says, "by this shall all people know that you are my disciples, in that you love one another." All people will "read" the congregation and in the congregation they will find meaning. What is love? How is it manifest? The meaning of love will have different symbols and relationships for people of different congregations, resulting in diverse "readings." When interpreting John 14, the expression of the Gospel is the community of disciples or believers. Newbigin says:

> The primary reality of which we have to take account in seeking for a Christian impact on public life is the Christian congregation.... The only hermeneutic of the Gospel is a congregation of men and women who believe it and live by it.... This community will have, I think, the following six characteristics.
>
> - It will be a community of praise.
> - It will be a community of truth.
> - It will be a community that does not live for itself.
> - It will be a community ... sustained in the exercise of the priesthood in the world.
> - It will be a community of mutual responsibility.

- It will be a community of hope. (Summarized from Newbigin, 1989: 227–233.)

Hermeneutics as a Re-presentation of Biblical Meaning

In traditional theology, there is a progression from personal Bible reading, to Bible study, and then to exegesis, and further to biblical theology. Exegesis works with the technical structure of the text: the words and the grammar. It seeks to establish the text from which meaning can be ascertained—exegesis accounts for what the words say, not what they mean. Synthesis increases through the progression from Bible reading to exegesis. Hendrikus Berkhof (1985) maintains theologians cannot do systematic theology unless they start by simply reading the Bible. Sometimes dogmaticians fail to do that. Exegesis is the product of understanding the words; hermeneutics accounts for the next step in the progression.

There is, then, a distinction between hermeneutics and exegesis. Propositional proclamation is a reflection of exegesis: what the words say. Yet we also know that the narrative is as revelatory as the words (Osborne, 1991: 149ff.). Together they create a word and deed combination that conveys both surface-level structure and deep-level meaning. The deed makes the word relevant, transformational, and concrete. The word explains the meaning, significance, and purpose of the deed. We must not work with the text only in terms of structures. We must move to the hermeneutic in terms of both the original context and present day contexts, including the circumstances of the communicators.

Hermeneutics draws us toward a deeper understanding of God's communication with the world. Once we start working with full text, we are at a hermeneutical level that calls for theological understanding and response to the meaning, which then forces us to go back and reread the text once again in light of what went before, and what comes after (as we discussed in chapter 1). So we need to ask about the deep meanings, that is, we need an approach that takes the text seriously and builds a theology out of it that is both true to the author's intent and still takes the contemporary context seriously. In short, we need to do biblical theology.

A Biblical and Theological Hermeneutic

The final approach we wish to emphasize involves an investigation of the authorial intent, what we understand the divine and human authors of the text itself to be saying in specific biblical contexts. Therefore we approach the text exegetically in order to be theological.[8] Properly done, this progression leads to a hermeneutical exploration of the context of God's revelation. In this process the emphasis is not so much on what it says (exegesis) but rather on what it means (hermeneutics). Traditional exegesis tries to get at the original meaning in terms of the author's intent. However, every message enters into a context that in some measure shapes the meaning. Therefore, exegesis becomes a progressive search for surface-level manifestations of the text, the forms that were necessary in order to convey the meaning as the authors of the Old and New Testaments (what we will soon define as horizons I and II) intended. In contrast, hermeneutics is always context-sensitive and searches for the deeper meanings. Since every message is communicated in a context, the focus is primarily on the implications of the set of circumstances within which the text was presented. This understanding allows communicators to project the message of the text into new contexts: their own and that of a people receiving God's Word (horizons III and IV).

If this is true, we must ask questions pertaining to the nature of the sources' contexts, involving the variety of cultural situations found throughout the Bible. Similarly, the communicators' context and its impact on how they understand Scripture, and the receptors' context in which the message will be understood, must be taken seriously. The communicators' task is to understand the original intent as discerned in the text and pass that on to the receptors without inserting overly intrusive personal assumptions that emerge from cultural, ecclesiastical, and theological biases. Theologically appropriate communication is interested in meaning at every level, in every horizon.

From a hermeneutical encounter with particular passages, we attempt to discern the original theological intention of a biblical author. That author, in turn, must be considered not in isolation but in relation to the rest of the Bible. It is not acceptable for pastors or translators to take a book and preach from it or translate it in isolation from the rest of the Bible, failing to associate the material with the original intent of the writer and with the rest of biblical revelation. This broader kind of association requires an understanding of the sweep of biblical history, as each book has its place in the context of both a particular time and place and as a part of a whole within the canon as accepted by those who held to the canonical criteria we presented in chapter 2.

This is why references to other parts of the Bible within a particular text are so vital to the message of the author. In the author's time, these references served to verify the authenticity of a particular writing as it related to the whole. A book of the Bible can never be fully understood in isolation. Arthur Glasser strongly warns us that the work missionaries and other communicators do as an expression of contextualization today must reflect a disciplined effort to submit to the whole word of God. Otherwise, communicators become like the false prophets in the Bible whose efforts reflected distortions of truth and destructive deviations from God's central concerns (Glasser, 1989). Issues of deviation and authenticity, of course, take seriously the whole concept of discourse analysis, which we develop in appendix B.

An example of this broader hermeneutical approach can be found in Luke's two-volume work in the New Testament. The full meaning of Luke's message cannot be grasped adequately without the communicator working with Old Testament prophecy, Old Testament theology of history, and the Old Testament conjunction of word and deed in God's actions. Unless we understand the original intent of the prophets we have no way to see how Luke, guided by the Holy Spirit, utilized those texts for the benefit of his listeners. We have no way to appreciate how Luke used those prophecies throughout the Luke-Acts corpus if we fail to first exegete them in their own context.

Similarly, an understanding of Mark as the memoirs of Peter is seriously lacking unless a person appreciates Peter's story and spiritual pilgrimage in conjunction with his writing in I and II Peter. Without that, the book of Mark cannot be fully appreciated.

There is no such thing as a stand-alone text, isolated from communication. We cannot preach one book of the Bible by itself, treating it as a self-contained entity isolated from the rest of the Bible. The author or authors of each book of the Bible clearly had other parts of revelation in mind when they wrote (see figure 2.2 for an example from II Peter). If this referential intent of the author is true for whole books, it is much more important when considering specific passages. We must avoid pulling passages out of context to support a particular viewpoint or theological view. Each part of Scripture must be seen in its broader sociolinguistic and theological context.

Based on this process of theological hermeneutics, we take the next step by considering the meaning that others have seen in the text throughout the history of the church. How do their ideas "translate" into the life of Christian people—the Church? This question relates to the historical development of dogma that we noted in chapter 3. How do historical interpretations interact with other ideas to develop a theology? How do they relate to the societies in which Christians now reside? How do they direct the church in interfacing with the world around it? The answers to these questions add to our understanding of the meaning of specific texts in particular and of Scripture in general—moving the discussion to a wider hermeneutical arena that includes all of the contexts in which the Gospel finds itself. Hence, as we presented in chapter 2, we must consider the nature of the source text and then (as developed in chapter 3) connect the text in relation to the context of the receptors, both ancient and contemporary.

This process was evident in Hosea's handling of God's proclamation to the People of Israel. Peter's preaching to the crowd on the day of Pentecost serves as another example. Peter exegeted a text from the prophet Joel and applied it to the specific issues faced by the Pentecost crowd. Peter was convinced he was faithful to the text, and yet he developed meaning that had a new impact on his audience—and three thousand people were added to the church that day. A further example comes from the concept of Jesus as the Lamb of God. See appendix A for an extended discussion of the biblical and theological development this concept provides as a demonstration of a biblical and theological hermeneutic. Furthermore, we applied this dynamic to present-day audiences in the Samo and Mayan contexts. Sam Hofman discovered a new understanding of "wisdom" because of his Tzeltal translation experience. These examples bring us to an appreciation of the need to focus on the communicability of the message, a key concept that pervades this book. The meaning communicated must be the same as the meaning in the source text—but that meaning comes in a totally different package because it is a totally different time and place. We must now apply our hermeneutical approach to the development of theologically appropriate communication.

THE HERMENEUTICAL SPIRAL

In this book we emphasize the re-presentation (making present again in the here and now) of the intended meaning of God's self-revelation in a variety of contexts. As we read Scripture, it is possible to seek out root metaphors that conceptualize both the biblical and the present contexts.

Development of the Spiral Concept

Juan Luis Segundo developed a hermeneutical circle based on reality in terms of the questions that emerge from biblical and contemporary Latin American contexts. These fresh questions and insights provide a rationale for new action. Segundo allowed for progressive development in theological investigation. As a post–Vatican II Roman Catholic, his thesis was grounded in the possibility of historical development of dogma. Based on his model, there emerges a new way of experiencing theological reality because reality is seen with new eyes (Segundo, 1985).

Orlando Costas (1976) developed a praxeological approach to interpretation based on a hermeneutical spiral. He began with the context of the poor in Latin America. Having interacted with them, he felt their pain in the context of economic, social, and political oppression. Steeped in this perspective, he reread Scripture. In doing this he "discovered" the place of the poor in Scripture: "The poor you have with you always" (Matt. 26:11). Once he re-read Scripture, he discerned the preferential option that God has for the poor, which moved him to solidarity with the oppressed that stimulated a further rereading of the Bible. Theologically, great care must be taken here. As one progresses along the spiral, it is easy to lose sight of the centrality of God's self-disclosure in the text. But the process does provide a model for connecting present-day contexts with Scriptural contexts in which similar themes are evident, a spiraling that may contribute to new theological development in contemporary contexts.

Grant Osborne also presented the idea of hermeneutics as a spiral structured to incorporate ever-broader contexts that lead from the text to the initial receptors of the text. He then continued to expand from that source to impact contemporary receptors who interpret the meaning with respect to their own context (1991: 323–326). Osborne recognized the need for the entire process to be grounded in the text, not primarily in the context. Here is where the Evangelical appreciation of inspiration informs and shapes the interpretation of Scripture and the theology that flows from it. The primary source must be the first author, God, who, through the thought-forms and context-specific actions and worldviews of human authors, communicates with human beings in a particular time and place for a particular purpose. Once this perspective is understood, the message from above can be applied to any context. Because of the particularity of each context, a reexamination of the text is necessary in order to enable communicators to appreciate anew how the Bible speaks to people everywhere—down through the ages in always-new circumstances that give expanded meaning to the old, old story.

We suggest taking this process one step further to better understand the biblical text and sociolinguistic contexts in which we communicate the Gospel in order to make a missiological impact. Drawing from Segundo's circle and Costas and Osborne's idea of spiral, we can identify the text of Scripture as that which ultimately points to Jesus Christ. If we then connect the text with contemporary cultural contexts, we begin a conversation between text and context, a dialogue that informs our understanding of each. By so doing we move from old (text) to new (context), shaping our understanding of the old while at the same time moving understanding forward for our day.

Here we caution that we do not intend this spiral to be read specifically as theology either "from above" or "from below." What we see in the spiral is culture on the one hand and revelation on the other, and each informs the other. As we go deeper, we draw new water from the same revelational well. Each swing of the spiral brings new understanding of text and context, thereby depicting a bigger picture of an awesome God and a greater appreciation for God's creation. This sets up a kind of spiral as represented in figure 4.5.

Missional Intent of the Spiral

The spiraling process of missiological hermeneutics begins with missional intention. The purpose is Gospel proclamation through crossing barriers. Like Jesus, Gospel communicators "go down" as they enter the context, what we have long called "incarnational mission," which leads to identification with the receptor. Kraft called this "receptor-oriented communication" (Kraft,

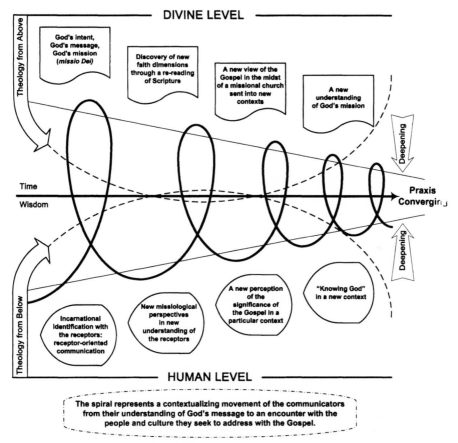

Figure 4.5.   The Hermeneutical Spiral

1979: 147). Whatever the name, such identification leads to a discovery of new faith dimensions as it forces us to reread Scripture based on what we have learned from the context. Rereading Scripture leads to a new missiological perspective of the understanding of the receptors, creating new solidarity between communicators and their audience. Both step forward incarnationally, leading to further receptor-oriented communication and a new rereading of the text. Enhanced receptor-oriented communication creates a new perception of what the church (the community of faith) is to be about in a particular context, which leads to a missiological reading of the text, including a new understand of God's mission and thus a new appreciation of the reality in which God's mission takes place. Mission in turn leads to a new appreciation of the dynamics of an ongoing hermeneutic. Spiraling such as this progresses through text, context, and missional proclamation to reach a hurting world that desperately needs the reconciliation found in Christ in order to become the People of God.

Another way to look at the hermeneutical spiral is to work with the semantic flow of the text, thinking of worldview themes (as reflected in metaphor or semantic constellations, as discussed in chapter 3) as pathways of the spiraling between text and context. This is the externalization of a movement that is still centered in the text. We cannot get away from the words and the grammar. We need to deal with them. The text remains text. Yet we must also consider the semantic structures that draw heavily from the context. Sociocultural and linguistic constraints helped shape the text in the first place, and will also impact what people in the contemporary context understand. If, in the text, the Gospel communicator discovers deeply human root metaphors, these metaphors may provide pathways to let that truth explode outward to shine from the text through narrative, through biblical theology, through new questions, to the present context. This in turn sends us back to reread the text with the new context in mind (now we are spiraling). In so doing, we are still being faithful to the text. Yet we have deepened our understanding of what is happening in the hermeneutic of the interaction of text and context. Thus we gain new insight, new perspective, in keeping with our original definition for hermeneutics.

We have now moved beyond the hermeneutical circle. We are not superimposing the agendas of the context on the text. Rather, following Osborne, we bring the text to a context. We do this, however, mindful of the issues in the context, seeking similar contexts in the Bible. By interacting with the issues, we seek to bring God into the situation—God did this before and God will do it again, thus illuminating God's People concerning God's will for them. What has God said about the issues at hand? What are the contextually appropriate root metaphors? We can search the Bible to see where similar metaphors appear and re-present them (make them present tense once again) in the new context. We find where God, in fact, had something to say about the issues facing people in today's world, and allow the biblical text to speak to people in their circumstances.

However, we must also keep in mind that the receptors of Gospel presentation perceive the Bible's meanings through their own understanding of reality, their worldview, and the contextual glasses with which they read the text. The text does not change, but the local interpretation of it does. The resulting theology flows from the interaction of their perception of reality and the intent of the text. Hence, proclaiming a message or translating Bible passages that reflect, to a large degree, the issues or circumstances that people bring to their understanding of the text is a valuable exercise, enabling them to get it right. Through this process communicators gain new information, a new understanding of Scripture. Such a new perception comes as the fruit of the hermeneutical spiral we have been developing. Another way to describe this hermeneutical process is as the interaction of four horizons.

THE FOUR HORIZONS AS A
MISSIOLOGICAL HERMENEUTIC

Drawing from Friedrich Nietzsche and Edmund Husserl before him, Hans-Georg Gadamer, professor of philosophy at Heidelberg from 1949 to 1968, suggested the notion of "horizons" as a way of describing and relating (a) a person's perspective within a particular context of history and (b) the text that arises out of a past historical context that person may be studying. Gadamer's work moved beyond the historicism of European (especially German) thought of the nineteenth century. Gadamer, however, proceeded to make the case that such historical studies involve a "fusion of horizons" that bring together the reader's present horizon and the horizon of the text as the reader studies the past historical context (see Kurt Mueller-Vollmer, 1985: 269–273). Jürgen Habermas critiqued Gadamer from the point of view of what Habermas called "the ontological construction of hermeneutical consciousness," since it would appear that Gadamer's two "horizons" often were melded and confused (cf. Mueller-Vollmer, 1985: 294–319).

Avoiding Gadamer's unfruitful "fusion of horizons," Anthony Thiselton proposed keeping the two horizons of the biblical text and the interpreter-in-context separate but interactive. Both are affirmed, both exist in their own right, and both affect the other: "The goal of biblical hermeneutics is to bring about an active and meaningful engagement between the interpreter and text, in such a way that the interpreter's own horizon is reshaped and enlarged" (Thiselton, 1980: xix). Grant Osborne summarizes Thiselton's viewpoint:

> Thiselton finds four levels at which the "illusion of textual objectivism" becomes apparent. (1) Hermeneutically, the phenomenon of preunderstanding exerts great influence in the interpretive act. This subjective element cannot be denied. (2) Linguistically, communication demands a point of contact between the sender and the recipient of a message, and this distinction provides a major barrier to recovering a text's meaning. The differing situations of the hearers remove any possibility of a purely objective interpretation. (3) These problems are magnified at the level of literary communication, where other factors such as narrative-time, plot development, characterization and dialogue enter the picture. . . . (4) Philosophically, meaning is never context-free but is based on a large list of unconscious assumptions between sender and receiver. When these connecting links are not present, "literal meaning" becomes extremely difficult if not impossible, for meaning can never be context-free." (1991, 386)

Subsequently, Osborne drew heavily from Thiselton in developing what he called "the hermeneutical spiral of biblical interpretation" (1991). Osborne's spiral goes beyond the "two-horizon" perspective and recognizes that there is a dynamic, continuing, constantly changing interaction of text, community, and context through time in relation to meaning. Osborne gives a helpful overview of the issues of meaning as they relate to the problem of the relationship of author-text-reader (1991: 366–415).

Finally, D. A. Carson entered the fray and added a third horizon—the audience. Also borrowing from Thiselton, Carson pointed out:

> Any Christian[s] who witness cross-culturally must concern [themselves] not only with *two* horizons, but also with *three*. [They] must attempt to fuse [their] own horizon of understanding with the horizon of the text; and having done that, attempt to bridge the gap between [their] own horizon of understanding, as it has been informed and instructed by the text, and the horizon of understanding of the person or people to whom [they] minister (Carson, 1984a: 17).

This sounds very much like the Gospel communication problem we have addressed throughout this book, linking the author with the text as well as the receptors. The audience, however, may be both ancient (reflected in the original recipients) or contemporary (reflected in present-day receptors). Therefore, the model needs further refinement.

We wish to expand the horizon concept a step further by suggesting four horizons. By "horizon" we intend to emphasize differing worldviews represented in the various contexts, rather than an epistemological perspective, as Gadamer did. Four horizons, or viewpoints, of meaning seem to inform the Christian understanding of what God has said: (I) God's context-specific intended meaning in revelation found in the Old Testament, (II) God's revealed intended meaning in the New Testament that involves a new understanding of the Old Testament, (III) the Gospel communicator, and (IV) the contemporary receptors. In the next series of diagrams we build the "four-horizon" approach through a series of steps. The four-horizon approach provides the springboard for the remainder of this book. Readers should pay close attention to the diagrams as they read the text. Each step unfolds a new understanding of both the four-horizons concept and its application to an effective hermeneutic for communicating God's Word in our complex world.

Step One

We begin, then, with the recognition of two complementary facts about humanity: all humans have much in common and yet human cultures demonstrate a phenomenal degree of diversity. Common humanity, cultural diversity. As we demonstrate in subsequent chapters, these two complementary characteristics of being human, when applied to matters of culture, linguistics, and communication, form the basis of our recognition that there is a great deal of difference between surface-level structures of meaning (including cultural symbols and manifestations) and deep-level structures of meaning (including cultural themes and metaphors). (See figure 4.6.)

We must also take into account the fact that the deep-level structures are closely related to the surface-level structures and vice versa, because surface-level meanings derive from, and yet shape the worldview of, people within a culture. Thus, although we need to differentiate between the deep-level and the surface-level, they are dynamically and intimately interconnected. In the figures that follow, the reader will note that each "horizon" represents the interconnected constellation of meanings that draw from both the surface- and deep-level structures. People living in different cultures handle pregnancy, birth, rites of passage, and death differently. They handle spiritual understanding in a wide variety of ways. The economic, social, political, and linguistic structures are all immensely different. All of these manifestations, however, reflect deep-seated beliefs and values that not only motivate appropriate behavior (for each society), but also bind them together with all other communities, past, present, and future. We believe this is related to being created in the image of God and to sharing a common humanity. This is why Scripture is communicable in all human languages and relevant for all peoples. It reflects in human contexts messages about God the Creator of all. The Holy Spirit is at work enabling human beings in every context to understand what the God who created them intends for them. So Scripture provides a connecting point, continuity with all of humanity, extending back to creation in Adam and Eve and forward to the culmination of all human history in the New Jerusalem. God interacts in the midst of God's People today, just as he did in

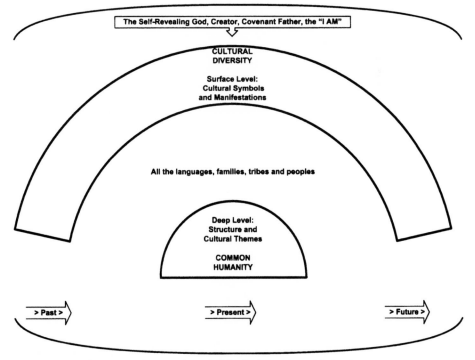

The Self-Revealing God, Creator, Covenant Father, the "I AM"

CULTURAL
DIVERSITY

Surface Level:
Cultural Symbols
and Manifestations

All the languages, families, tribes and peoples

Deep Level:
Structure and
Cultural Themes

COMMON
HUMANITY

> Past >   > Present >   > Future >

Figure 4.6.   The Four Horizons of a Missiological Hermeneutic: Step One

biblical times. The biblical narrative unfolds the story of God's presence through time and space, serving as an example of what God can do in any other context.

Step Two

The second step in the process of building a four-horizon hermeneutic includes recognition of the divine origin of the text of Scripture. As we emphasized in chapter 2, we approach the Bible as a text that has dual authorship: divine and human. So we want to encounter God's intention in the text, while at the same time recognizing that God's message to humanity has always been conveyed through humans, in the midst of differing cultures.

Such duality forces a recognition of the discontinuity and continuity of God's revelation. The diagram in figure 4.7 is meant to show the movement of time from left to right: from past, through the present, on the way to the future. As time progresses, there is discontinuity as God's message takes on different surface-level symbols among different cultures that each reflect different worldviews. The arrows in the diagram are important. They represent progressive revelation and, post-Scripture, the historical development of the church's understanding of God's revelation.

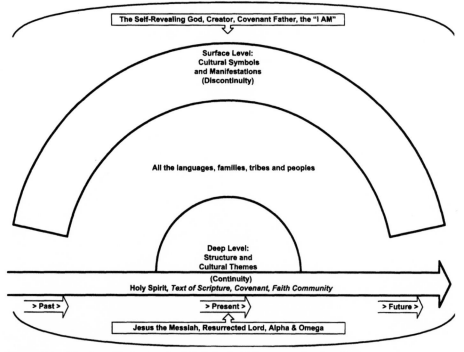

Figure 4.7.   The Four Horizons of a Missiological Hermeneutic: Step Two

Yet there is also continuity, as attested in the biblical text itself. The phrase, "I am the God of Abraham, Isaac, and Jacob," (Exod. 3:6) presupposes continuity. Throughout the Scriptures, it is the same God who speaks, from Genesis to Revelation. The content of the Scriptures themselves purport to be cumulative, building one on another, thus assuming continuity. We add to this the Bible's christological affirmations regarding Jesus, the Alpha and Omega, coupled with the continuity of the Holy Spirit throughout.

All of these indicators point to a unity and continuity of the text—predominantly in terms of the deep-level themes, metaphors, and meanings—shaped and expressed through ever-changing and ever-different surface-structure cultural symbols. Thus God's revelation in Scripture appears to involve continuous discontinuity over time.

Step Three

The third step calls for a recognition of all of the "horizons" in which God's revelation occurs. Imagine with us that we are on a large ship in the middle of the ocean. We look out from the ship and see nothing but water. If we look as far as possible on a clear day, we may see the slight curving of a line far away in the distance. This is the curvature of the earth. And where the water of the ocean seems to meet the sky, we see this curving line as a horizon. But imagine that some days later we look out from the prow of the ship and we see a large, dark mass rising up above the curved line of the water. We recognize that we are nearing land. A few hours later we look out and notice that the ship is beginning to approach land, where we can see buildings at the foot of the mountains. Another hour or two brings us close enough to see that there is a seaport, docks, other ships, warehouses, hotels, restaurants, and people.

Now in each of these four views we perceived a horizon. Each horizon was different. All four horizons were true. And the four did not contradict each other. Yet the object of our interest, the data we considered important, the way we reacted to the sight, the perspective from which we observed what we saw differed markedly.

This is the case with our approach to biblical hermeneutics, as shown in figure 4.8. The reader should notice that we have drawn four horizons. The figure is a graphic attempt to demonstrate the interconnected constellation of meaning that involves both the surface-level and the deep-level meanings of each horizon. We conceptualize these horizons as (I) the Old Testament, (II) the New Testament, (III) the communicator, and (IV) the audience. Within each horizon there are a variety of contexts, each with its own perspective and understanding, as we demonstrated in chapter 3 when we spoke of the Bible as a tapestry. Clearly God's Word must fit a multiplicity of diverse contexts that, despite their individual discontinuity, express commonality of origin and relationship to God.

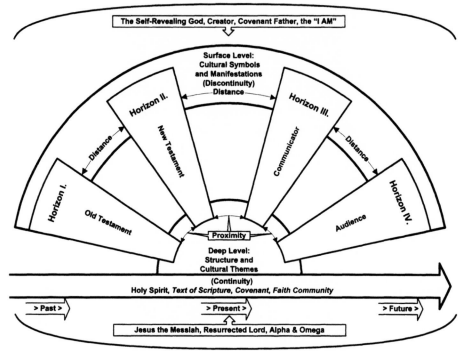

Figure 4.8.   The Four Horizons of a Missiological Hermeneutic: Step Three

In figure 4.8, the four horizons are in the middle of the diagram and are shaped by elements from below and above. At the upper, wider end of each horizon, the reader will see what we call surface-level structures composed of the symbols and variety of phenomena through which the deep-level structures (the lower part of the diagram) are formulated in a culture. The horizons represent the interfacing of both deep and surface structures.

Step Four

At this point in the development of our model, we need to recognize that the four "horizons" are not all of the same order. In figure 4.9 horizons I and II are qualitatively different from horizons III and IV, due to the uniqueness of God's revelation, as found in the canon. As we noted in chapter 2, as Evangelical Protestants, we are not willing to open the canon. We know the New Testament (horizon II) represents a distinct set of horizons as compared with the Old Testament (horizon I). Yet I and II, together as God's Word, comprise the canonical Scriptures that are normative for us, our only rule of faith and practice. We dealt with this extensively in the first two chapters of this book. Horizons III and IV represent the process necessary to ensure appropriate commu-

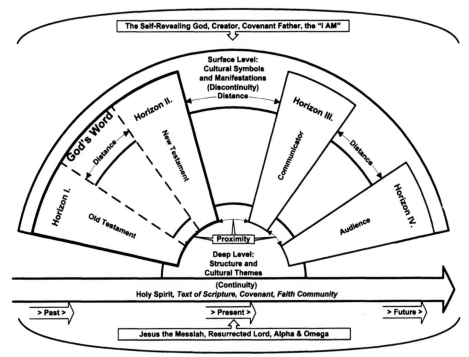

Figure 4.9.   The Four Horizons of a Missiological Hermeneutic: Step Four

nication regardless of where or when a message originates and who responds. We turn now to the fifth step.

Step Five

We can view the hermeneutical process as a progression of four movements. In figure 4.10 the four movements can be presented as an interaction between horizon III and horizons I and II. Following the patterns of the New Testament authors' interpretations of the Old Testament, the communicator in horizon III approaches the text at the surface level of symbols expressed in the discourse-level semantic flow of the text.

Movement 1 (III: 1 to 2)   In this first movement we read the text at face value as a context-specific communication of God's self-disclosure. Communicators here are aware of the distances of history, culture, and worldview between themselves and the world of the text of Scripture being read. However, as communicators interact with the text and are immersed in the thought-world of the text, they begin to participate in the second movement.

Movement 2 (III: 2 to 3)   The second movement requires a consideration of all of the contexts (human, social, cultural, historical) in which God's self-revelation took place and from which the text emerged. As communicators

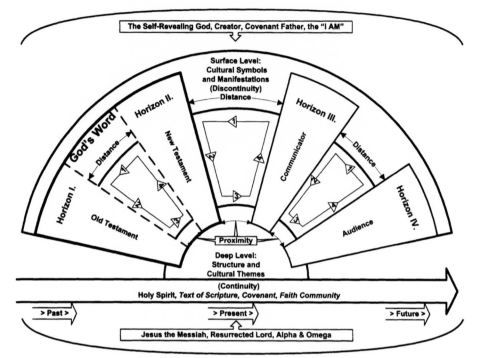

Figure 4.10.   The Four Horizons of a Missiological Hermeneutic: Step Five

immersed in the biblical thought-world of horizon I and II, they delve deeper into the meanings conveyed by the text as related to both the divine and the human authors' intentions in a particular time and place.

Movement 3 (III: 3 to 4)   The third movement begins the process of relating the deep-level structures of meaning in the text with comparable (and relatively close) deep-level structures of meaning in the communicator's thought-world. An example of this is Jesus' commandment regarding agape, self-giving love. Drawing from the thought-world of Deuteronomy whose surface-level structures were distant from those of Jesus's day, Jesus brings to bear in his own world the deep-level meaning of self-giving love committed to the welfare of the other. Although the surface-level acts of such self-giving love might differ in Jesus's day as compared with our day, the deep-level injunction is nearly the same in all of the horizons: God's self-giving love in Jesus Christ transforms the disciples of Jesus into persons who live out their lives in self-giving love for others. "By this will all people know that you are my disciples: if you love one another" (John 3:35). This is true for all time and for all cultures, yet this truth is lived out at the surface-level in very different ways in diverse cultural settings.

Movement 4 (III: 4 to 1)   The fourth movement allows the deep-level structures of meaning to be transferred into the communicator's context to transform the surface-level symbols and manifestations in the communicator's horizon in accord with the communicator's new understanding of the Gospel.

Missional Movement between Horizons III and IV

How, then, do we go about the process of interpretation and missional communication? These four movements begin all over again when the communicator seeks to make that meaning relevant in the context of new receptors. However, the direction of the movements differs because they begin with the receptor (IV) and not the communicator. As shown in figure 4.10, there is a specific relation between horizon IV and horizon III. As Gospel communicators begin to interact with the new receptors, they will seek to listen and learn how the people in the context understand their world. Here there is once again a hermeneutical spiraling of the interaction between the receptors-in-context, the communicator-in-context, and eventually with the text-in-context. The progression should be clear. The desire to know God sets up a process that leads to an appreciation of the horizons in which God has communicated and in which God continues to interact with human beings through the work of the Holy Spirit.

When we get to the new receptors, the direction of the arrows in figure 4.10 is important. If communicators are receptor-oriented, their starting point involves an encounter with the receptors' surface-level structures. Once communicators begin to understand the new receptors' horizon, at least on the surface, the communicator may participate in the second movement. By seeking to associate the receptors' questions with deep structural meanings, communicators enable receptors to move toward an understanding of horizons I and II with reference to the theme, metaphor, question, or issue at hand. The new context of horizon IV forces communicators from horizon III to reexamine their own reading of the biblical horizons I and II. This process helps to restate or re-create the root metaphor or issue examined. This second movement begins on the surface and moves to a deep examination of the perspectives and root metaphors that can then be presented as new metaphors in a different context. Our human commonality allows for this to happen meaningfully.

From the perspectives of their own horizon, Gospel communicators cannot understand the questions of others (including both Scripture and the contemporary context) without relating them to their own experience, to their own symbolic systems and their own understanding of reality. The text comes to the present context and brings new understanding. By following through from text to context and back again, we encourage the historical development of dogma. This process is a product of the continuity of revelation, presenting the same God, the same covenant, and the same community of faith. Yet always in new contexts God is known and understood in new ways. Everyone knows God in context.

As this deep-level reflection progresses, communicators begin to draw inferences as to what may be the deep-level structural meanings in the receptor's horizon related to the issue at hand. This is the third movement (IV: 3 to 4). Hopefully, the third and the fourth movements involve a shared conversation between communicators and receptors. Hopefully communicators will avoid simply filtering biblical knowledge to receptors who need to appreciate the text for themselves. Once the communicators and the receptors participate in such a conversation, they will begin to discern the fourth movement (IV: 4 to 1), whereby the deep-level structural meanings discovered in the third movement are given new expression in the surface-level meanings of the receptor community.

To some degree the process outlined here must take into consideration the historical discontinuity of each context. Yet in each new context there is a restatement of the same divine revelation. And there is an ongoing illumination as a result of that restatement. Thus Christians from majority world cultures and contexts can inform westerners as to how their new contexts have provided them with a new appreciation of the text. The Gospel communicator will need to continually ask new questions. Jesus himself said, "Unless I go away, the Comforter will not come to you; but if I go, I will send him to you. . . . When the Counselor comes, whom I will send to you from the Father . . . he will testify about me" (John 16:7; 15:26).

The process we have illustrated from the point of view of the communicator's horizon can be shifted to the horizon of new receptors. This shifts the focus but the process remains the same. Members of the new church seek God's intended meaning. They bring their questions to the text of Scripture and they test their understanding of that revelation within their structures of plausibility. They do not need to rely on what communicators tell them; they can go to the text and benefit from what communicators already know. Here is the infinite communicability of God's Word in process. The receptors can also listen to God. They can also tell others what they hear.

Thus the process begins again, drawing new understanding from each of the previous horizons. The Old Testament perspectives are interpreted through the viewpoint of the New Testament. The New Testament authors draw the ancient Hebrew texts into conversation with Greek- and Latin-speaking Roman contexts. The Scriptures of the Old and New Testaments are then reread by Gospel communicators who seek to pass the meanings on to their receptors. Over time, the receptors themselves become Gospel communicators. And today new audiences hear God speak and marvel that they, too, are included in a plan that extends back to a time before the foundation of the earth.

A BIBLICAL EXAMPLE OF
FOUR-HORIZON HERMENEUTICS

Luke 4:21–30 illustrates how the Gospel writer applied the four horizons to missional communication. This is a critical passage in that it captures the whole semantic structure of Luke's text. It is the primary place where Luke presents Jesus' mission, so we are interested in both the theological and missional implications of the passage. After Jesus' reading of Isaiah, Luke tells us that the people were amazed at what they heard—they were awestruck. Then Jesus began his homily. "A prophet has no honor in his own country" he said (4:24). He continued by briefly mentioning two stories they all knew: Elijah's interaction with the widow of Zarephath, and the healing of Naaman the leper.

At the conclusion of this brief sermon Luke tells us that the people dragged Jesus out of the synagogue and were ready to throw him off a cliff. What changed their view of him in those brief minutes? Referring back to the texts that Jesus cites gives a clue. Jesus emphasized that there were many widows in Israel, but Elisha went to a foreigner; there were many lepers in Israel, but a foreign general was singled out for healing. Jesus was saying that the recipient of God's grace and the agents of God's mission are sometimes people on the periphery. In fact, in the cases that Jesus cites, they were not Israelites at all. For the ethnocentric Jews of first-century Palestine, this was unacceptable. At the beginning of the story the folks in Nazareth were ready to have their favorite local son tell them how great they were. They opened their arms to him. But then Jesus told them he came for the outcasts and the foreigners. The reflection on the stories reinforced Jesus's reading from Isaiah, and the people of Nazareth understood exactly what Jesus was saying to them. So much so, that they were ready to kill him.

With this background in mind, we can now apply the horizons model. In this passage, Luke proceeds with his narrative by recounting Jesus's interaction with the people of Nazareth and their response to his talking about Naaman the leper. This requires the analysis of two texts: Luke chapter 4 and II Kings chapter 5, each with a different context. The surface-level difference between Nazareth and where the Naaman story took place is great: different locations (hill country versus the Jordan River), different times (at least six hundred years separate the two), different languages (Aramaic versus Hebrew), and different cultures (classic peasant Hebrew and Syrian city-state societies versus Hellenized Greco-Roman Palestine). Yet, the matter of being marginalized or oppressed (the little girl who was taken captive by Naaman; the poor widow of Zarephath) is exactly the root metaphor of Israel under the domination of Rome. In fact, the people of Nazareth could easily put themselves into the story. All Jesus had to do was mention the Old Testament stories and the people understood he was speaking about issues of power and belonging, marginality and ostracism—of lepers, foreigners, and strangers. Those deep themes of Israel are all in the story. They are part of the text. The people of Nazareth tried to kill Jesus because they knew exactly what he is saying, and they did not like it.

Knowing both the Old Testament and the contemporary contexts, Luke tells the story in order to bring out the juxtaposition. He says that Jesus said,

"During Elijah's time there were many widows in Israel . . . and during Elisha's time there were many lepers" and the implication is that there are many widows and lepers here, now, in Nazareth, in the first-century. Jesus picked up on this and essentially affirmed that the ones chosen as recipients and agents of God's mission would be outsiders, the estranged and the marginalized. Later, Luke would show how Jesus was frequently accused of spending time with the poor and the fringe elements of the society (tax collectors and sinners) rather than acting like a rabbi and frequenting holy places (Luke 15:1). Luke acts as a translator here, not only between Old and New Testament contexts but also between these and his audience.[9]

Now we can move to horizon III, the communicator. What Luke did for his audience, Gospel communicators must do for theirs today—proclaim previous revelation to new audiences. Gospel communicators cannot do this without a thorough knowledge of the receptor context. People living in colonized places of the world, especially the oppressed, understand this much better than people who have not felt this pain. The marginalized peoples of the world understand metaphors of oppression and may receive the message more readily than those who do not. What are the root meanings?

We must be careful here. We do not want to disconnect the deep structures from the surface structures so completely that the deeper meanings become merely metaphorical or allegorical. The canonical flow of the text must reveal the root meanings. The text takes the lead. We cannot go in the opposite direction. We cannot ask: Given a metaphor what text will buttress it? Instead, we must let the text encase the root metaphor and then let that metaphor speak to us as well as to our receptors.

Various contexts reveal different metaphors about oppression. Yet each expresses the same deep-level meanings in different forms. The root metaphor speaks to them all. Regardless of the circumstances, Jesus cared about all people. When Jesus told his hometown crowd that what they heard in the Isaiah passage had been fulfilled in their presence, they were in awe. But when he told them that he had come to minister to the oppressed and excluded, they were ready to push him off the cliff. Translating that emotion and symbolism is essential for this proclamation to be understood in a present-day context.

Furthermore, communicating the missiological implications of this passage in the overall context of Luke's writings is essential for appropriate communication of the Gospel. Jesus sends some crucial signals here about his mission—"to the Jew first but also to the Greek." Outsiders, even non-Jews through all time and space, are included—God so loved the world. And it is this world that makes up the fourth horizon: the contemporary, the disenfranchised, the marginal, the poor, and the refugees.

The Four Horizons as a Hermeneutical Process

Where does this leave Gospel communicators today? If Luke can do what he did with the Old Testament text in his context, can we do it too? We must make a distinction between revelation and illumination. We dare not say we are under revelation. Even the apostle Paul was careful on this matter, making a point of mentioning when he was writing on his own, apart from divine revelation. Yet the same text and the same Holy Spirit illumines our minds to understand the Scriptures.

The sixteenth-century Reformation affirmed the priesthood of all believers. The Reformers rightly stressed that all people who believe in Jesus can go back and check to see if the reading of Scripture is correct. Thus the community of faith is to carry out Gospel communication. We need the Holy Spirit in the midst of the faith community. All Christians around the whole world, representing many cultures, need to consult with each other as to what they understand when they read the Scriptures. They need to work in concert, all together drawing out the meaning of the text.

Today this means that the same Bible is read, interpreted, and understood in multiple ways by 1.5 billion Christians around the world who speak many languages and derive a deep understanding of Scripture in the midst of global diversity. The same God, the same Lord, the same Holy Spirit call on the Church to reread the same Bible in infinitely different contexts, languages, and worldviews. Those who read the Bible are part of a worldwide hermeneutical community gaining new and deeper understandings about God as the Scriptures impact dynamic cultural contexts. Here is the wonder of the infinitely communicable Gospel of Jesus Christ.

As represented in figure 4.11, on a global scale, Christians together, equally, read the text. The whole world Church becomes a hermeneutical community. The whole Christian Church as a hermeneutical community is involved in proclamation as mission: proclaiming everything we have understood about God to people in many new contexts (Matt. 28:20).

SUMMARY

When we consider what God did as God spoke in Holy Scripture, it is truly marvelous in our eyes. We start from God's view of creation as God sought to communicate through it—the creator talking with the creatures including the crown jewel—human beings—created in God's image. Communication, the Word, not only produced creative acts but also served as the means of ongoing interaction. God spoke in the midst of God's People. God spoke to Abraham who pulled up

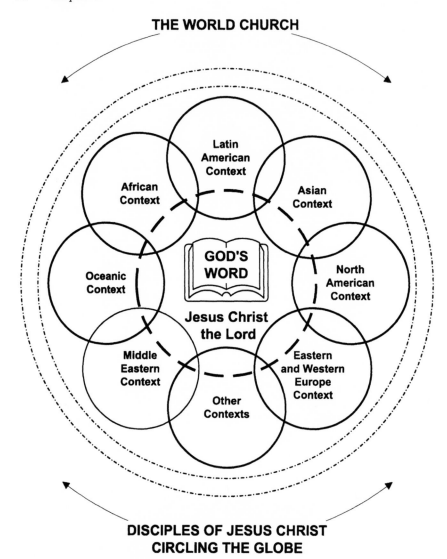

Figure 4.11.   The Global Hermeneutical Community

stakes and went looking for a land that God would show him. God talked to Moses and a ragtag crowd of refugees gradually became a nation. And so it went through the Bible. God proclaimed God's intent to and for humans. Gradually, as we continue reading, a pattern emerges: the covenant, a root metaphor that characterizes relationship through the communication process. "I will be your God, you will be my people and I will dwell in your midst" (Ex. 6:7).

As communicators who desire to declare God's Word in a complex world, we face the challenge of understanding what God said on the one hand and how to communicate it in present-day contexts on the other. We have shown that it requires a host of skills and wisdom drawn from a variety of disciplines that traditionally have not been considered part of the task of communication. This complexity is best understood as a dynamic interaction of horizons. At minimum, there are four horizons that convey the meaning of the message. Above it all is the supracultural God, the source, the originator of the whole process. God, in turn, spoke to people in particular contexts, so we must analyze the contexts into which God originally communicated. The context of the communicator impacts the assumptions made and the meaning the communicator gives the message. And the context of the new receptors with their particular experiences and their understanding of the world shapes the way they hear God speak to them. The role of the trinity in the process (revelation, incarnation, and illumination) provides a guide for today's communicators as they seek to present unchanging truth in a changing world. Herein lies the value of seeing the historical development of dogma as a process of discovering an increasingly deeper understanding of the Gospel: new information from particular contexts brings new perspectives to ancient texts.

God also took note of the contexts into which God communicated and made appropriate adjustments to them. If God did that, so must those who seek today to proclaim God's Word to others. This conversation continually expands as new receptors hear and respond to the biblical message and provide a new perspective, a different horizon that Christians have not seen before. This is the view given in Revelation chapter 7 where every nation, tongue, and people are represented. Each adds their perspective, and collectively they give praise and honor to our Savior and Lord.

Drawing from Thiselton's horizons model, and given the theoretical focus of this book on theological, communicational, and cultural issues, we have presented the four horizons in an effort to create a new appreciation for mission. New understandings are now possible because of the expansion of the Church in our day. What Christians have seen and heard they should make available to others so they too may know God in the fullness of truth as revealed across time and space. Because of human commonality and yet incredible cultural diversity, Gospel communicators have the privilege of learning from their receptors; receiving new insights about the sense of an ancient text. Because every context predisposes the people in it to perceive the text in a particular way, each can learn from others and gain new appreciation for what God intended that human beings understand about God in their midst. Each new understanding will, in turn, enrich the appreciation others may have of the mighty works of God. Sam Hofman learned new things about wisdom from the Tzeltals who, in their turn, benefited greatly from Sam's contribution to their understanding about the wisdom of God.

If God intended all people whom God created to be in relationship with him, how can they "have faith in the Lord and ask him to save them if they have never heard about him? And how can they hear, unless someone tells them?" (Rom. 10:14) The message will be manifest always in a particular context. The Gospel is understood always in a specific cultural matrix. God uses language and culture in unique ways in each particular time and place. The issues involved in developing a communicationally and culturally appropriate proclamation require our attention in the next two chapters.

NOTES

1. Telephone conversation between Charles Van Engen and Sam Hofman, July 12, 2002.

2. For excellent summaries of these developments in philosophical and linguistic approaches to hermeneutics, see Osborne (1991: 365–396); Thiselton (1980: 326–356); Kaiser and Silva (1994 chapters 12–13); and Mueller-Vollmer (1985: 1–53). For a theological reflection on these developments, see Otto Weber (1981: 308–345).

3. In this vein, Osborne mentions Paul Ricoeur, David Tracy, Brevard Childs, and James Sanders. Also David Kelsey and the later work of Ludwig Wittgenstein are important, as is the work of E. D. Hirsch, who "separates 'meaning' (the act of comprehending a text on the basis of the whole semantic field) and 'significance' (the act of inserting that meaning into different contexts, such as modern culture)" (Osborne, 1991: 393).

4. See, for example, Clodovis Boff (1987: 63–66; 132–153); Leonardo Boff and Clodovis Boff (1987: 32–35); Guillermo Cook (1985:104–126); Severino Croatto (1987: 36–65); Samuel Escobar (1987: 172–179); Dean Ferm (1986: 25–26); Ismael Garcia (1987: 12–16, 28); Gustavo Gutierrez (1974: 13); Roger Haight (1985: 46–59); Jose Miguez Bonino (1975: 90–104); C. Rene Padilla (1985: 83–91); Robert Schreiter (1986: 75–94); Juan Luis Segundo (1976: 7–38); Gordon Spykman et al. (1988: 228–230); Jon Sobrino (1984: 1–38); and Raul Vidales (1979: 48–51).

5. In Segundo's thought there are four decisive moments or factors influencing the hermeneutical circle:

1) There is our way of experiencing reality that leads us to ideological suspicion. (Mannheim's three elements are involved in Segundo's understanding of this first stage: (a) a concrete evaluational experience of theology; (b) an act of the will on the part of the theologian with respect to his/her theology; (c) a direction in treating new problems that derives from this act of the will.)

2) There is the application of our ideological suspicion to the whole ideological superstructure in general and to theology in particular.

3) There comes a new way of experiencing theological reality that leads us to exegetical suspicion, that is, the suspicion that the prevailing interpretation of the Bible has not taken important pieces of data into account.

4) We have our new hermeneutic, that is, our new way of interpreting the fountainhead of our faith (i.e., Scripture) with the new elements at our disposal (Segundo, 1976: 7–38).

6. This is the thesis of Fletcher Tink's Ph. D. dissertation (1994).

7. Van Engen and Tiersma applied this methodology to a missiological hermeneutic related to mission in the city. See Van Engen (1994: 241–270); Van Engen (1996b: 90–104).

8. See Karl Barth (1958, I. 2, p. 466). This is mentioned also by Otto Weber (1981: 310).

9. Luke was probably a Hellenized Jew, a God-fearer, and therefore reflects the Greek perspective but understands at a profoundly deep level the Hebrew worldview. The way he writes, his humor, how he organizes his work, are all Hebraic and he draws heavily on the Old Testament. In Luke 4, he presents Jesus in an Aramaic, hometown context interacting with the Hebrew background, specifically the prophets.

Communicationally
Appropriate Communication

Understanding the communication situation colors the way communicators read the text and transfer the message into contemporary contexts so that receptors may hear "the word of the
Lord."

*Coauthor Dan Shaw's Bible study group meets every Tuesday evening. They are
an irreverent bunch and it is often difficult to get them to settle down and reflect
on the impact of the Bible on the world's problems they often discuss. One
evening, one of the members (who happened to be a seminary student), came prepared to discuss the story of David and Bathsheba, found only in II Samuel 11
and 12.[1] The facilitator introduced the subject and the seminary student took over.
It was more than an hour before he got to II Samuel 11 and 12, and to Dan's
surprise everyone sat spellbound as this skilled communicator walked the little
group through the fundamentals of exegesis and hermeneutics without ever mentioning the words—it was masterful. His presentation went something like this.*

*In order to appreciate what a particular passage means, we must see it in the flow of
the whole of Scripture. II Samuel fits into the Jewish historical books designed to help
the Jews answer some very important questions: Where did the priests come from?
Where did the temple come from? How did we get Kings? Where did the prophets
come from? If we understand the history of the Jews we can make a lot more sense
out of the Bible. The Jews began their history in Genesis 12 with God calling Abraham. They came out of captivity in Egypt, wandered in the desert, and finally took
over the land God had promised to Abraham and were ruled for a period by the
judges. Now we get to the history of the Jewish nation beginning in Samuel.*

*Our fearless communicator then proceeded to describe how Old Testament
books were written, cut in half to fit on a scroll and then numbered: I and II
Samuel, I and II Kings. He explained how the position of authors with respect to the exile was also very important, as their agenda was quite different*

on either side of this significant event in Jewish history. He described how David was a highly revered king included in genealogies throughout Scripture, beginning in Ruth in anticipation of his birth, and included in Jesus' genealogy in Matthew. Then he presented some specifics about Samuel, his relationship to Saul and to David, and the rationale for including this story of David and Bathsheba only here—because of the author's focus on the questions he was trying to answer.

The emphasis was on God who lifted up kings and put them down—God was in control, not kings. Understanding why Solomon was the king after David, rather than his older brothers, as culture would dictate, is very important and cannot be seen without introducing Solomon's mother, Bathsheba. Samuel, as both priest and prophet, anointed David, even as he did Saul. In the text, he, like God, could not show preferences. He had to "look at the heart," not just at what others could see—he had to tell the story. And David, like all human beings, was mortal and subject to temptation and sin, which always has consequences. Therefore, this story, in this context, is very important for understanding the remainder of Jewish history, including the dividing of the kingdom, the exile, and the people's response. Now, finally, our gifted teacher arrived at the passage in focus. I looked around, time was passing, but there were no yawns, no droopy eyes. There were, however, lots of questions and comments of amazement at understanding the Bible in a new and exciting way. Now rather than detailing II Samuel 11 and 12, the communicator gave a quick lesson on how to read Scripture that ended with an assignment. This is what he said:

When we read Scripture, we must put ourselves into the flow of history: What was happening? Who was involved? Where was it? Why is the story included here? Our first objective is to understand this story as the author meant his audience to understand it. Then, having understood what it meant to the original audience, we need to try to understand it from our own perspective in light of our relationship to God. If God was the true author of Scripture, and used various people to communicate his message, and by extension we today are the people of God, then what is the message God intends for us? Ideally, we should read Scripture aloud because it was originally presented in an oral mode. So go home and read II Samuel 11 and 12 aloud. Then read it five or six more times as a story. Don't stop when you get to the end of a chapter; keep reading because there were no chapter breaks when it was written. Then begin to ask questions about the text that comes out of each sentence or two: Why did the Kings go to war in the Spring? Who was Joab, and why did David "send" out the army instead of leading it? Who were the Ammonites they destroyed, and how far away was Rabbah? Look at a map. And so the questions go, verse by verse. Furthermore, pretend this is a drama full of characters. As you read, put yourself into the scene, play-act each character—how do you feel? What can you learn about the details of the story? Play this game during the week and we will talk about the first five verses of chapter 11 next week.

The presentation was brilliant! The following week, everyone was back, and more besides, except one woman who was embarrassed to come because she had not had time to read the passage several times as assigned. She was encouraged to attend regardless, and she never missed during the next six weeks as II Samuel 11 and 12 came alive for this little group. The communicator focused on proclaiming an important message that, in turn, led people into crucial topics dealing with family relationships at a new and important level, concluding with what God wants us to do about these relationships as we live our lives today. This Bible study group would never be the same! They learned to appreciate Scripture in a new and vital way.

This experience introduces the topic of appropriate communication. It encompasses both the biblical community, which was the occasion for en scripturation, and communities today that must grapple with the reality of life in a world in which God has something to say about how people should live. What follows takes a serious look at both the nature and the process of appropriate communication. We draw heavily on communication theory and apply it to the theological foundations presented in earlier chapters.

THE NATURE OF
APPROPRIATE COMMUNICATION

Throughout history, missionaries have often missed the connection between their proclamation of the Gospel and communication theory. Often Gospel proclamation and even Bible translation have been considered basically a matter of language learning, establishing lexical equivalence, and then, through an intuitive process, hoping it would all work out to get the message across. By getting the words into the new language, somehow the Holy Spirit, the reasoning went, would bless it and everything would be fine. Such an approach may also account for a lot of misinformation about the Gospel and may contribute to so many unused Scripture portions and even Bibles sitting on dusty shelves in near-abandoned warehouses.[2] Gospel communicators need to do everything possible to enable people who receive God's Word to understand it. Clearly, from our perspective, understanding the nature of the communication process will facilitate the receptors' grasp of the message regarding God's intention for them.

Standards of Appropriate Communication

In discussing communication, the whole text, the complete discourse, must be taken seriously. We pointed out in chapter 1 that the Bible must be viewed as a whole, as well as each part seen in the context of the flow of salvation history and the theological development of the people of God—just as the seminary student tried to make clear to the Bible study group.

In 1981 Robert deBeaugrande and Wolfgang Dressler published a landmark work on the nature of text in general and discourse in particular. They presented the importance of understanding a text within a context, both in terms of the text initiator and its recipients. They define text as "a communicative occurrence that meets seven standards of textuality." If any one of these standards is not satisfied, the text will not appropriately communicate (1981: 3ff).[3] These seven standards for appropriate communication are:

1. Cohesion: The parts of a message must go together. "The surface components *depend* upon each other according to grammatical forms and conventions" (deBeaugrande and Dressler, 3).[4]

2. Coherence: The message communicated must make sense. Components "which *underlie* the surface text, are *mutually accessible* and *relevant*" (4).

3. Intentionality: For a message to communicate an audience needs to understand the author's purpose—"the text *producer's* attitude that the . . . text [be] instrumental in fulfilling . . . a *goal*" (7).

4. Acceptability: As people understand the message being communicated and the intent of those communicating, they are able to respond appropriately. Response serves as a demonstration of how well intentionality was understood. This concerns "the text *receiver's* attitude that the . . . text [has] some use or relevance" (1981 :7).

5. Informativity: How new information is presented so people can relate what they already know to understanding new information. Information flow—"the extent to which the occurrences of the presented text are expected vs. unexpected or known"—is crucial to processing a message (8–9).

6. Situationality: A message must be tied to the contextual expectations of an audience. This "concerns the factors which make a text *relevant* to a *situation* of occurrence" (9).

7. Intertextuality: No message stands alone, but is tied to other messages, which, when combined, form a repository of human knowledge from which people can decipher a particular message. This "concerns the factors which make the utilization of one text dependent upon knowledge of one or more previously encountered texts" (10).

Each of the seven standards is necessary for a text to be presented and understood in order to produce a response in ways appropriate to the intentions of the communicator or author. Added together these seven standards of communication create an appropriate text. The focus is on the ability of a communicator to present a message in such a way that it gets the point across effectively. In other words, all of the aspects must combine and recombine to present a viable, communicable text. Without all of these standards interacting together, communication cannot take place. deBeaugrande and Dressler (1981: 11) call these standards "constitutive principles," following Searle (1969: 33). These principles both define and create an understanding of a text and inform the relationship of a text with its context.

For example, for those receiving the Pauline letters written from prison, the context was very important. These letters reflected the effort it took for the Apostle, who was suffering for the sake of the Gospel, to write and maintain contact with the new believers. They also spoke of the importance Paul placed on instructing people in churches scattered throughout the lands where he had journeyed. Despite his suffering, for which he requested prayer, he gloried in his calling, which was far greater than the immediate pain of his circumstances. All of this is implied in his opening salutations where he identifies himself (and often those with him) and designates his addressees. This surface style grabbed their attention and focused on the deeper issues and needs of interest to them. As the communicator, Paul provided (1) cohesion, (2) coherence, and (3) intentionality that initially set the agenda of the communication. The topic and intent then, come largely out of the source context. The structure of a text is the focus from which the rest of communication takes place.[5]

Acceptability is the transitional standard of textuality in deBeaugrande and Dressler's constitutive principles. Ensuring communication is a transitional task performed by a person who understands both the source and receptor circumstances and attempts to ensure that the objectives and acceptability of the source communicate to a new audience. The communicator is the primary agent in this process. This person is given the task of ensuring that what was understood and acceptable to the original audience will also be appropriately communicated to the new receptors—an ancient biblical author needs to be understood by a contemporary audience. In Ricoeur's terms, communicators *re-describe* the circumstances so that they make sense to a contemporary audience (Ricoeur, 1991: 177).

The remaining standards of textuality—(5) informativity, (6) situationality, and (7) intertextuality—relate to the whole idea of transfer into the particular context of the contemporary receptors. As people receive a message, they are the ones to interpret the situation they know back into the text. For example, the Samo would not begin a letter with a formulaic, "Dear . . . " as in North America. Endearment is not an issue for them. Identification of the sender is the key issue much as it was for the apostle Paul. For years the only letters the Samo received were from men who had been sent to jail because of breaking some government regulation, often cannibalism in the 1960s, and later for adultery, which became more common after pacification. While in jail, some of them learned to read and write, and they occasionally tried to send a letter home—most never arrived. Those that did were brought to coauthor Dan to read, and always the salutation went, "In order for you not to forget me, my name is . . ." In other words, I'm not dead yet even though I've been gone for several years now. I'm still one of your relatives. I'm alive. I don't want to be forgotten.

That opening line for a letter turned out to be very useful when translating Paul's epistles for the Samo. It was particularly meaningful when the Samo learned that Paul was often writing from prison. So the letter to Thessalonica begins in Samo: "You people in Thessalonica, in order that you not forget me, my name is Paul." Can you imagine what that does for the Samo appreciation of what Paul is saying to the Thessalonians in the rest of the letter? There is so much implied information unpacked in that opening statement. When the Samo hear that opening line, they know what is going on. And because they understand the context, it makes sense to them just as it did to the first recipients, the Thessalonians. The Samo could understand Paul's intention, though Dan also had to ensure that they understood why Paul was in jail. For them, using "Dear," as in some contemporary English translations, would only confuse them with respect to the intentionality of the author.

If the communicators know that the information in the text assumes circumstances different from what the recipients can supply, sufficient material must be provided to help them understand. For the Samo living in virgin rain forest, the environment of the biblical context posed a major problem. Early in Dan's translation experience, he tried to choose stories that were not context-specific in order to avoid an explanation of the environment. This, however, could not last. Dan tells the story.

> When we translated the story of Jesus feeding of the five thousand in John chapter 6, the first question the Samo asked was "what kind of grass did the disciples tell the people to sit down on?" This was not a question I had anticipated and, of course I did not have an answer. We solved the problem by going for a walk, and collecting grasses. By doing an analysis of the way the Samo categorize grasses I discovered that the Samo classify plants (as well as most other things) based on placement in the environment: in the forest or in open places. After much deliberation, the Samo decided that the hillside in Palestine must have been an open space for that many people to sit down. The grass must have been soft enough not to hurt anyone sitting on it. Therefore, the grass name used in the translation is the same as that found on airstrips—one of the few open spaces Samo know. That type of grass matched their expectations and enabled them to make inferences that avoided images of people sitting in the forest or other inappropriate places. Using the right nomenclature met with audience expectations and allowed them to focus on the miracle rather than on the type of grass in that place (adapted from Shaw, 1988: 155).

Taken together deBeaugrande and Dressler's standards of communication provide a message-centered, user-friendly, and receptor-oriented structure that can be applied throughout the communication process. They accomplish this by applying "regulative principles (again, following Searle) that control textual communication rather than define it."

REGULATIVE PRINCIPLES
OF APPROPRIATE COMMUNICATION

While deBeaugrande and Dressler's standards of communication define the nature of proclamation necessary for an audience to consider the message relevant, their regulative principles serve as a control on the communication process it self. They call these controls efficiency, effectiveness, and appropriateness.

1. Efficiency ensures "a minimum of expenditure of effort by the participants" (deBeaugrande and Dressler, 1981: 11). The focus here is primarily on regulating the context in which messages are created and understood.
2. Effectiveness "of a text depends on its leaving a strong impression and creating favorable conditions for attaining a goal" (11). Communication should make an impact that forces an appropriate response.
3. Appropriateness regulates the relationship between what is said and what is meant. It ameliorates the tension between exegesis and hermeneutics. This principle strives to ensure "agreement between [a text's] setting and the ways in which the standards of textuality are upheld" (11).

This triad of principles connects old and new information and relates to the cognitive environment of both communicator and receptor. These principles serve as the communication generator, the deep-structure concerns that must be met by the more or less universal standards necessary for communication to take place in any context. This "text grammar" impacts the surface-level linguistic and cultural forms used to manifest how these communicative standards and principles work in a particular language. These three regulative principles are language-specific and must be independently analyzed and understood. The people themselves automatically use them and intuitively respond to their presence or lack thereof in the communication.

In the Samo language, for example, sentences are tied to each other in a chainlike pattern: The last part of almost every sentence is repeated as the first part of the next sentence. When the first part of the next sentence is repeated, people are able to assimilate the information. If they cannot assimilate the information, the communication load is considered too rapid and the discourse will not be conveyed as intended. And if the discourse is not appropriately conveyed, they will not pay attention to what is presented. If they do not pay attention, there is no point in communicating.

To continue this pattern in English, however, is not acceptable. Speakers of English place a high value on literacy and on a reasonably concise, logical, well-presented, linear flow of information. To communicate in English using Samo repetitive, oral-based patterns would quickly render English speakers (or more appropriately, readers) bored with this pedantic style. But if the Samo (like people in most oral societies) do not receive information in this way, they soon feel overloaded and are unable to process the glut of information.[6]

These regulative principles help organize the use and application of the communicative standards that serve as criteria for effective texts. What is true for text also pertains to the more general category of communication. Together these criteria and the principles that make them operative set the stage for a presentation and critique of communication models.

MODELS OF
APPROPRIATE COMMUNICATION

Understanding how communication works is essential for all who seek to initiate relationships with other human beings. God began the process by speaking the creation: God "said . . ." and it happened (Gen. chapter 1). God then created human beings in God's own image, people who were able to establish relationships with God and with each other. This reflects both the rationale for our creation and the way we were created—for relationship. There is much we can learn about communication from watching God in action, connecting with real people and the reality of their lives and transforming them into God's own image, as was the original intention. Therefore, while understanding deBeaugrande and Dressler's criteria for and regulative principles of appropriate proclamation is critical to a formal presentation of what communication is, how communication works is a very different matter. The focus needs to be on process over and above product. Here we present two key models in a radically abbreviated form in order to help communicators appreciate both the complexity and necessity of appropriate communication.[7] These two models are generally known as the "code model" and the "inferential model," or relevance theory. We briefly present them here in order to aid in understanding the nature of appropriate communication as it serves the criteria and regulative principles (presented above) for effective communication.

The Code Model of Communication

In the years since World War II one primary communication model has been in vogue, based on the idea of the telegraph and popularized by Shannon and Weaver (1949). This mode of communication came to be known as the "code model of communication," derived from the linguistic work of Wilhelm von Humboldt (1971) and Ferdinand de Saussure (1959, originally published in 1916), who both emphasized the importance of signs as they apply to an appreciation of human cognition. Shannon and Weaver divided signs into internal mental images of meaning and outer expressions with their focus on forms. This form-meaning composite impacted Berlo's (1960) development of receptor-oriented communication, was the centerpiece of Nida's (1964) translation theory, which later came to be known as "dynamic equivalence," and Kraft's (1979) application of all this to missiological issues in general. In his discussion of the multiplicity of communication channels, Hall (1959: xiv) noted that verbal communication was a relatively small part of the code, which could also be carried by paralinguistic aspects: body language, proxemics, environment, and other context-specific modes. All of this created "noise" as Shannon and Weaver called it, and had a considerable impact on the understanding of receptors who decoded a message, often in ways that an author did not intend. Thus voice inflection, gestures, clothing styles, and a host of other "signs" were juxtaposed with verbal communication and affected the way a communicator was understood.

This, together with the theory behind the code model, provides a major rationale for language and culture learning. To the extent possible, communicators must interact in ways appropriate to the receptors' context. The more a communicator relates to their receptors' field of experience, the more suitable the feedback becomes and the more dynamic the encoding for maximum decoding becomes. Besides the linguistic aspects of the "code" we have added "field of experience" to represent contextual issues that further impact the codes used in communication. This is in keeping with Hall's effort to be holistic. Figure 5.1 is a simplified diagram of the code model.

The focus of this model based on meeting the receptors' expectations enables Kraft to reflect that God always takes the initiative in communicating to human beings in their context (1991: 173ff). The object is to create as much overlap as possible. It is this overlap factor that resembles the incarnation and places the onus on the communicator to overcome the noise factors and make the adjustments necessary for communication. The argument is that if God took this approach with those whom God created, those who follow God's example and seek to magnify God's name should do the same.

However, the emphasis of the code model is on the presentation of the message. Gospel communicators tend to reproduce the forms in which the message was initially presented as closely as possible in order to ensure a product that hopefully transfers the same meaning. However, these "form-meaning-composites" (to

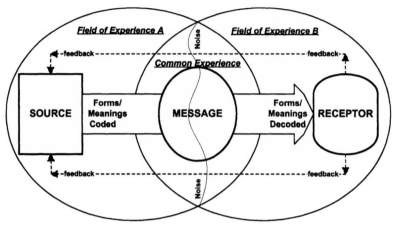

Adapted from Shaw 1988: 29.

Figure 5.1.   The Code Model of Communication

borrow a term from the tagmemic theory of linguistics (cf. Pike, 1967: 63) carry a heavy information load that presumes receptors understand both the source and the communicator's presuppositions. Less emphasis is placed on how the message is understood or what happens to it after it is received. This often results from an exegetical approach that attempts to maintain the original forms wherever possible. Furthermore, this approach can easily result in receptors being held accountable once the message has been presented to them, regardless of what that communication might mean in their time and place. This focus on how receptors understand the message leads us to seek another model that complements the code model.

The Inference Model of Communication

In the mid-1980s Sperber and Wilson pointed out the importance of considering how an audience perceived an author's intent. Their insights reflected the work of Charles Pierce who, in the early 1940s, noted that signs are culturally created categories that not only have form and meaning, but also refer to something in reality (Pierce, 1955), and Paul Grice who, in a series of lectures at Harvard in 1967, argued for the necessity of intentionality based on pragmatic theory (Grice, 1989). Since many signs, including the words and phrases used to communicate a message, are tied to some objective referent, it is possible to test how they fit within the real world at large. That world has a context, and it is out of that context that communication emerges with a particularity of intent and the need for "an audience to recognize the intention behind the utterance" (Grice, 1989: 213–14). For Sperber and Wilson, communication takes place when the signs used in communication fit with both the communicator's and the receptors' sense of what, for them, is reality—that is, there is a context that provides understandability of communication. When an author's intent matches the recipient's inferences, Sperber and Wilson call the message "relevant" (1986).[8] Hence, the model came to be known as "relevance theory." This theory "argues that the recovery of contextual information is essential for comprehension and that communication is largely an inferential process" (Green, 2001: 2).[9]

For Sperber and Wilson, communication requires (1) communicators who make their intention (they use the term "ostention") for communication clear, and (2) receptors who are able to determine, through a process called "inference" what a communicator intended. This requires that a communicator have a deliberate intent to convey information, which receptors are able to process for its intended message while using contextual information available to them, what Rountree calls "the conceptual text" (2001: 6) (relevance theorists call this the "cognitive environment"). deBeaugrande and Dressler's standards of communication and regulative principles are essential to this process. The closer the two contexts are in terms of understanding intent and potential meaning, the more appropriate or "relevant" the perception of the communication. As Blass notes, "context is a set of assumptions brought to bear in the interpretation of an utterance" (Blass, 1990: 31). This expectation of relevance within a context encourages people to make an effort to process the information. In other words, people assume a meaningful exchange when someone goes to the trouble to communicate with purpose and intent. If, however, they must expend what seems to them to be an inordinate amount of effort to understand the communication, they will no longer focus on the message and only hear the noise generated by issues that may have nothing to do with the communicator's intent. Background assumptions and shared assumptions, then, are crucial to the communication event. Figure 5.2 is an attempt to represent the theoretical issues behind the inferential model while at the same time presenting it in a way that can be compared with the code model in figure 5.1.

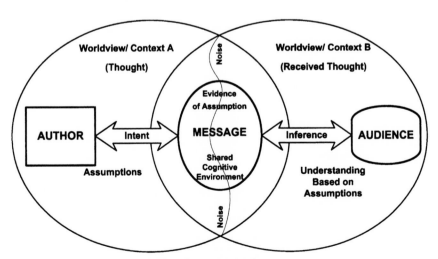

Figure 5.2.   The Inference Model of Communication

Relevance theory recognizes the importance of transferring an intended message in such a way that a new audience can make sense of it. In this model, communication does not focus on the forms and meanings used to present the message. Rather it concentrates on the thought processes necessary for communicators to ensure that receptors understand their intent as clearly as possible. Though transferring biblical intent across the chasm of time, space, and culture separating biblical and present-day peoples is very difficult, it is essential for appropriate communication. As we noted briefly in chapter 1 and developed further in chapter 4, the way Scripture interprets itself is a canonical approach that demonstrates the hermeneutical method we espouse in this book. The inferential model forces communicators to enter into the communication process for the purpose of ensuring an understanding of a message—how would it have been communicated using the present context? The focus is on presenting a message so that an audience is able to interpret the intended meaning of the author as expressed in a text.[10] This is dynamic and process-oriented, and demands an interrelationship between everyone (or at least all the ideas) involved in the communication. The interaction between source and receptor, intent and inference, is relational and can be traced back to God's intent in creation.

The inferential model has had a considerable impact on Ernst-August Gutt, who has specifically applied the concepts to Bible translation:

> [T]he interpretation of a stimulus is always relevance-determined, and hence context-dependent. It is therefore not always possible to take some given "meaning" or "message" and produce a stimulus that will be able to communicate just this "message" to some particular audience. Whether or not this is possible will depend on whether the "message" in question is communicable to that audience in terms of consistency with the principle of relevance. The view that the main problem in translation is that of finding the right way of expressing the content in the receptor language has tended to obscure the problem of the communicability of the content itself. (Gutt, 1991: 98–99)

The difficulty with the inferential model is that effective implementation requires considerable time and research of both the original context and the circumstances into which the message must now be presented. This often becomes problematic in crosscultural situations that demand an effort to learn another language and culture. No wonder Bible translation demands a lifetime commitment. Yet current trends shy away from long-term involvement of outside communicators and toward adequate training to equip those who know and understand the receptors' language and culture to present the message themselves.

While the code model more adequately represents the exegetical side (what God said) the relevance model is more hermeneutical (context-oriented with respect to God's intent), emphasizing how authors would have communicated had they used the receptors' context. However, the exegetical-hermeneutical duality is critical and must not be ignored. It is not a matter of either/or, but rather of both-and. Both outside exegetical specialists and inside language and culture bearers must work side by side to ensure appropriate communication. Nor must insiders be forced to accept outside input regarding the content of Scripture and God's intentions for human beings. Rather, insiders must be trained to apply the principles of these communication models in order to appreciate God's relationships with creation and present them appropriately within their context. Ultimately this comes down to a team effort that leads to decisions and testing done within a hermeneutical community by those who know that community best. Relevance theory is central to understanding reality, not to the forms and meanings necessary to present that reality. It forces an amalgamation of both sides of the communication equation with respect to deep understanding and, to the extent possible, mutual appreciation of the cognitive environment held by both. In the case of translation, the communicator/translator serves as the means to bring the respective contexts together, enabling a new audience to utilize their cognitive environment to make a connection with an unknown environment, which, for the purpose of understanding a message, they must appreciate in order to make sense of the intended message. This is the communication task.

Therefore, in order to ensure appropriate communication, the process of exegeting text and connecting it to a hermeneutical community (both with respect to the source and contemporary receptors) is important. Both the code and inferential models can be brought to bear. We are not endorsing one communication model over another. Rather both the code model and inference/relevance model, with their respective emphases, can be applied to the entire communication context of source, communicator, and receptor. We must avoid the simplistic pitfall of substituting a newer, cognitive-linguistics informed model for one that has solidly impacted an entire generation of theoreticians—the former is more content-based, while the latter is more context-based. We must value each for its contribution to our understanding of communication in general in order to maximize the strengths of each and thereby minimize their respective weaknesses.

For Gospel communicators, the objective in approaching the Bible is to adequately understand the context into which God initially communicated God's intent for human beings, and apply that understanding to contemporary audiences. As both models stress, there are two sides to the equation and both must be fulfilled before deBeaugrande and Dressler's standards of textuality and regulative principles may be met. If a message, no matter how well formed and thought out, is not comprehensible, it will not be understood and will probably be ignored. No matter how comprehensible the message may be for receptors, if they do not perceive it as relevant, they will probably not give it sufficient attention.

Finally, if the forms the communication takes are clear to the present audience but do not adequately represent God's intention for human beings, they are not faithful to the message of Scripture and may lead receptors into heresy. Therefore we must move beyond forms and meanings as such and focus on the authorial intention and audience perception necessary to ensure understanding. All of this is implied in the four-horizons model presented in chapter 4.

RELEVANT INFERENCES IN
APPROPRIATE COMMUNICATION

Communication in deBeaugrande and Dressler's terms may include all sorts of styles and forms over and above some manifestation of the verbal (including literacy). It includes ritual, dance, music, dreams, prayer and other genres considered relevant in a local context. These nonverbal aspects supplement and contextualize the relatively small percentage of communication encased in actual words. As we have commented often, these forms and styles work on two levels: horizontal and vertical.

Vertically, nonverbal aspects of communication are used to communicate with what Hiebert calls the "transempirical": any spiritual force, beneficial or detrimental, to human beings (Hiebert, 1982b).[11] At issue here is an appreciation of spirituality and the need to respond in appropriate, culturally recognized ways established as relevant for interaction with the cosmos. Communication associated with an appreciation of spirituality is often related directly to individual or group survival in what people often perceive as a hostile world—one frequented with spiritual forces that can wreak havoc on crops, bring disease, or cause division within a culturally defined social unit. Human beings seek, in some way, to control these transempirical forces and bend them to their will, thereby improving the human condition, extending life, or simply leaving humans alone to live as they please.[12]

Horizontally all human beings seek to communicate with other imminent or "empirical" forces, often other human beings, where the emphasis is on interaction patterns that stress interpersonal relationship. While these patterns vary from one society to another, they are very important because communication usually takes place in the context of human interaction. So, for example, knowing how fathers communicate with sons, the circumstances under which they are allowed to communicate, and what they may communicate about are all subsumed under an analysis of expectations within the father-son dyad. The same can apply to any other relational structure, as well as with the inanimate world surrounding people and subsumed in their particular context.

When combined, the vertical and horizontal planes create the environment for communication. An objective of horizontal communication involves corporate survival in the midst of many social and cultural forces. And an objective of vertical communication involves corporate survival in the context of spiritual forces. The apostle Paul makes it clear that the real battle is spiritual not physical (Eph. 6). Both types of forces have been in place since creation (Col. 1:16) and they enter into all communication. Notice that we see these concerns in the multiplicity of human experience throughout history, both in Scripture and in our contemporary, complex world.

Suppose a group of people change their allegiance from fear and placation of local spirit-beings to an allegiance to the one true God. Can we assume that their worship styles and ways of expressing spiritual interest will suddenly be null and void? Of course not. The same rituals and meaningful vertical communication they used before their new understanding of the "transempirical" can now, by and large, be used in worship, although the focus of their allegiance will have changed. What is important is their understanding of God and the inferences they make about the supernatural in their context.

By way of example, we might consider how the people of a culture might introduce a local myth. As noted in chapter 2, a literal translation of the Samo mythical introduction, *omu kogowa,* is "long before the ancestors." Now, if that introduction were to be used in Genesis 1:1, what inferences would the Samo make? They would immediately know that this is an important message—something that would validate their understanding of truth. Using Sperber and Wilson's terms, it would validate God's original intent within the particularity of the Samo language. It would say pay attention, you are about to hear something important—a myth, a story that rings true. Using this mythical style within the context of Scripture connects the vertical with the Samo understanding of the horizontal and serves as a means of connecting the Samo to ultimate truth. As with God's intent in communicating with human beings, the Samo acknowledge the same purpose for their mythology, communicating truth that impacts the way people live.

Or perhaps a group uses dance forms that they incorporate into an all-night ritual. Such holy dance may be the appropriate communication vehicle to associate the vertical and horizontal planes of the communication environment. Scripture is full of such dancing. This principle could apply equally well to musical forms, dreams, or prayer. Certainly all of these forms are in the Bible. Yet westerners, in their dichotomistic, particularistic approach that emerges from the Enlightenment, have largely dismissed these forms of communication as irrelevant. In English, the word "myth" implies untruth rather than origins of truth, as it does both in the Bible and among many groups around the world. By being rationalistic, westerners have removed deBeaugrande and Dressler's regulative principles that allow their standards of communication to take effect.

In short, they have removed the means for relevant communication as presented by Sperber and Wilson. When that happens, for many people in the majority world, all that is left is irrelevance—the message does not communicate because it comes cloaked in the wrong sociolinguistic structures.

During a consultation in Papua New Guinea, coauthor Dan Shaw was part of an inquiry to determine why a particular group of people took Scripture so lightly. A mission church had been established in the area many years before and there was a considerable amount of nominality. Church leaders had invited the translation team to come so that the people could apply Scripture to their lives. How could they get people to see the new translation as something important? Dan tells the story.

> As we analyzed this social context, we asked a lot of questions both of the translators and the local believers present at the workshop. We asked about their social structure, about what they considered important, and how important subjects were communicated. As we probed these issues of meaningful communication style some very interesting points surfaced.
>
> In the past, among these people, it had been customary that when someone was upset and wanted to reduce his or her stress, that person would stand in the middle of the community and berate other people, often in positive terms but with deep sarcasm. Everyone knew, however, that the display was just a culturally appropriate way to reduce tension. When the mission first came into the region, the pastors, not yet having a church building in which people could gather, would stand in the middle of a village and preach the Gospel. This form of communication so reminded the people of their cultural custom of reducing stress that they paid little attention to the message. They reasoned that this Gospel in general and Jesus in particular could not be a very important if presented in this manner. Important messages were communicated by the elders talking quietly around the fires in the evening. This fact brought up another problem: the pastors were mostly young and well educated—but ignorant of cultural values.
>
> The solution, it turned out, was to teach older men the stories so they could tell them to their people in the solitude of their homes. When combined with a literacy program that enabled people to quietly read the stories and apply them to their own lifestyle, this new practice greatly increased interest in translated Scripture. The communicational styles simply had to be right before the people gave credence to what was being presented. Messages and their intent were bound to the styles of communication chosen to present them as well as to the words used in the proclamation. When the ritual used reminded people of a form that signaled a private matter that could be politely ignored, the message was treated as unimportant—the Gospel was viewed as irrelevant. However, once it conformed to the way important messages should be presented, the response changed as well.

Understanding the nature of communication and applying principles for appropriate communication is essential to effective proclamation. Cultural and linguistic understanding must be brought to bear in a particular context for people to appreciate the message from God and relate it to daily life. Gene Green says it well:

> Authors speak, but readers truly do contribute something to the interpretive process. They are active and called upon to make inferences, but only those for which the author has given evidence and which are consistent with the communicative principle of relevance. Meaning is, therefore, not simply subject to readers and politics but rather the ones who speak are given full voice while readers enter into communication with them. A gap exists between a biblical author's semantic representations and the meaning he wished to convey. We, as the first readers, fill that gap by an inferential process. This does not suggest that language is unstable but simply that meaning is linguistically underdetermined. Relevance constrains the inferences made in understanding. (Green, 2001: 53)

This moves our discussion from the use of communication styles and symbols to the nature of communication and how that is tied to community.

THE PROCESS OF
APPROPRIATE COMMUNICATION

Following Sperber and Wilson, and working through deBeaugrande and Dressler, Christeena Alaichamy (1997) approached the communication task as a consultant interested in enabling national translators in India to understand the translation process as a form of appropriate communication. To accomplish this, she developed a "tri-dimensional model" involving what she calls "coupling," "commonality," and "bridging." These concepts closely compare with deBeaugrande and Dressler's regulative principles, but she developed them for the purpose of enabling communication rather than regulating communicative standards. This process now draws our attention.

Coupling

For Alaichamy, "coupling" connects a new message with receptors' preexisting assumptions. In crosscultural communication, coupling strives to recreate an author's assumptions such that those who receive the message do not react as though it were foreign. Coupling serves to mediate between the content and context so that receptors can understand an author's intentions while at the same time applying it to their own context, thereby enabling an appropriate response.

Commonality

The second aspect in the process of appropriate communication is "commonality"—what is shared by both author and audience alike. Within a cultural context there is considerable commonality—people share assumptions, worldview. However, across cultures the focus increasingly becomes that which is common to humanity rather than within a society. Much within a culture may appear similar at the surface level, but the rationale for understanding may be radically different at the deep, assumptive level. All human beings laugh and cry, but what causes them to laugh or cry may be very different. Maslow (1954) notes common needs that must be met in order for people to survive. But how they meet those needs varies greatly in different cultures around the world. What of an author's experience or assumptions is common to the particular audience that first received the message? What information must be provided in order for a new audience to understand what was originally assumed as common knowledge? These questions lead to the third concept of "bridging."

Bridging

For Alaichamy, "bridging" across the sociolinguistic gap is a difficult and technical process. She used the concept to show that appropriate communication is the responsibility of the author. However, when that textual author was a biblical personage who not only lived a long time ago, but in a strange and far off place, the responsibility falls on a present-day communicator—a "translator." The communicator's task is to build a bridge between what the textual author originally assumed on the basis of a particular worldview and what is assumed by the people of a very different, contemporary context. For receptors to understand sufficiently and make correct inferences involves the provision of what the author's original audience assumed.[13]

Bridging different sociolinguistic contexts requires considerable research pertaining to the original communicational context. The new context spans considerable time and space and involves providing the missing pieces in order to allow that audience to make proper inferences upon which they can act in response to the message. As Alaichamy noted, it is the responsibility of the communicator to work through this process (1997: 115). Neither the textual author, who is no longer around (except through the presence of the Holy Spirit who illuminates Scripture), nor the contemporary audience, who is largely unable to investigate the original context, is able to do this. Bridging, then is the unique role of the communicator. The danger comes when proclaimers filter the message through their own worldview and biases and thereby create communicative noise that may be theological, ecclesiastical, cultural, or anything else that may cloud understanding. We raise this issue again in chapter 6, but make the point here that great effort must be taken to avoid a filter effect on the part of communicators so that an audience can ultimately hear God and not the contemporary communicators' biases.

When the communication pertains to the way people relate to God, the source of Scripture, the process is all the more crucial. Through this process, people will make inferences about God that will influence their thinking as well as the decisions they make about relationship with God. It requires considerable motivation for people to abandon what they know from their own understanding of the "transempirical" and come to trust a new message that, if followed, may draw them into uncharted spiritual territory. The devil is very good at playing on natural, human-centered fears that would keep people from changing their allegiance.

To ensure that communication takes place, Alaichamy incorporates linguistic and cultural information from each horizon into a technical structure summarized in figure 5.3. This technical dimension involves three crucial steps necessary for appropriate proclamation: analysis, synthesis, and presentation of the message. These concepts are derived from Alaichamy's tri-dimensional approach. Those who would proclaim the Gospel must make a conscious effort to thoroughly analyze the source documents in order to synthesize the author's message and present it to a new audience in such a way that people are able to grasp what was originally intended and act upon it in ways appropriate to them. This is a difficult task. Our intent here is to present steps based on communication theory that will reduce this complexity and enhance understanding on the part of communicators as well as receptors.

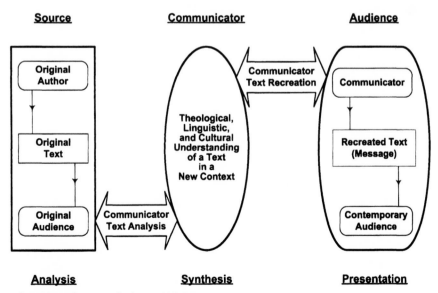

Adapted from Christeena Alaichamy, 1997: iv.

Figure 5.3.   The Technical Dimension of Appropriate Communication

Step One: Analysis

Analysis of the source text is the first step, including familiarity with the language and culture of the original context. It demands an appreciation for the rationale behind the communication and what the author assumed about the text, as well as an understanding of the receptor audience and their inferences. The entire communicative context of the original text must be considered at this juncture and relevance theory is of great help.

There is considerable biblical precedent for building relationships that facilitate the discovery of a message or apply textual understanding to a new context. For example, Ezekiel (18:2) speaks of children being allowed to relate to God on their own and not only through their parents. That passage repeats an ancient Hebrew proverb that says, "Sour grapes eaten by parents leave a sour taste in the mouths of their children" (18:2). It then goes on to say that parents need to give their children freedom to relate directly to God. Despite the proverb as it came to be used, Ezekiel points out the need for recontextualization in each generation. In the end, "good people will be rewarded for what they do, and evil people will be punished for what they do" (Ezek. 18:20).

New relationships that offer new understanding of a message can also be seen in the concept of re-presentation introduced in chapter 1 with reference to Abraham's context. First, God established a covenant with Abraham, and over a considerable period of time demonstrated the value of their relationship. As soon as Isaac left Abraham's tent, however, God renewed the promise of the land and many descendants by recommitting to the covenant with Isaac (Gen. 26:23–25). Then, when Jacob left Isaac's tent, God entered into a new relationship with him that reaffirmed the covenant with both Abraham and Isaac (Gen. 28:13–22). Years later God spoke to the children of Israel from Sinai and said, "I am the God of Abraham, Isaac, and Jacob." Then God reestablished the ancestral covenant through a new relationship with them. Through covenant Israel became "God's people," and Yahweh became "their God." Such analysis enabled an understanding of the source text and context that could then be appropriately communicated in a new time and place. What does this kind of relationship mean to the Samo? To the Maya? To Dan Shaw's Bible study group? To you, the reader?

Step Two: Synthesis

The second step of appropriate communication draws on the first step and yet avoids introducing personal bias or assumptions. Synthesizing an understanding of the source in order to pass it on to a contemporary audience is the objective, not presenting theological or personal biases.

Coming from different worldviews and theological perspectives, however, it is only natural for a multiplicity of communicators to read the text differently. However, as pointed out in chapter 4, the starting point is critical. Is the understanding of the text what God intended to communicate to all human beings or is it something people have read into the text? If a communication in its full measure (including an incarnational lifestyle) becomes simply a mirror of the proclaimer's agenda, it is not a faithful presentation of an author's intention. Appropriate proclamation is more than merely informing others what a communicator thinks ought to be known—passing on information. If, on the other hand, people receive God's intended message and apply it to their lives, a transformation process will begin, conforming people to God's image.

Communicators, then, learn from others, even as they learn from the text, and this, in turn, is transformative. Rare is the crosscultural communicator who returns home unchanged by the context of ministry. Communicators must be willing to allow people the freedom to learn something about their relationship to God that could not be know given the communicator's worldview. We can only allow this kind of freedom if we truly trust the Holy Spirit and allow God's power to draw people to the truth of the message. For it is God's truth that will set them free (John 8:32), not what others tell them.

There is a need to bring together the deep contextual assumptions implied in the text to see how human commonality can be manifest in the particularity of a new context. The cultural expectations of horizontal relationships within any given society inform the nature of vertical relationships, but must do so in light of God's intentionality through scripture. So, for example, what relationship-oriented terms can be used to refer to God? What terms best reflect the relationship between believers and Jesus Christ? Are the Father-Son adoption metaphors common in the Pauline corpus best, or do cultural issues set these terms apart as negative or irrelevant for the people who receive the message? Adjustments are required in order to reflect God's intended communication while a particular community must receive the information in ways that match their conceptual map. Perhaps, for example, the mother's brother-sister's child dyad (so familiar in parts of Africa, Australia, and Melanesia) should be used to reflect a relationship to God. How free are communicators to make such adjustments? The answer to this much-debated question takes on new character when relevance theory and the horizons model are taken into account. The answer, in large measure, takes us back to the starting point, the text.

Remember that God never spoke in a vacuum. God entered into contexts in which language and culture were in place and, therefore, required God to fit into and use the terminology of each setting. We must determine, then, whether God's intent was to focus on fathers and sons as genealogical relationships with a prescribed set of interaction patterns or on relationships between God and human beings, however those relational patterns might be reflected in a society. In other words, was the original communication a culturally-specific message in which the meaning of the text was bound to the context, or was it a generalized communication ultimately destined for all human beings regardless of their context in time and space? We think the latter, and therefore, believe the text must be analyzed in light of the coupling stage for God's intent. It must then be processed through de-Beaugrande and Dressler's communicative principles. But—and this is a crucial point—we must consider the text as God's Word first, and then work from there, never the reverse. There is a directional flow to the hermeneutical spiral (as we discussed in chapter 4) that is crucial if we are to avoid heresy. And we must always begin with the text, never the context. However, we must not downplay the complexity of intertextuality; a text can never be isolated from the context that precipitated the communication in the first place.

As missiologists, we are increasingly convinced that even in revelation the primary focus goes beyond communication to relationship. If that is the case, then Gospel communication becomes an introduction of the text in a new context from which, because of different assumptions, new understanding emerges. Communicators introduce God to receptors who in turn gain new understanding of God via the presentation. People build a new relationship with God because of how they perceive the text vis-à-vis their context. And relationships are dynamic. They are always developing through history, deepening and growing. Yet there are some basic values and assumptions as to how those relationships work. There are some givens and the givens of relationships are manifest in highly cultural ways. If knowing God is the objective, then the focus must be on communication of a relationship rather than simply the transfer of information. The academic emphasis on technical expertise in typical western contexts needs to be complemented by competence in the local context. It is the people of a particular context who know and understand their situation and are comfortable interacting in ways an outsider will never be. Westerners can enable local pastors and translators, not by doing it for them, but by working alongside them and providing expertise that gives them confidence in knowing the nature of the source text.

Finally, we must note once again the role of the Holy Spirit in the explanation of the text—its synthesis or appropriation in a new context. Jesus said, "I will send the Comforter and he will remind you of what I have said and help you understand what I have said" (Jn. 16:14). In both the initial presentation and the process of synthesis, the Holy Spirit's illumination is necessary for the receptors to understand and participate in this new relationship. The Holy Spirit brings an understanding to the communicator of the message and to the receptors who must apply it in a new way to their circumstances. This illuminating interaction between the Holy Spirit, communicators, and local recipients of the message makes for great synergy, a team effort that enables greater appreciation for God's communicational intent as well as the content of the message.

Step Three: Presentation

The third step in Alaichamy's model relates to the communicator's ability to "bridge the gap" and assimilate into or appropriate the message to the receptors' context (1997: 113ff). Without this information it is impossible to recreate the original message in the new context. This knowledge is assumed in the horizons model as presented in figure 4.10 in which each horizon interacts with the one on each side of it to re-present the one in the new context of the other. The bridging process takes each horizon into account and implements the entire transference of a message from an ancient context to a contemporary context. The attention is on communication with its emphasis on the message, not on the baggage (linguistic and cultural forms and meanings as well as theological, ecclesiastical, and even personal issues) that communicators bring to the process.

For example, evangelical missionaries have tended to look at the text primarily as "command"—the Bible is something to be obeyed. With that as their concept of the Bible, they unconsciously told people what they thought they needed to know and what that meant in terms of their behavior. The problem was that their view of what God said was impacted by their cultural assumptions, not necessarily by what God intended to communicate. This communicator-centric position was then unconsciously passed on to receptors. It demonstrated the impact of the code model, with its focus on text rather than context, on word-for-word translation rather than on communication. Ensuring a transfer of information was the focus. The Bible, then, simply became a source of information that often resulted in people not understanding the nature of relationship—relationship with God as well as with other believers.

Even today, western missionaries seem to feel compelled to explain who God is. The difficulty is that in doing this they explain their own view of God, which emphasizes Enlightenment arguments that provide an apology for God's existence. Such arguments, however, are often irrelevant for nonwestern or pluralist audiences that are relationship-oriented. Instead, it may be good for missionaries to listen to the people they seek to reach and learn more about God from them.

Unless the people's views are considered when communicating the "old, old story," communicators will simply pass on information with little relevance, which, following Sperber and Wilson, may result in little or no communication. The end product of this approach is a task orientation: ensure a message is communicated, a translation is completed, or a church is planted. It becomes more important to "get the job done" than to have the people hear and respond to God's intended message. It is as if the end product in itself is what God wanted. But when we look at the biblical pattern, God always began by interacting with people: being in their midst, relating to their needs and interests, and then speaking to them in their context.

Once this biblical perspective is understood as an appropriate approach to communication, the task becomes less important and the relationship becomes central. As we noted in the introduction to this book, communicators may be the ones chosen by God to exemplify that relationship. In their person they seek to present God as well as the uniqueness of the Scripture God indwells. This is what sets the Bible apart from all other texts. If the biblical text is to have relevance within a particular context, and be appreciated as the panoramic, historical, and dynamic communication it was intended to be, then it must proclaim the nature of God and the uniqueness of Christ. This comes in the form of a relationship between God and God's People. It is both revelational and descriptive of how God developed relationship—of what happened beginning at creation and moving throughout history down to the contemporary context.

Because the message comes wrapped in interactive, relational modes, new receptors are able to appreciate the ongoing progress of God's developing relationship with those who populate horizons I and II. With that understanding they can then appreciate their own relationship with God as well as with others in horizons III and IV. The message becomes relational—not just information people need to know. They are forced to ask questions about their knowledge of God and how they interact with the "transempirical." Is their god too small for the biblical view, or did they know about the God of the Bible all along, yet the truth had been hidden to them?[14]

Appropriate proclamation of the message requires interaction of each horizon with the next. The technical dimension takes place through God's interaction with the biblical author who transmitted the message to a human audience in a particular time and place. When applied by communicators to the audiences they seek to inform of God's message, the process must be reworked to provide a new audience with everything necessary for them to make appropriate inferences about God's intentions toward them without ignoring the relevance for the original audience. And while the focus here is on presentation, analysis and synthesis, have obvious implications within the context of this third step. Applying these three steps enables communicators to view the issues in the biblical text through new eyes. That understanding can then be passed on to contemporary audiences in such a way that they too gain new appreciation for the totality of God's message to them. And, throughout the process, the "evangelists," those who proclaim the message, draw "new" water from ever deeper in the well of understanding.

SUMMARY

The relationship between God and God's People is infinitely communicable. To present such an important message takes an attachment approach. The communicator needs to connect with the people so they may better reflect on the truth about God. This, of course, forces communicators out of their comfort zone and away from familiar scientific assumptions and processes. Because of their own relationship with God, they end up not being in control. Incarnational presenters, then, should try to communicate a relevant and meaningful message to the context, thereby bridging the gap by means of a presentation that accounts for analysis of the source and synthesis of information pertinent both to the source and to the receptors. The objective is to present a message that encourages people to make a decision regarding both vertical and horizontal relationships and subsequently follow through on the consequences of that decision as it impacts their lives.

We began the chapter by looking at standards of communication. What must be included for a message to be transmitted with the author's intended meaning when received by others? As a community of believers forms in a particular society, people begin to build relationships with God and with each other. However, new Christians do not need to reinvent the wheel. There is a larger community of believers—the worldwide Church. Over the centuries the churches have had wild ideas about what God intended in the text, but there was always a community that judged the reception of that word by a particular set of standards: a closed canon set in the historical events of Israel and Jesus and the Apostles.

This places the new receptors' understanding of the text within the broader context of the church. There is only one Bible, but its message runs throughout history. It has changed people's lives, it has resulted in the historical development of dogma, and it has produced a global church. Furthermore it changed the lives of those in that little Bible fellowship group. Led by a talented communicator, they took the message of David and Bathsheba and allowed it to shine into their own lives. They allowed it to illuminate their own familial relationships in a new and exciting way.

Beyond the communicational concerns for appropriate presentation of the Gospel with its focus on hermeneutical issues, we must also consider the critical issues that impact particular people in their time and place. This leads us, in chapter 6, to a discussion of cultural concerns that affect the formulation of a text and the communication of it in radically different and unexpected contexts.

NOTES

1. In chapter 3 we addressed the consequences of this story, noting how God used the prophet Nathan to get David's attention. Here we look at how a communicator can use this tragic story to impact the lives of people in a Bible study group.

2. It seems too facile and misleading to fail to take seriously the entire "communication context" (source, translator, and receptor) and then say, "God, bless it." We both know of too many translations of Scripture that have been properly checked,

printed, bound, and dedicated but, unfortunately, are largely unread and unused because people can't make sense of it in their own context. Gene L. Green addresses this issue in an excellent review of relevance theory as it pertains to hermeneutical issues. He makes the point well: "Our recognition of the humanity of Scripture must take into account the nature of human communication as well as the cultural, linguistic, temporal, geographical and situational gap between the contemporary reader and the ancient authors and readers" (Green, 2001: 41).

3. The contrast made in chapter 1 between the Bible as text (with a focus on what it says) and the Bible as Scripture (with a focus on what God as the original author intended people to understand) is not reflected in deBeaugrande and Dressler's definition. However, their standards of textuality clearly indicate a need for both exegesis and hermeneutics. This forms the two sides of the communication equation for Sperber and Wilson (1986).

4. All emphases in these definitions are from deBeaugrande and Dressler and indicate their concern for the importance of these concepts.

5. This assumes a particular style, or genre, of discourse as discussed in appendix B.

6. The interaction between principles of communication and the regulative principles relates directly to relevance theory, a key model for communication.

7. This is not an attempt to give an exhaustive history of the development of communication theory. Nor do we desire to give a detailed contrast of different communication models. Rather we seek, here, to give evidence necessary to support our argument that the theoretical issues of communication are important and must be taken seriously by all who would effectively present the Gospel. A considerable literature has recently burgeoned around the core values of these models and their application to the practice of contemporary mission. Bible translators have been at the forefront as they seek to relate translation theory to communication processes. Ernst-August Gutt led the way with his seminal transfer from relevance as a theory to application (1991, 1992), Ragina Blass (1990) has connected relevance issues to understanding discourse in West Africa, and Gene Green has reviewed the literature and summarized it from a hermeneutical perspective in order to understand the application of biblical texts to the contemporary circumstances in which we live in the twenty-first century (2001). Dave van Grootheest has written a Masters thesis exploring some of the debate raging around relevance theory (1996) and Harriet Hill has written a Ph.D. dissertation focusing on the implications of relevance theory for ensuring that African recipients understand God's intentions for them (2003).

8. In understanding communication, we largely reject the dualism and oversimplification of Humboldt and Saussure, which leaves meaning in people's minds without objective external referents. This leads to cognitive relativism, which Pierce's triadic view of signs rejects. For Pierce (1955) the *object* represents reality out there (real trees), the *representatum* involves the signs people use to represent that reality (the word used to talk about the tree), and the *interpretant* is the mental image these signs stimulate (the intent and inference in the mind of communicators and recipients when they think about and respond to trees). McElhanon discusses symbols in the context of prototype theory with a focus on how abstract images, or gestalts, reflect the way human beings experience life (2000). For further insight into how the theory of signs impacts religious understanding and symbolism see Hiebert, Shaw, and Tiénou (1999: 231ff).

9. Relevance has a technical definition that goes beyond what appears to be important or pertinent to a particular conversation or text. Following Wilson and Matsui (1998), Green defines it in relation to cognitive effects and processing effort:

> *Relevance*
>
> a. The greater the cognitive effects, the greater the relevance;
> b. The smaller the effort needed to achieve those effects, the greater the relevance . . .
>
> In order for an utterance to achieve relevance, it must be processed in a context which will yield for the hearer some cognitive effects without undue or gratuitous processing effort. (Green, 2001: 27)

Thus the best communication takes place when the processing effort is low (inferences are easily made) and the cognitive effects are high (relevance to the receptor's environment is clear).

10. Green picks up on this point by noting: "Relevance theory affirms that within the process of interpretation, the recovery of the [communicator's] informative intent is at the very heart of what communication is all about. 'Intention' is far from being some opaque cognitive mystery which is inaccessible to the [receptor]. According to relevance theory, the informative intention of the communicator is deemed recoverable and its recovery is essential for successful communication. This notion, however, is not the same as mutual knowledge, which is an impossible goal to obtain" (Green, 2001; 43).

11. We are intentionally not using the term "animistic" because beliefs associated with these ideas permeate all religious traditions and form the basis of "folk religion" (Hiebert, Shaw, and Tiénou, 1999: 75ff).

12. This is an immense topic far too complex to handle here. For more detail and information, see Hiebert, Shaw, and Tiénou (especially section two, 95ff).

13. This is the essence of Harriet Hill's research as she investigates what the Adioukrou of Côte d'Ivoire understand of the biblical context (more than she realized) and what material must be supplied so they can draw proper inferences. Once the latter is identified, the issue becomes how best to supply information that will fill the cognitive gap between the original text and Adioukrou understanding. Hill developed tests to establish this and in so doing learned much about the Adioukrou worldview as well as her own understanding of Second temple Judaism, which undergirds so many assumptions in the New Testament text (Hill, 2003).

14. Communicators may be surprised to discover that the people to whom they communicate the message suddenly go beyond them theologically. By this we mean the receptors know something about God that other Christians never saw before. What is important, however, is that the receptors discover this out of the text presented to them as they relate the message to their particular context, to their own lives—just as God spoke to Abraham, Isaac and Jacob.

· 6 ·

Culturally Appropriate Communication

> The communicators' culture and worldview influence the way
> they skillfully draw the message from a source text and pass it on
> to contemporary contexts. In doing this, communicators of the
> Gospel must avoid being the filter through which the receptors
> hear God.

*Coauthor Dan Shaw was enjoying the revelry among a group of Samo men
during an all-night ceremony. The kava drink was flowing, the men of the local
longhouse community were enjoying the company of their visiting allies, and
everyone was having a good time. Shaw continues the story.*

*In the midst of this camaraderie I noticed a middle-aged man sitting alone and not
entering into the festivities. The rest of the group totally ignored him and he, in turn,
paid no attention to what was going on. As the night wore on, he pulled up his bark
cape and went to sleep despite the noise around him. Finally, I asked someone,
"what's the matter with Hiyanbi?" The response was,* diyę fini diyoo, *"his spirit
him." I knew the words: a possessive pronoun, the word for indwelling spirit or life
force, and a referential pronoun. But strung together the phrase meant nothing to
me—I could not make sense out of the phrase. Why would the response to my question about a non-participatory man who was usually friendly and engaged in household activities be "his spirit him"? It made no sense.*

*Days later, after many questions that precipitated considerable discussion, I learned
that the group could not account for Hiyanbi's solitude in the circumstances and their
response was to leave him alone to work out whatever it was he was brooding over. In
other words, the culturally appropriate Samo response was to leave a person to the dictates of the spirit within and when ready to reengage with the group the rationale behind the behavior would come out. This response served to demonstrate the tension between corporate relationships within the household on the one hand and a person's
individuality and identity on the other. My question about him prompted a response
which, loosely translated was, "it's his business, talk to him if you must know." This
idiomatic phrase characterizes a culturally appropriate response that seems contradictory
to the normative expectations in a collectivist, kinship society. Loners are rare, and this*

*was not normal behavior for Hiyanbi. Yet, those around him seemed to be saying, "it's
his problem not ours—we are going to enjoy this event with our alliance partners and
when he's ready, he will come out of himself and join us." As I gained familiarity
with the Samo language and culture, queries about how I should respond were frequently answered with nε fini noo, "your spirit you." In other words the decision
was mine—I had to make up my own mind and act accordingly. It was a response
to listening to the spirit in me and yet not ignoring the collective good of the community. Fortunately, the Samo were always happy to give me relevant assistance when
I asked, and teach me the implications of my response and the tensions it might create.* (Shaw, personal journal)

As a discipline, anthropology has contributed in very important ways to
mission. Understanding the fundamentals of the discipline can contribute
to a theological appreciation of God's creative acts. It can also impact the
presentation of the Gospel in particular cultural contexts. The more we understand about the context of the biblical cultures in which God communicated as well as the contemporary cultures into which we seek to present
what God said, the more effective our proclamation of God's intentions will
be. On the other hand, missionaries have contributed to the study of societies around the globe, providing the information that initiated anthropology
as a formal study in the late nineteenth century. In the 1950s, Eugene Nida
and a group of United Bible Society consultants found themselves writing
and researching anthropological subjects in their translation work, and the
journal *Practical Anthropology* was born. Eventually this insightful publication
merged into the present-day *Missiology*.

Charles Kraft's book *Christianity in Culture: A Study in Dynamic Biblical
Theologizing in Cross-Cultural Perspective* (1979) was a landmark attempt to
take theology and anthropology seriously as disciplines that intermingle
within the whole of missiology. In essence, anthropology must be allowed to
reinterpret theology and vice versa as an ongoing process. So, for example, in
his research of Christianity in the Solomon Islands, Allen Tippett tried to ex-
tract a church's theology by analyzing their hymnody. When he reiterated
what they themselves could not articulate, they nodded and said, "Yes you
understand, that is what we believe" (Tippett, 1975). The more we appreciate the contexts into which God formulated a message, the more effective
will be our transfer of information, thereby enabling present-day recipients
to infer the message God intended for them as they live out their lives in the
context of their horizon.

In this chapter we seek to apply cultural theory to the particular contexts in which we wish to communicate. We appropriate anthropological
theory in the form of helpful models that enable greater understanding of
any social context in which human beings relate to each other and demonstrate, through living their lives, what Ruth Benedict so succinctly called

"patterns of culture" (Benedict, 1934). Such cultural awareness creates a greater appreciation for the way people live, which, in turn, enables communicators to be more culturally appropriate in an increasingly complex world.

CULTURAL MODELS

If communicators are able to approach a text by asking culturally sensitive questions of both the text they seek to present and the context into which they desire to communicate, their presentation will have a greater impact. Like the theologians and communication specialists discussed in the preceding two chapters, anthropologists also use models to help them understand the people with whom they interact. By applying theoretically generated anthropological models, communicators can more effectively analyze the entire communication context and use that understanding to be more effective in their mission. Inasmuch as these models have been extensively developed elsewhere (Hiebert, 1983; Shaw, 1988), and this is not a textbook in anthropology, we will only briefly summarize them here.

Culture Types

People all over the world approach life in very different ways. It is these vast differences that have for centuries attracted the interest of explorers, missionaries, and anthropologists. This diversity, however, can be made manageable by applying a model anthropologists label "culture types." By observing various lifestyles and the things people consider important, E. R. Service noted that societies could be grouped into what he called "levels of socio-economic adaptation" (1962). The similarities among societies of the same type could be easily contrasted with differences among the types. Instead of being faced with a confusing morass of behavior, anthropologists look for distinguishing characteristics that serve to identify each culture type and then, as they learn the particular language and observe people's behavior in that particularity, they iterate the cultural issues that set that society apart from others. Using Service's insight, we can organize societies around the world today into four large, generic classes or "culture types": Kinship, Peasant, Industrial, and Post-Industrial.[1] Each culture type exhibits profoundly different approaches to life and, therefore, to God.

Within each culture type there is, obviously, a wide range of cultural variation. Yet, within each, people seek to solve life's problems in similar ways. It is this similarity of approaches to life that enables peoples of each type to make broad, sensical assumptions about others in the same type. This highlights the ability of people of the same culture type (regardless of where they live) to understand others who share that type and are, therefore, able to communicate more effectively. Applying the concepts of relevance theory to culture, people's inferences within a type are more likely to match the intentions of others. If communicators understand something of the character of each culture type, they are more likely to be sympathetic to the concerns central to the people, and be able to identify issues that will enable appropriate proclamation. We look now at some of these issues in an effort to familiarize readers with the diagnostic characteristics of each culture type.

Kinship Societies   In kinship societies, such as the Samo, the emphasis is on group orientation and consensus that reflects interpersonal relationships. These societies tend to be holistic, with spiritual influence prefacing almost everything. The idea of God as a pervasive force is reinforced by their mythology, ritual, and ceremony, all of which influence spiritual powers that affect life. Myth also serves as a rationale for a people's origin as well as a way of understanding how things are. Religious ideas express an emphasis on magic and ritual as ways to solve life's problems. Religious specialists (shaman) assist people in their rituals and ceremonies as they seek to draw family groupings together against spiritual and physical enemies. From this perspective there is little incentive to share what they know with others. So when the Gospel comes to them, they receive it and interpret it in light of their myths, magic, and rituals, and it becomes something that gives them power over others. Why should they share it? Hence, kinship societies have tended not to be very evangelistic.

In the Bible, we find a kinship-type orientation in the early books, from Genesis up to the introduction of the Kings of Israel. We find hunters and gatherers, the early subsistence-type agriculturists, and a strong interest in the ancestors—Abraham, Isaac, and Jacob. Kinship peoples today tend to strongly identify with these passages (cf. Shaw, 1988: 121ff). When Dan Shaw began translating for the Samo, he started with Genesis—translating the myths to which the Samo responded by recounting their own mythology. The stories created an immediate point of identification.

Peasant Societies   We find peasant societies, like the Maya, throughout Latin America as well as much of Asia and Africa. In these contexts the marketplace, barter systems, and interaction between people within different strata of society are central to life. In such societies a small elite often occupies the top social strata, while a large number of peasants, artisans, and others are arranged hierarchically between the elite and the peasantry. These social distinctions are also reflected in a bifurcated religious experience. Thus a high (or state) religion often coexists with more personalized folkways of dealing with the transempirical.

In such a society God is somewhat removed yet somehow also involved, often as a troublemaker. He is enjoined to be on the people's side fighting for their group or protecting their nation. The group is larger than the family focus of kinship societies. Mythology for people in peasant contexts is not just a rationale for the way things are; it is raised to a cosmic level with an emphasis on who people are with respect to God and what God is doing in the universe. Magic and ritual are still important, especially for individuals and small groups, whereas state religion and matters relating to a high god prevail for the society as a whole. This produces a contrast between shamans, who handle the individual and small-scale concerns, and priests, who serve as large-scale religious specialists or even as political figures. How people live their lives and where they go for help (to shaman or priest) depends on the nature of their concern and their understanding of how supernatural power relates to the problem at hand. Supernatural power, then, often becomes a means to gain status or improve one's position in the social hierarchy.

Insight about peasant societies provides a way to look at Israel among the nations. During the time of the kings before the exile, Israel was very much a people in relationship to each other in contrast to other peoples—this provides the surprise in the book of Ruth when Ruth followed her mother-in-law and exclaimed, "Your people will be my people and your God my God" (Ruth 1:16). The Israelites settled on the land and specialized their skills. An elite emerged composed of the kings, the priests, and their families.

Mission outreach for this type of society emphasizes evangelism within the group or nation. The Jews went into exile but did not evangelize very well because this Gospel was for them, God was their God, and they did not see the relevance of sharing God. Throughout Israel's history, their identity was tied to their land; after each exile they sought to return and rebuild. So, as a peasant people, the Maya of Southern Chiapas understand the nation of Israel and appreciate their struggle to balance the physical attraction of the land with the spiritual saga God took them on. They are now seeking their fortunes in larger towns but returning home for fiestas. They recognize that resources are finite and their relationships in the social hierarchy are central to their survival.

Industrial Societies   Industrial societies (what we in the so-called west are more familiar with) emphasize productivity, commerce, and the distribution of goods and services. Industrial productivity takes place in a highly structured but individualized way, rather than with a group emphasis as in kinship and peasant culture types. Large centralized corporations rule the economy and utilize a labor force to accomplish their purposes. For such people, God is highly personalized. God is primarily "my God," and the relationship reflects some aspect of culturally appropriate interaction. However, because of the highly specialized economic and scientific orientation, supernatural concerns are the province of religious specialists assigned to study such things. These ideas emerged out of the Enlightenment and have carried over into the industrial-ization and modernity of Europe and North America. The age of discovery in-stigated an exploitation of others and a supremacy that impacted all cultural ac-tivity, including missions. Science tends to rule until every other avenue has been exhausted—God is often little more than a last resort.

The urban context of the Pauline epistles strongly resembles this indus-trial perspective, as Wayne Meeks made clear (Meeks, 1983). The individual-ism, urban environment, rapid expansion of an empire, and centralized gov-ernments all look familiar to industrial societies today. Perhaps that is why so many people in the industrial culture type love the logic and argument of the Pauline corpus.

Postindustrial Societies   Finally postindustrialization, as it is manifested in the early part of the twenty-first century, encourages high productivity with a focus on the distribution of ideas and globalization that reduces the focus on boundaries and the people within them.[2] Such networking is exemplified in regional and international trade agreements. This culture type is typified by a global renaissance of the arts, the emergence of free-market socialism, and con-cerns about human rights, especially with respect to eliminating sexism and all forms of hegemony that place one person in control of another.

In such societies God is viewed as a pervasive force that, although ulti-mately related to each person, allows for individual choice and initiative— "may the force be with you." Such interest in the connection (call it a net-work) between the empirical and the transempirical is contributing to an upsurge in cultural and religious revitalization. And while supernatural issues are the emphasis of spiritual specialists who are not the doers but the teach-ers, supernatural power is no longer mythologized but considered real, even if it cannot be explained. The excitement of the new millennium has generated a rise in religious fundamentalism, as every nation impacted by the major world religions (Judaism, Buddhism, Hinduism, Christianity, and Islam) is ex-periencing revival. Thus it is no surprise that Native Americans are increas-ingly interested in their language and cultural heritage, and why an interest in prophecy has reinstated the book of Revelation as an international bestseller as indicated by the *Left Behind* series (LaHaye and Jenkins, 2000).

We do not find postindustrial societies as such in the Bible, but Gnosti-cism and the millenarian cults that prevailed following the fall of Jerusalem bear some resemblance. When it comes to missions, postindustrial perspectives place a premium on reaching people everywhere, as reflected in Ralph Win-ter's hidden people focus and Mission 2000, which are both particular and global in their conceptualization and outreach. However there is also a coun-termission emphasis generated by the relativising of religion; everybody is part of a network, and despite their particular beliefs is striving to reach the same spiritual goal.

While these descriptions of each culture type are obvious oversimplifications, the model lays out key principles that help shape our thinking. They allow cross-cultural workers to apply the model to ascertain a greater appreciation for those peopling the Bible as well as how the particular society in which they minister fits into general cultural patterns. This culture type model can be paired with the cultural subsystems model to develop a powerful tool for cross-cultural understanding.

Cultural Subsystems

In the same way that anthropologists use a model to group societies into broad culture types, they also seek to group the various behavior patterns of people within each type. The cultural subsystems model does this. Every society, regardless of what type it is or where in the world it exists, must answer five fundamental questions:

- How do we survive?
- Who are we and where did we come from?
- How do we interact with others?
- How do we control each other's behavior?
- How do we interact with the supernatural?

Anthropologists variously categorize these questions into basic cultural subsystems: economics, kinship, social structure, political organization, and religion. These aspects of culture help a researcher focus on one subsystem at a time, although anthropologists recognize a considerable amount of overlap and integration among the subsystems. While there are obviously other key questions each society must answer, the model provides a focus for research as well as a set of theoretical assumptions that help direct anthropological study. The various cultural subsystems interact with and on each other both within and across societal barriers.

Economics   Economic concerns are dominated by a society's ability to respond to their environment by developing technology and a means of exploiting their circumstances through a division of labor, distribution of wealth, and forms of exchange. This, of course, is drastically impacted by the culture type of the society in focus, each type differing in the way they relate to the ecology, focus their technology, and develop processes to make it all work for them.

For our purpose of appropriate communication, we are interested in the economic issues that pertain to the source (What is the environment in Scripture and how did people respond to it?) as well as those of the receptor (Are the circumstances of today the same or different from those encountered in the Bible?). Living in the rain forest, the Samo could not fathom a place where there was very little rain and yet there were large bodies of water. While the biblical context is arid and marine-oriented, the Samo know only a wet, riverine environment. The boat economy of the fishermen disciples creates a communication load across cultural types and social barriers and creates the need to describe physical and environmental differences. This required some creative adjustments without changing the meaning of Scripture in a new context that is far removed.

Kinship   People establish identity by answering the question: Where did I come from? Kinship is really about identity. Who am I?—or for most of the world's peoples, Who are we?—is a crucial question. Here the ancestral interests of kinship and peasant culture types are a constant reminder throughout the whole of the Bible that origins are crucial to human development. Whenever Paul entered a synagogue, he began his remarks by citing the ancestors, Abraham, Isaac, and Jacob. Later, when speaking to Gentiles, he reminded them of their spiritual heritage as children of Abraham, children of faith. It is no surprise, then, that the central relational metaphor throughout Scripture is the parent-child dyad, and particularly the father-son relationship. Believers are born, through faith, into a heavenly family and thereby enter into relationship as children of the Father (John 1:12, 13) and joint heirs with Jesus (Rom. 8:17). Drawing on Goodenough (1965), the nature of relationship subsumes rights and duties that are culturally defined: parents, so identified within a society, are to behave in particular ways (cultural ideals), and when they do not behave within those boundaries, they may be viewed with disdain. Similarly, children are to behave in accordance with culturally expected patterns but their actual performance may not conform to those expectations. These are kinship concepts that westerners, coming from the individualistic perspective of industrial and postindustrial societies, understand quite differently from their contemporary receptors.

Social Structure   Questions of relational structure, especially between groups, dominate the aspect of social structure. While people in kinship societies tend to be egalitarian with small groups centered on the family or some culturally defined extension of it, peasant societies group people with respect to social prestige or status in an economically structured pyramid with the elite at the top. The caste system in India is a classic example of this kind of structuring. Industrial societies also tend to group people with respect to economic structures often related to professionalism or religious affiliation, whereas postindustrialists focus on networks often impacted by political control.

Group organization and structure often dictate who can marry whom since marriage is often viewed as an opportunity to unite families, social groups, or even nations. The biblical kings maintained alliances with other nations through the exchange of concubines. Perhaps this was one of the reasons God did not want Israel to have a king—women from foreign lands brought their idols, religious ideas, and cultural expectations with them and impacted Israel accordingly. People in the west may or may not understand such positioning within and between groups, so social structures must be somehow explained.

Political Organization   Questions of social control are crucial in establishing how people, both positively and negatively, sanction each other's behavior and determine who their leaders are, and appropriately respond to violations of cultural norms. Early in Israel's development, under Moses, the political structure was simple. People interacted within a family structure under the leadership of the father (exemplified by their ancestor Abraham), who in turn related to other heads of households within a tribal structure (Gottwald, 1979). Later, as these people entered the promised land, the tribal focus lessened as they built towns and cities in which a peasant-type structure reflected both religious and political leadership. Israel's dealings with the nations around it also reflected the nature of internal relationships expanded to the international scene in the form of warfare, taxes, and being subject to the king as culturally defined. All of this changed dramatically under Imperial Rome, when a distant emperor governed local affairs through far-flung procurators. So, for example, the circumstances surrounding the birth of Jesus were dictated by imperial decree and set political intrigue in motion; the wise men's arrival, Herod's jealousy, and Joseph's flight to Egypt to protect the young Jesus. How will postmodernists—who tend to be global and networked in perspective and desire to understand their particular place in the process of decision making—read these events? The implications are crucial to how people understand God's ultimate goals for the world and the place of each people's story, their mythology, in that universal structure.

The impact of political sanction gives rise to the issue of sin, which is crucial to communicating the message of the Bible. Every society has a moral code, a set of cultural expectations that people are supposed to live up to. In the first three chapters of Romans, the apostle Paul demonstrated how people exchanged truth for a lie and began to worship creation rather than the creator (1:21–23). Eventually, people will judge themselves according to their inability to live up to their own conscience because there is no way they can live up to the standards God built into creation (2:14–16). Finally, in his argument, Paul shows that all people, regardless of ethnicity or moral code, are guilty before God (3:23). However, condemnation is only half the equation; the other half focuses on the importance of redemption: accepting God's provision for salvation. Understanding this broad sweep of redemptive history is, in part, an appreciation for what God is doing in the universe, as each story contributes to the whole. Over time each cultural narrative impacts the rest, bringing new ideas while enabling people to hold fast to the truth of the old—the hermeneutical spiral comes into play once again.

Religion   Finally we come to a crucial question: How do human beings relate to the transempirical? Notice that we dealt with the question of sin in the political section, which follows Paul's treatment of it as a matter of conscience, an expression of cultural values and worldview themes manifested in various types of behavior. However, people relate those values back into the supernatural realm. In their heart of hearts, most human beings know the answer to the question of sin is a supracultural (beyond culture) concern. The ultimate authority is not of this world, but is beyond the human realm in the structure of supernatural power. Recent expressions of so-called power evangelism in the west reflect what the rest of the world has known all along: spiritual powers beyond the confines of this world strongly affect human activities and patterns of interaction. That is why spiritual specialists from shaman to priests to pastors and seminary professors have long focused on assisting people in their search for God. From the beginning of time, some sort of mediation has been recognized as necessary: Abel brought a better sacrifice than Cain and it cost him his life. God, in infinite wisdom and knowledge of creation, provided a mediation through Christ. But before Jesus's advent God applied the incarnation principle, interacting directly and indirectly with human beings. After Jesus's ascension the Holy Spirit filled this role of enabling people who had faith to become more like God. This is the mystery to which Paul frequently alludes and that humans, regardless of cultural identity, are much in need of learning (Col. 1:26, 27).

Taken together, we can combine the culture types model and the cultural subsystems model to develop a matrix for comparing the key differences among cultures. Figure 6.1 is a somewhat reductionist grid designed to highlight these crucial contrasts. If communicators approaching a society other than their own are aware of the culture type of the people with whom they seek to interact, they can appropriate this model and anticipate the issues that will confront them. Once in the context they can look for local idiosyncrasies that show how the people diverge from the expectations of the model and reflect their own particularity. It is the emphasis on the rationale behind the response of people in each culture type to the various subsystems that leads to a discussion of worldview.

Worldview

A third model of vital importance for culturally appropriate communication centers on worldview. We have already used the idea frequently. It goes back to the famous anthropologist Bronislaw Malinowski, who wanted to get inside people's heads. In fact, he desired to understand what was important to people and why. What lay behind people's behavior patterns? In short, he desired to "grasp the native's point of view" (Malinowski, 1922: 25). Later, Robert Redfield (1953) was the first to use the term *worldview* and projected fourteen universals that all societies had to deal with in some way. More recently, Michael Kearney (1984) recategorized these universals and Charles Kraft (1989) redefined them to include values. Drawing from a more cognitive perspective, Paul Hiebert sees worldview as the interaction between explicit, or cognitive, awareness and implicit, or more value-based, assumptions (Hiebert, 1983: xix). The key issue for worldview studies is an understanding of perceptions of reality, as that enables people to interact with the totality of their world. In figure 6.2 we present a highly reductionist form of a basic worldview model. The worldview universals, as represented here, are quite different from the five basic questions people ask, as we noted earlier. The

CULTURAL SUBSYSTEM	Kinship	Peasant	Industrial	Post-Industrial
Economics Survival Material Culture Labor	*Subsistence* – Relationship – Basic – Gender/age	*Market Based* – Status – Specialize – Status	*Commercial* – Wealth – Accumulate – Education	*Multinational* – Knowledge – Cooperate/Network – Knowledge/Information
Religion Deal with Transempirical Practitioner Institution	*Animist* – Magic/Ritual – Shaman – Community	*Dual Religion* – Magic/Ceremony – Shaman/Priest – Community/ Religion	*Science* – God is dead/Seek in failure – Pastor/Priest – Organized Religion	*Mystical* – Spiritual Presence – Guru – Personal philosophy
Kinship Focus Dominant Dyad	*Face to Face* – Relational – Sibling	*Social Hierarchy* – Group focused – Intergeneration	*Individual & Impersonal* – Job related – Husband/Wife	*Individual & Personal* – Cooperative group – Varies with family
Social Structure Rationale for Group Marriage	*Community* – Relation/Territory – Alliance	*Family* – Caste/Group identity – Family maintenance	*Individual* – Job/Prestige – Sex & child care	*Small Group* – Knowledge/Group ID – Companionship
Political Organization Sanctions Leadership	*Community* – Informal – Achieved	*Kingdom* – Informal/Formal – Ascribed	*Republic (Independent)* – Formal/Government – Elected	*Global (Interdependent)* – Formal/International – Benevolent Dictator
Dominant subsystem	Kinship	Social-Structure	Economics	Political Organization

CULTURE – TYPES

------- R E L I G I O N -------

Each culture type places emphasis on a different cultural subsystem. This subsystem becomes the dominant focus for that culture type. Religion is not dominant for any culture type but impacts each type in different ways. This has profound implications for appropriate communication of the Gospel message.

Figure 6.1.   Contrastive Features of Culture Types and Subsystems

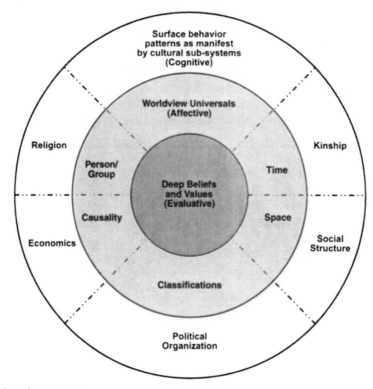

Adapted from Shaw 1988: 108.

Figure 6.2.   Beliefs and Values Impact Surface Behavior Patterns

main difference relates to cultural behavior reflected in the subsystems and the rationale for that behavior, which emanates from the deep structure of each culture. The contrast between deep and surface structure, then, is central to a discussion of worldview.[3]

The linguist Noam Chomsky noted that a relatively simple set of basic concepts could be communicated in a wide variety of linguistic and cultural forms. He then posited that "deep structure" ideas could be manifest by a wide range of expressions he called "surface structure." The rules necessary to produce speech from basic ideas he called "grammar." This understanding of deep and surface structure was immensely helpful to anthropologists who began to realize that worldview was the deep structure central to people's behavior. Deep structure ideas could be manifest in a myriad of ways, which anthropologists call "culture." This led Goodenough to define culture as what people within a society need know or believe (deep structure) in order to behave in a manner acceptable to its members (surface structure) (1957: 167). Put in terms of communication this could be rephrased: What do we need to know (about both the source and the receptors) in order to communicate an author's intent (deep structure) in such a way to ensure receptors make correct inferences (surface structure)? In other words, how do we ensure appropriate communication?

When we project an awareness of culture types and cultural subsystems onto an appreciation for worldview, we gain new insight into the nature of the context into which God originally communicated. To understand God's intended meaning we must first understand the culture type, its central themes (worldview), and how they are manifested in the behavioral patterns of the people. This serves as recognition of hermeneutical structures that enabled the original receptors to make sense of the message when God spoke. What God said always entered into specific cultural contexts that had an effect both on what and how God spoke as well as the inferences people made about what God said. That is why these models need to become an integral part of understanding a text. As soon as we include this element, we recognize how crucial it is to take seriously the cultural context into which God originally communicated in order to ensure appropriate communication of the message to those who receive it anew.

For example, take the idea of a place to worship. During the days of the Pentateuch, with its relational, kinship focus, there was no temple building. When Abraham wanted to worship, he set up an altar (often beneath a clump of trees). Only after the Israelites' sojourn in Egypt where their culture was impacted by Egyptian worldview did the tabernacle evolve. The desert environment provided the focal point for sacrifice and worship, and special practitioners were appointed to facilitate its benefit to the people. Much later, during the time of the kings, the temple was built. By then a peasant society had begun to emerge and an elite group of priests built their lives around maintaining this place of worship. Only in that context were the social structures available—plenty of people to build the elaborate structure and its varied artifacts and to support a priestly elite. The temple then served as the focal point for centralized worship.

By New Testament times there were increased economic and commercial institutions epitomized by urbanization. In that context there was a shift from the temple to the synagogue that made worship more widely dispersed and individual. The rebuilt second temple was still important but its function had changed—this was part of Jesus' frustration when he drove out the merchants and money changers. By the Apostle Paul's day there was almost a postindustrial mindset. He says believers are the temple (I Cor. 3:16,17); in other words, it doesn't matter where people worship so long as they are being conformed to God's image (a point similar to the one Jesus made to the woman at the well).

Now listen to what an African pastor had to say about the place of worship:

> The class roared with laughter. But the tall solemn African pastor declared he had not been joking. "Brother Chuck, you asked what is the least we would need to still have the Church? I am serious when I say all I need is a bell. I can walk out into the bush in my country, stand under a tree, begin ringing the bell, and the Church gathers. (Van Engen, 1991: 15)

Admittedly this pastor was talking about people gathering together for worship because they have heard the ringing of the bell. And they gather where there is shade, under a tree. In terms of the surface level it appears the primary significance of the tree is that it gives shade. But is that the end of the story? Is it possible that the tree has a deeper meaning that we can begin to appreciate when we connect the significance of a place of worship for the Israelites to the importance of trees in different times and contexts, with climates similar to sub-Saharan Africa as places for encountering God? This was true of the tabernacle and the temple and even a synagogue. It is not mere coincidence that this African pastor would gather the people together for worship under a tree. His congregation may understand the significance of events that took place under other trees better than those of us who do not see trees as a primary place of worship.

Looking at all of these worship contexts as symbols, we see a root metaphor centered around God's presence (the deep-structure idea) expressed very differently in varied cultural contexts (the surface manifestations). The themes running through the progressive development of Scripture represent, in effect, God's worldview: issues God wanted to communicate in every context, such as "worship me in spirit and in truth" (John 4:24). However, the way those themes are expressed in particular contexts is very different because each focused on a different time and/or space. This introduces the need to understand the impact of cultural change as a final anthropological model that affects the communication process.

Cultural Change

There is no such thing as a static culture. Over the years, people's experience, both among themselves and with the world at large, forces them to constantly evaluate their circumstances and accept or initiate changes that enable them as a viable group of people to maximize their resources and deal with the realities of their life in ways that ensure the survival of their society. The Bible, as we note throughout this book, is full of examples of cultural change. Over the course of history the Israelites shifted among all of the culture types and thus relate to each of the major cultural questions in very different ways as they processed their basic assumptions through the changes manifest in their surface culture.

The history of mission is a tale of cultural change. In our lifetime we have seen the west shift from a primarily industrial-type culture dominated by a colonial emphasis to postmodern structures that emphasize synergy. Missionaries find themselves shifting their job description from telling people about God, to encouraging people to tell others in their context about God. A focus on equipping and enabling local people to do ministry in their context is very different from primary evangelism. This represents relatively rapid cultural change in the approach to doing mission in our day.

Tippett, following Homer Barnett under whom he studied at the University of Oregon, developed an "advocate-innovator" model of cultural change that helps communicators of the Gospel understand what is taking place in the contexts where they work. Figure 6.3 diagrams the model. Advocates bring new ideas and instruct people in these ideas using the language and cultural knowledge of the people. The people, in turn, take these ideas and relate them to their experience, their understanding of life as they live it, their worldview. As they process this information (be it McDonald's hamburgers or different ways to think about God) they run it through their cultural grids (what we have called models): how does the new relates to their culture type, basic cultural questions, and worldview? While often not conscious, people within a society constantly rework information in order to ensure it makes sense to others in that time and place. These advocates then become innovators of these ideas in a new set of circumstances in which that information has not been previously implemented. The result is new behavior or a new set of ideas that they advocate to others, and so the chain of change ripples throughout an entire society.

The ramifications of this model for appropriate communication are tremendous. First, it calls for local adaptation of the communication models presented in chapter 5. Communication must take place in ways that allow people to not only understand the message, but also appropriate it to their context and precipitate cultural change. This is what contextualization is all about:

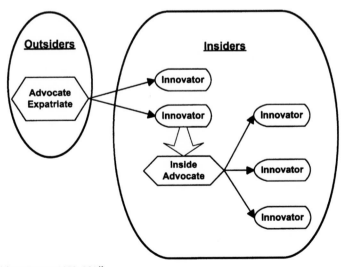

Constructed from Barnett 1953: 291ff.

Figure 6.3.   Advocates and Innovators

making ideas from a source outside the society understood and applicable to the circumstances in which people live. And so the hermeneutical spiral begins to sweep through a society as it applies God's Word to living their lives. Advocates, in turn, learn new things about God because of this new perspective and are themselves enriched.

We implement these models throughout the rest of this book in order to encourage appropriate communication. The message that people hear when they receive the Gospel should incite them to process the information through their entire cultural system and thereby plant desire among all of the people within that context to share what the believers in Jesus Christ have—an answer for the hope that is within them (I Pet. 3:15). That answer can only come from insiders who advocate new innovations based on an understanding of what God said. Outsiders cannot contextualize—only local people can do that. And it is an ongoing process, never a final product.

APPLYING CULTURAL PRINCIPLES TO APPROPRIATE COMMUNICATION

The type of society extant in a context is impacted by the worldview of the people—by the basic assumptions they bring to living their lives. These beliefs and values are buried in the deep structure, as contrasted with the forms or manifestations that are the surface vehicles of cultural expression. Unless all of those involved in the process (insiders and outsiders alike—advocates and innovators) understand the biblical root metaphors with their focus on panhuman experience, contextualization will be of limited value. It is at this deeper level that proclamation must take place. The message must be communicated on the basis of people's understanding of God on the one hand and themselves on the other. Change must take place at the worldview level, not just within surface-level forms. Unless this happens, syncretism or even heresy may be the result. Nominalism can similarly be avoided if these deep cultural factors are accounted for. The hermeneutical model we develop in this book is designed to address some of these issues. So appropriate communication is only the first step in a long process of enabling people to work through their experience and apply God's Word to their modes of thinking as well as what they consider effective living. We revisit this when we discuss enabling effective communication in chapter 8.

We can now apply deBeaugrande and Dressler's standards of textuality that we considered in chapter 5 to cultural structures. Culture is *cohesive.* All the parts go together, which is why anthropologists are able to talk about cultural as a system. Culture is *coherent.* If it were not, it would not be a culture.

It makes sense to those who apply its assumptions to appropriate living and use those assumptions to evaluate the lifestyle of other peoples. Each culture has a message that makes sense for a particular subset of human beings engaged in life as they know it.

Continuing through the standards of textuality, or relevance, culture is also *intentional*. People know how to behave appropriately, and when they are inappropriate there are sanctions that bring them back into line. This appropriateness often relates directly to a situation. It is culture that reduces the need for people to think through the implications of every behavioral experience. Being *appropriate* is automatic and allows the brain to focus on important things. It is this aspect of culture that is disjunctive for people who assume one set of behavior patterns as appropriate and then find themselves in another context in which people may consider behavior based on those assumptions to be inappropriate, thus precipitating culture shock. Culture is also *informative*. What the brain (conditioned by a particular set of assumptions) expects carries a high information load when responding to something new. If expectations are not met, receptors must go back and pay attention to the unfamiliar information. Focused attention to the unfamiliar can also bring about culture stress. This, in turn, makes any crosscultural interaction *intertextual* by definition. It is a crossing of barriers where the message, despite its similar objectives in terms of human survival and quality of life, communicates differently because people in each society have a different worldview. And so we must deal not only with words but also with actions. God's divine revelation in human words always involves different words and different actions.

As appropriate communication takes place across the boundaries of the culture types, interesting adjustments are required to reflect the shift in cultural and situational assumptions. For example, in the book of Ruth, the text presents an emerging peasant-type culture. The narrative is centered on economic issues (famine, harvest, gleaning) that serve as a means to convey kinship and family concerns—each affects the other. One objective of the book is ensuring the position of David in the right line of descent, which, though Ruth herself had no way to know it, ensured the genealogy of Jesus, as Matthew notes in the first chapter of his Gospel (Bush, 1996: 52–53). There, despite her Moabite lineage, Ruth's name appears as an ancestor of Jesus.

Now when we look at contemporary receptors, our objective is to enable them to understand the same message that God communicated to the people of Bethlehem through Ruth. To accomplish this we begin with a look at the respective culture types. Are the contemporary people we are communicating with primarily a peasant-type of society or do they fit into a different type? The answer will affect the way an appropriate proclamation is structured. Will we tell a story with a pastoral setting, or is it better to present the information as a myth (kinship society has a strong interest in origins), a sermon designed to help people in an industrial-type society understand the context of Bethlehem at the time of the Judges, or a more postmodern approach where the focus is on demonstrating relationships, especially between the people and the spiritual world in which they operated?

These questions imply that communicators understand the issues pertinent to each culture type as they are expressed through the cultural subsystems. Which subsystem is in focus and how can it be demonstrated? How do people receiving the message relate to this particular situation in the book of Ruth, where the emphasis is on a peasant people with economic and social hierarchical concerns? Are the receptors fully aware of peasant cultural constraints? If not, the communicator has a problem because the assumptions relating to the subsystems in the culture do not match what people in a peasant society expect. Communicators cannot ignore these differences; something must be done to implement Alaichamy's bridging concept.

Each culture type, each society, each worldview has both positive and negative aspects. Some help us in the task of listening and communicating. Some may create blind spots that communicators coming from a particular context are not aware of. Awareness is one of the most significant goals here. Just to be aware of the differences greatly reduces the automatic superimposing of the communicator's worldview onto the presentation.

Avoiding the Filter Effect

Historically, missionaries have served as the bridge between the source text and receptors. They were considered the guardians of source-text meaning: how it would be presented, and the forms to use in order to effectively convey that meaning in new contexts. In the process, however (and this is particularly true when the source text is a sacred text) the translators' understanding of source-text meaning is impacted by their own worldview, by those assumptions that they hold to be true about the world and apply to the source context. Therefore, a so-called translation is often an interpretation of what the bridge person thinks the text means and passes on what that worldview expects. As we pointed out in chapter 2, such interpretative communication can quickly place contemporary receptors on the slippery slope to heresy. By the definitions of communication we have used, recipients form a "conceptual text," from which they infer the original communicative intent.[4] They do this by applying their own circumstances and worldview to an understanding of the intermediate, or bridge, communication.

It is rather like the telephone game we used to play as children—passing a message around a human chain and noting what comes out in the end, a very different content than that expressed at the starting point. At issue here is avoiding this filter effect. How can communicators, trained to interpret a source text, and to apply communication principles, avoid bringing their own interpretive biases (both cultural and theological) to understanding a message new receptors will use to make their own inferences? Put another way, how can communicators appropriately proclaim God's intentions so that receptors receive the same information as the original receptors? Once the message is received are people able to utilize their understanding of the message for their own spiritual growth and the development of a local theology?

Here we can apply Alaichamy's "synthesis" step as discussed in chapter 5. The process begins by understanding the communicators' biases, what they bring with them, their basic values. Then we apply this knowledge in order to reflect on the impact these assumptions have on understanding both the biblical and receptors' horizons. All of these interactive contexts—the biblical, the communicators', and the receptors'—produce a new understanding that emerges from the interaction. All of the horizons are crucial to a hermeneutically sound and communicationally appropriate presentation, as we emphasized when discussing the four horizons in chapter 4. Finally, we need to take a serious look at the real task of equipping Gospel communicators to avoid theological and cultural imperialism while developing and encouraging an interactive approach to appropriate proclamation.

As human beings, we take our culture with us. Our ideas impact everything we do. This means that we can never get away from culture. There is no such thing as a culture-free existence, because culture is in our heads. It impacts the way we think, which in turn impacts how we behave. Furthermore, it impacts our interpretation of the behavior of others, both in ancient times as when we read the Bible and in contemporary contexts. The concepts we bring into another cultural situation (either in terms of understanding a source's concepts and behavior or the behavior and rationale of the receptor) impact how we transfer information. For this reason we have utilized the hermeneutical spiral in order to appreciate what we have called the "communication context." The baggage communicators bring to this task is unavoidable, but it must be consciously understood so that it may be laid aside as much as possible. The way communicators look at Scripture and transport that information into another cultural context must be as free of intervening biases as possible. Culture-free communication is, of course, impossible. So the task here is at least to make a conscious effort to allow the text to speak directly to receptors rather than filtering it through communicators' biases. An awareness of basic values helps reduce a communicator's filtering effect.

The Communicators' Basic Values

What do communicators bring to the study? They bring their own presuppositions from their culture, background, and experience. So considering theological issues involves thinking about God with respect to culturally defined experiences and assumptions. People are largely unaware of these assumptions because they lie deep in the presumptive level of what we have called worldview—they are in the deep structure. People tend not to question these assumptions because for them, they are cultural givens. For the members of a particular society, these values represent unquestioned reality. Presumption such as this makes communicators not only monocultural, but also ethnocentric. Everything they encounter will be filtered through that grid.

Lingenfelter and Mayers (1986) supply a basic values profile that is useful in helping communicators appreciate what they assume but find so difficult to articulate. They lay out six dichotomistic contrasts that serve to raise awareness.

Time/Event   Value is placed on schedule, organization, and structure, in contrast placing value on what is happening—the activities, issues, or human concerns at hand.

Task/Person   Value here is placed on the nature of an activity with a focus on getting it done, in contrast to emphasizing individual or corporate need, viewing people as central rather than a means to accomplish something.

Dichotomy/Holism   High value is placed on either/or thinking with an analytical approach—lay everything out and reach solutions. People with a holistic worldview have a both–and approach: they seek to make sense of the whole picture and they want to see all the parts together.

Crisis/Noncrisis   Value is placed on handling events as crises, meeting deadlines, or dealing with problems by using trained experts to solve the crisis. In contrast, noncrisis orientation is more relaxed as people try to handle things themselves.

Achievement/Status   High value is placed on what one accomplishes in contrast to one's position in the society; success is based on individual achievements rather than group relationship structures.

Vulnerability as Weakness/Vulnerability as Strength   Strong individualism and a focus on success leads people to consider vulnerability as a weakness. People want to be self-sufficient, not vulnerable. In contrast, vulnerability may be considered a strength in communal, interactive contexts where individual contribution to the collective good is highly valued.

Each of these "basic values" is culturally defined and varies from one society to the next. As a whole, they do not represent all "basic values." Similar contrasts could be established for generosity and stinginess, attitudes toward relationships and the unknown (including eternity), and a host of other things human beings tend to value. However, the model serves to portray the need for approaching crosscultural involvement with an open heart and mind. Communicators need to be flexible, go with the flow, and relate with people on their own terms whenever possible. The attitude these characteristics portray to those who would receive the message communicators seek to present will go far in proclaiming a Christ-likeness that others will desire to know. This attitude stretches any communicator's ability to put one hand on the source context and the other on contemporary contexts, where ideas and concerns are very different. Understanding these basic values raises the consciousness of communicators about themselves as well as the issues in the source and receptor contexts. This understanding serves to reduce the filter effect, allowing the message of God's Word to permeate into yet another context in which a different set of basic values is no less valuable in God's sight.

While within any society there is considerable variation with respect to these basic values, there usually is a consensus that leads to what Mayers calls "modal scores" (Mayers, 1982). These modal values reflect general tendencies that can help people with one set of values establish certain expectations for people in other societies with a different set of expectations or worldview. Communicators must be cautious, however, to avoid cultural stereotyping (overgeneralization projected onto all members of a community) and projecting their rationale upon others. The benefit of being aware of one's own basic values is the ability to adjust readily to constrating values. Raising one's assumptions to some level of consciousness is the objective. Keep in mind that the extreme forms of these values are rare. People adjust the emphasis to the particulars of situations as they live out their lives, sometimes tending in one direction, while in different circumstances tending to emphasize issues that would indicate a very different orientation. Making situational adjustments within a set of values is not right or wrong. While "basic values" may be just that, there should be no value judgments attached to any of these positions. Rather they simply form two extremes of a dichotomy designed to point out contrastive cultural elements that often prove troublesome in crosscultural interaction.[5] These contrastive sets must not be seen as either/or values, but rather both-and perspectives. Both must be there, both have value, both are ultimately necessary for effective relationships of communicators who seek to communicate values from the Biblical text with people in contemporary contexts.

In Mayer and Lingenfelter's view, the more contrastive the values of people from different cultures, the greater a role that value will have in their interaction. When people from different societies find themselves in agreement with respect to a particular value, it does not necessarily signal compatibility. At issue may be the rationale for that position. When the rationale for holding a common viewpoint is different, that may prove to be as conflict producing as having very different profiles. Studying the meaning of these values may be crucial for appropriate communication. As communicators interact, basic values play a role in their success or failure. Adaptability and willingness to interact in terms that make sense to local people is essential. People need to understand the source of their values and seek a commonality based on God's expectations. People do not expect outsiders to be just like them, but attitude is so important. As external strengths are blended with internal strengths, a new product emerges, a new set of value-oriented responses that reflect a Christ-likeness.

Communication Distance

An application of Winter's (1975) and later Wagner's (1983) development of cultural distance in evangelism is appropriate here. They discuss E_1, E_2, and E_3, as an evangelistic model that calls for those who are most similar to serve as the primary evangelists in a culture. Following the culture types model, we can clarify this evangelism typology by noting that those in the E_1 context share the same culture, those in E_2 share the same culture type, and those in an E_3 relationship are of different culture types (Shaw 1990). We can apply this same set of principles to effective communication and posit that C_1 communicators (where "C" stands for communication) will be most effective because of their shared knowledge—their shared values with an audience. Traditional missionaries, in contrast, have generally been in a C_3 relationship that represents the greatest cultural distance possible. They have crossed cultural and linguistic barriers in order to communicate.

This distance factor is one reason why career missionaries need to change their primary responsibility to training local people to be missionally effective in their own context. The emphasis in our decolonialized world is to work alongside those who know the local context, partnering with them to complement the knowledge they have with what they often lack. But it takes time to develop the biblical knowledge needed to appropriately apply communication principles and skills in their own context. In the meantime, communicators and others in mission roles have a responsibility to provide the part of the equation local people have not yet adequately acquired. The goal is to ultimately enable them to accomplish the communication task within their context and then develop crosscultural skills to expand into C_2 contexts—to be missional and reach out to other cultures of the same culture type. This is the point of Ajith Fernando's call for an adjustment of relationships between western and nonwestern communicators (Fernando, 1986). Taken to its logical conclusion, cooperation between outsiders and insiders leads to interaction patterns and ways of functioning that reflect a team approach.

A Team Approach

The "real" presenter in a meeting of two cultures is not the crosscultural enabler. Rather, it must be a local person equipped to do the job. No one person can do everything necessary to appropriately communicate the Gospel. An outsider cannot carry forth this process in its entirety. Nor can a local person or even the local church carry through on all aspects of the communication process. While it is true that God enters into the process through the power of the Holy Spirit, it takes a collaborative effort to ensure culturally appropriate mission.

By working alongside local people, outsiders can function in mentoring and equipping roles. Most people of the majority world tend to learn best by doing rather than memorizing principles and applying them later (Sanders, 1988:206). The pedagogy of learning biblical principles and applying them to communication through involvement in the process enables those who participate to grasp the principles through direct experience, thereby bringing them to effective involvement despite their lack of academic credentials. Thus the advocate and innovator model for change can be applied as outsiders appropriately equip inside practitioners who can then accomplish the task of local proclamation in the right context. Local pastors and other communicators using communication styles that make the most sense to the audience will quickly create excitement about having God's Word among them.

SUMMARY

There is a missional application of the models we have developed and presented in this and the other chapters in part II of this book. Mission agencies can use these models to unite local expertise with outside expertise. People on both sides have much to learn about this process, but the focus should be on using outsiders to equip insiders who know the local context with the means for communicating the message. This is not to say that outsiders do not need to learn the language and culture or connect with the cultural values of their receptors. Insiders know this and need to enable the outsiders to understand it, thus bringing the two sides together. Communicators of God's message (regardless of the form used) need feedback from the receptors as well as from Scripture, in the power of the Holy Spirit. Outsiders cannot be asked to eliminate or even radically change their worldview, nor should they want to. Rather, they need to appreciate the limitations their worldview places on the total communication context and realize their role as enablers of understanding. From this position they may consciously seek to avoid being the filter through which information flows. Rather than filters they should be enablers.

Outsiders are rather like a catalyst in a chemical reaction. They serve as the means for the initial communication to take place. They are not the filter or the medium of communication. In the process, crosscultural communicators serve as a means for God to communicate to an audience that has not yet responded to their Creator as God would like them to.

The cultural models informed by theological and communicational input lend themselves to appropriate communication influenced by the Spirit of God working in the midst of people in their particularity. As the Samo learned, God wanted them to conform to the desires of the Holy Spirit in their midst, not just their own spirits. God's approach to this aspect of their worldview was contrary to the Samo perspective and linguistic constraints. The Samo had to change their perspective of God. Yet, both the horizontal and the vertical dimensions are complementary. The objective is that people may hear and respond to God's call. The Apostle Paul understood this team approach when he penned Romans 10:14, 15. "How can people have faith in the Lord and ask him to save them, if they have never heard about him? And how can they hear, unless someone tells them? And how can anyone tell them without being sent by the Lord?" All of the horizons are there. Similarly effective communication in our world must include all of the elements in this part of the book. What local people learn about God through this process enables them to survive in their world with God's help, an understanding that enables Robert Schrieter to develop what he calls a "local theology." It is to this application of God's Word in the midst of God's People to which we turn in part III.

NOTES

1. The post-industrial has only recently burst on the scene and is thus, for all practical purposes, nameless. Shaw has used the term in an attempt to deal with a conceptual shift identified by global pluralism and increasing complexity (1990). Eventually a representative name that is self-characteristic rather than simply "post" will emerge as the details of this culture type are better understood. "Postmodern" as it is used in literature identified an era that comes after the modern context from which contemporary, global pluralism is emerging.

Service's model is not to be confused with an assumed evolutionary progression from basic, rudimentary societies to highly complex, sophisticated peoples. It is more like a sliding scale that provides a first best guess for the purpose of narrowing down the number of things to look for and how a particular group of people may organize those aspects of their lives.

2. A large and burgeoning literature is developing in conjunction with this cultural phenomenon. It is not our intent to discuss the details here. Rather we seek to utilize the literature to present the issues and show the relevance to our topic. For excellent definitions and summaries of postmodernity, see Stanley Grenz (1996) and Dennis McCallum (1996). For theological implications of the phenomenon see Middleton and Walsh (1995), Leonard Sweet (2000), and Nancey Murphy (1997). For a historical understanding of missiological implications, see Wilburt Shenk (1999). For a perceptive discussion of the church in postmodernity, see Eddie Gibbs (2000).

3. Paul Hiebert views worldview as the interaction between levels of response to cultural stimuli: cognitive responses (surface-level), affective or emotional responses (mid-level) and evaluative responses (deep-level). The entire structure encompasses be-

liefs, feelings, and values that enable people to interact with the world around them and perceive reality (Hiebert, 1985: 46; 1989b). Nishioka has done a masterful job of comparing Hiebert's and Kraft's approaches to the study of worldview as applied to doing missiological research (Nishioka, 1998).

4. In her dissertation, Catherine Rountree presents the idea of a "conceptual text" from her research of cognitive, linguistic, and cultural factors that impact a people's understanding of the message encased in a particular communication. She uses this conceptual understanding to focus on issues central to effectively testing how receptors understand a text and the necessity of making adjustments to the communication in order to ensure a match between the author's intent of a message and the receptor's ability to make the proper inferences about that text: the "conceptual text" (Rountree, 2001: 6). To the extent possible, as Sperber and Wilson (1986) note, the two must match. We contend that an intermediate communicator must understand both sides of the communication process and avoid being a conceptual filter, thereby clouding the communication intent as well as the inferences receptors will make based on their conceptualization.

5. Notice that Lingenfelter and Mayers portray their cultural propensity for dichotomistic thinking in laying out these values as contrasts—two ends of a continuum. Clearly there are other ways to present these values that would force reflection on a particular perspective. The point, however, is to encourage reflection, and by using a grid structure and limiting questions to human commonality, respondents are able to interact with the values and place themselves with respect to their cultural expectations. These expectations, in turn, will tend to reflect and enable compatibility with other members of their society. Armed with such information, communicators are then able to adjust their activity to be more reflective of the ministry context rather than their preferred modal values as per expectations in their home culture. Hiebert develops this idea in his concept of the "bi-cultural bridge" (Hiebert, 1982) where both expatriate communicators and members of the local culture interact and create new combinations of behavior patterns based on values to which both can relate.

III

RELEVANT COMMUNICATION

The Receptors' Understanding of God's Intended Message: Contextual Issues

> The receptors will hear God speaking to the degree that the communicative event is relevant to them at a specific time and in a particular context. Part III suggests how a model for relevant and effective Gospel proclamation could be constructed.

In part III, we explore what happens when a new group of receptors comes to understand God's intended meaning in their context. Here we emphasize the perspective of the receptors in determining the relevance of God's revelation in the midst of God's People. The nature of a communicative event establishes the way the people of a particular context will seek to develop a theology they can apply to their lives in a way that is pleasing to God. This establishes the missional issues essential for relevant proclamation in pluralist contexts around the world. We seek to communicate the Word of God effectively by remaining faithful to the intent of Scripture (chapter 7), appropriate to the audience (chapter 8), and relevant in the use of media and styles of communication with reference to particular receptors (chapter 9). This is the application section of the book that projects our missiological passion and synthesizes the theological and theoretical issues necessary to bring authenticity and vibrancy to communicating God's Word to people in a complex world.

· 7 ·

Seeking Relevant Communication

Receptors bring an understanding of their world that creates certain theological assumptions on their part. These assumptions influence the way receptors hear the Gospel in their own context.

*In the fall of 2000, Kwame Bediako gave the Payton Lectures at Fuller Theo-
logical Seminary, "Africa in the New World Christian Order." In the second of three
lectures, entitled "New Tongues, New Images," he spoke of the impact of Scripture
on the mother tongue of the peoples of Africa. He spoke of the value of the text of
God's Word in the new contexts of languages and cultures that had long experienced
God, but that now, through the translation of Scripture, could make the stories of
the Bible their own. Each language has a distinct way of expressing truth, he maintained, and that expression has theological implications.*

*To illustrate this adaptability he pointed to Hebrews chapter 11. In the con-
text of discussing the "great cloud of witnesses" in Hebrews 12:1, Bediako drew
a connection between the ancestors and us. Waiving off the sensibilities of his
largely western audience, Bediako spoke as an African preacher giving us a window into his worldview. "The patriarchs join us, he said, "they are here. Look
around you; the ancestors have joined our company—do you see them?" He then
illustrated his point by telling how in his language, Akan from Ghana, terms of
address indicate relationship. Within a household, the most longstanding and
meaningful relationship is with nana, "ancestor." In prayer, then, the most intimate and meaningful address for Jesus Christ was nana. When using English,
the Akan do not pray to "ancestor Jesus," but when they use their mother tongue
they do, and in so doing they recognize a different conceptual understanding of Jesus that goes far beyond the words and their semantic meanings. His point? "Language is theologically significant. And if you don't understand that," Bediako
said, "you can't understand God."*

*Dr. Bediako recognized that Scripture was given in a multiplicity of languages
and each one presents a different view of God. Bediako's presentation resonates*

with the intent of this chapter: the theological implications of seeking relevant com-
munication.

Having developed an understanding of the biblical context, the horizons into which the true source of Scripture communicated with human beings, and the communicator's context that enables a self awareness of personal horizons, we are now ready, in part III, to consider the context into which God communicates in our day: the receptor's horizon. As noted when we presented the culture types model in chapter 6, we live in a complex world in which representatives of all culture types are present. Each society, in its turn, is trying as best it can to handle life's major questions and organize its world in a meaningful way. Into such contexts (whether they be in a New Guinea village, a Mayan peasant town, an urban ghetto, or a refugee camp) God breaks in and makes an impact on the human condition. In this chapter we want to reflect on how people in our complex world interact with the biblical text.

GOD BREAKS INTO CULTURE

In his book *The Word Among Us,* Dean Gilliland begins his presentation of New Testament contextualization by exegeting John 1:14: "The Word became a human being and lived here with us."[1] Without Christ's advent, the culmination of thousands of years of theophanies and progressive revelation, we as human beings cannot truly know God. At the birth of Jesus, the heavenly hosts sang, "Peace on earth and to everyone who pleases God" (Luke 2:14). The lowly shepherds praised God and told everyone they met wonderful things about Jesus (Luke 2:17). The Magi bestowed the "king of the Jews" with their wealth (Matt. 2:1–12). And through it all, Mary "kept thinking about all this and wondering what it meant" (Luke 2:19). Simeon marveled, "With my own eyes I have seen what you have done to save your people and bring honor to Israel" (Luke 2:30–32). Anna praised God and told everyone that the salvation of Jerusalem had arrived (Luke 2:36, 37). Later John would declare, "Our ears have heard, our own eyes have seen, and our hands touched this Word" (I John 1:1). What they saw physically has been revealed to us through the record of the written word, through the power of the Holy Spirit, and through the faith experience of believers down through the ages who in word and deed testify that the "Word has dwelt among us." The task of relevant communication is to make the word of God relevant within the particularity of the context in which Gospel proclaimers find themselves. This means that the communication context (the source, the communicator, and the receptor) will vary from situation to situation and demand analysis and understanding that is unique to that set of circumstances. There Christ, through his word, is made manifest in the life of a society and enters the hearts of the people in order that they, too, may be conformed to Christ's image. Gilliland states it well:

> Theologians today whose first concern is mission find their task is really no different from that of the first apostles. The central truths are absolute, while communication and application fit local needs and questions. This does not mean that we make Jesus over to fit every situation or need as it arises. It does mean, however, that while firmly anchored to the Christ of apostolic witness, there must be an immediacy about the Gospel. There must be a recognizable identity for Jesus and clarity about what he taught, so that persons in this place and time can say, "My Savior and my Lord!" (Gilliland, 1989c: 53)

It is to this task of ensuring a recognizable identity for Jesus and clarity about what he taught that captured our imagination as we have written this book. Now in part III we focus on how this information may be utilized to communicate God's truth without heresy or loss of understanding of what God intended people to know about their God.

COMMUNICATING GOD'S INTENDED TRUTH

In theology we use the concept of vestiges of truth—vestiges of a knowledge of God. For example, when Joseph ends up in Egypt and interprets Pharaoh's dream, Pharaoh does not question the identity of the superior being who provided Joseph the interpretation. He recognizes Joseph as the spokesperson for that being. He understands this being to be somehow in control of nature and, in response, is interested in matters of stewardship and care. For Pharaoh there is a vestige of an understanding of the God above gods. Later, there is a change of dynasties. The subsequent dynasty did not know Joseph. They intentionally went against the vestiges of Egypt's rudimentary knowledge about the God above gods and began a movement of deification of the pharaoh. At that juncture the Exodus happens. The whole point of the Exodus is not so much the freedom of the Israelites. Rather it serves as a means whereby that particular Pharaoh might come to know that "I am God" (Exod. 7:17; 8:10). Moses's message actually harks back to the vestiges that had been there in Joseph's day, long before Moses entered the scene.

The Apostle Paul says God has never left himself without a witness. In every cultural context there is some indication concerning God's greatness and goodness (Rom. 15:7–13). Thus communication involves linking up with that which God has left in the receptors' culture regarding vestiges of knowledge about God. This process creates a new appreciation of God that impacts the communicators as well as the receptors. We return to the implications of this in chapter 8.

The idea of vestiges recalls Richardson's approach to redemptive analogies (1974). We can find redemptive analogies in Scripture as well as in culture. They serve as a means of bridging between the biblical horizons and the cultural contexts of today's receptors who represent horizon IV. It is a way of showing people how they, in fact, culturally fit into God's plan. Establishing a word for God, as Bediako discovered, is a crucial early step in the communication process. Interestingly, and Sanneh makes this clear, the word may already be there. And whatever is adapted will be infused with a high degree of local intentionality, thereby ensuring one of deBeaugrande and Dressler's elements of textuality presented in chapter 5. People will make inferences about God's intent to communicate with them that relate directly to spiritual experiences they have already had.

As people receive God's Word in their respective contexts, communicators want to communicate, not just present, information. Receptors do not have to understand all of the informational content encased in a message. The overall message is more important than the details of the informational load. As Sperber and Wilson point out (1986: chapter 5), understanding based on a "conceptual text" is important but of little use if the relevance of a message is not assumed. When God is communicating with human beings through God's revelation, exciting things come through. But what is exciting for one cultural context may be dull for another. The communication principle here is this: what excites people relates directly to their culture type. People in kinship societies get excited about relationships, particularly with regard to human beings and the powers and principles of the universe. People in peasant societies get excited about structural issues that demonstrate interrelationships between groups. People in industrial societies get excited about economic issues as they impact individualism. And people in postindustrial societies get excited about seeing interconnectedness, especially as it impacts global networks and the distribution of information. Scripture as God's revelation to human beings is related to what excites them. Perhaps this is why Campus Crusade's "Four Spiritual Laws" with its emphasis on the individual ("God loves you and has a wonderful plan for your life") was such a success in late–twentieth-century America. By noting the culture type, we have a starting point for communicating God's revelation in terms that are relevant to people with certain built-in assumptions about how things really are, or how they ought to be.

Scripture, then, is more than information, despite the perspective that emerges from western enlightenment. In fact it is communication to individuals or groups. The canon is closed, but God still reveals himself through people's experience of God. Through the Holy Spirit, God illuminates people with insight and understanding that enables them in their context to understand the message more clearly. God provides information in order to stimulate action, calling for a response. This communication is a combination of word and deed. It is both deep-structure values and concepts as well as surface-structure behavior. So it is important for us to ask how God would present his word were God doing so among the receptors we may be addressing today. Asking "How do we translate this?" forces a form-meaning dichotomy largely the result of focusing mainly on surface structures, not the deep-level intent of God's original message. Asking "How can my receptors know God in their context?" is to emphasize deep-level structures of meaning.

G. C. Berkouwer emphasizes our inability "to discuss Holy Scripture apart from a personal relationship or belief in it. . . . [T]he pure correlation of faith is decisively determined by the object of faith, namely, God and his Word" (Berkhouwer, 1975: 9, 10). That theological perspective is based on a people's ability to understand what God is saying, which in turn provides a strong rationale for an accurate "translation" that reflects the importance of "fidelity" in Nida's terms. We must be faithful to the text. But at the same time we must present God's Word in a form of communication that makes sense to the receptor and reveals God's intended truth in the new context. As a community of believers develops in faith, they will most probably begin to experience the hermeneutical spiral and the developing church will create a theological perspective that at once draws from, and contributes to, the historical development of dogma. Once conceptualized, these vestigial messages, along with their biblical rationale, can be more effectively communicated.

EFFECTIVE COMMUNICATION CONCEPTUALIZED

Effective communication is strongly rooted in the concept of incarnation. Following the communication models presented in chapter 5, we believe relevant communication is confirmed when those who receive it consider the presented word relevant. This means receptors are able to make inferences regarding the original intent with which the original communicator would agree. Inasmuch as the initial source is God who wants all human beings to acknowledge God and understand God's message, it stands to reason that enabling relevant communication is tantamount to presenting that message in a manner consistent with local language and culture as well as being coherent with God's intent for humankind. Maximizing this communication of God's intent is the objective of relevant communication. We begin with some definitional material and proceed to note the resulting theological development. This enables us to present a case study from Scripture that reflects this application in the second horizon. If Scripture itself conforms to the model we have developed, then we can be reasonably sure that we are on the right track in developing these issues in the contemporary context of an ever more complex world. By way of definition, we turn again to Gilliland (1989).[2] In the opening chapter of his book he notes: "The issue at hand is the way in which the Word, as Scripture, and the Word as revealed in the truths of culture interact to determine Christian truth for a given people and place" (10).

Notice how Gilliland interacts with the context of the source as well as that of the receptors. He associates these two worlds by pointing out that the word is in Scripture (special revelation, focused on a particular time and place) and is also "revealed in the truths of culture" (general revelation through the creation and cultural recognition of truth—preserved vestiges). God is in the business of revealing God's self to human beings—to God's creation. This is both-and, each side of the communication equation contributing to the other, not either/or, where only one side is in focus, often at the expense of the other. But Gilliland takes this one step further by emphasizing that these two contexts interact to create new truth. We probably would not make as strong a statement as he does, but the fact remains, and we have made the point earlier: when there is an encounter between the horizons, a new perspective, a new Christian truth comes into being for a given people in a specific cultural context. The result is a new understanding of truth. In effect, we will never have the whole truth until all of the nations are represented and people from every tribe and language stand around the throne praising the Lamb. Then we will see "face to face" and not "through a glass darkly" (I Cor. 13:12). This will be the moment when all truths combine to voice God's truth. Then and only then will all of the elements of cultural truth from particular contexts be brought together. This is what Hiebert calls "meta-truth" (1989). New meaning is created when relevant communication takes place. Gilliland couches this in terms of contextualization without which relevant communication is not possible.

> Contextualization [communication], therefore, is the dynamic reflection carried out by the particular church upon its own life in light of the Word of God and historic Christian truth. Guided by the Holy Spirit, the church continually challenges, incorporates, and transforms elements of the cultural milieu, bringing these under the lordship of Christ. As members of the body of Christ interpret the Word, using their own thoughts and employing their own cultural gifts, they are better able to understand the Gospel as incarnation. (1989:12, 13)

This new understanding builds a new theology that in turn informs the world church and gives all Christians everywhere a new understanding of God's message to the world. Such an understanding involves a hermeneutical appreciation of the contexts of the text and forces an understanding of the context into which the presentation takes place in order to seek increased communicability.

KEY QUESTIONS FOR
EFFECTIVE COMMUNICATION

In developing a methodology for bringing God's Word into particular contexts, Gilliland presents a series of four key questions that, in fact, serve to introduce a whole line of questioning in each area (1989: 64). The questions are: What is the general background? What are the presenting problems? What theological questions arise? What appropriate directions should the theology take?

Before we consider these questions in greater detail, notice the progression they follow within a particular context. The first question focuses on anthropological study of the Word in both ancient text and contemporary context. The second looks at the so-called felt needs of those who would receive the Word while requiring an examination of the needs and responses of those in the original context. The third question emphasizes how the entering Word will assist in helping people meet their needs. The fourth question looks at the impact of the first three questions in the development of what Schreiter calls "local theology"—the Word made flesh. These questions recall Mayers' prior question of trust (1987: 5–15), and Hiebert's process of critical contextualization (Hiebert, 1987; Hiebert et al., 1999: 20ff).[3]

All of these questions assume the validity of God's Word. They also assume that as Scripture enters a particular context it will make a difference in the hearts and lives of the receptors. When it enters a new culture, God's Word will impact human lives and become central in their theological development and it will be viewed as relevant. Notice that all of these questions deal with the receptors' context. Yet, they must be handled in light of the source text and the communicator's views and biases in the transfer process. Communication does not take place in a vacuum. It must always account for the entire communication context. For now, however, while recognizing the importance of the source message and context as we handled them in part I, here we focus on the communication issues that by their very nature emphasize the receptors' horizon.

What is the General Background?

Gilliland's first question presents the importance of focusing on the cultural context into which God's Word is to be expressed. In order to answer this question we need to apply the cultural models presented in chapter 6. Here are some questions that must be asked: What is the broad culture type of the receptor context? How does that type differ from the culture in the source text? What are the issues that pertain to the cultural subsystems within this particular society?

Often a particular subsystem will emerge as central and help focus cultural concerns on economics, social issues, political issues, or religious concerns—each of which calls for interaction with the others. Understanding these basic cultural issues creates an appreciation for the people's worldview, their basic values, and their propensity for change. Cultural anthropology, then, becomes an essential tool for establishing the general background for each particular context. This part of the study must not be short circuited, but rather considered vital to effective Gospel communication.

What Are the Presenting Problems?

In terms of the context in which the communication takes place, what are the people's issues or perceived needs? At this point we begin to deal with themes that share similar points with the ones reflected in the biblical horizons. How are these themes reflected in both the biblical context and the world of the receptor culture? The focus here is on what is similar and what is different. Are there any comparable root metaphors? Where in the biblical corpus can we find similar issues that enable contemporary recipients to have a greater appreciation of what God is saying to them?

What Theological Questions Arise?

In essence, all societies ask the same deep questions. The big questions of human existence have theological answers that reflect God's desire to interact with human beings. Yet the specifics of a particular theological agenda emerge from the cultural context. Once we know the context and can appreciate the people's felt needs, we can develop a Gospel presentation that demonstrates God's interest in these particular people. God is so concerned about them he is not willing to let any perish. God will do anything to bring people to knowledge of himself. God desires to respond to their human needs in spiritual ways that will make sense in their context.

What Appropriate Directions Should the Theology Take?

The operative word here is "appropriate." Given the receptors' circumstances (the reality of their cultural background, their presenting problems, and their theological questions) what could be the contours of their knowing God in their context? The answer can only come from the receptors who live out the developing theology. Theological development can only be a local enterprise. Nor can the answer to this question precede a response to the other questions. There is an order here that suggests a process leading a group of people into a close and ongoing relationship with their Savior and Lord. Although the primary focus here is the receptor, we must also consider the source and receive cultural and communicational information about the context in order to shed light on the way people in that context may know God. Utilizing the hermeneutic of the four horizons model, the communicator's understanding of these worlds will impact how the message is presented.

As we saw in chapter 4, theology and the concomitant development of commentaries must incorporate the four horizons of a hermeneutical approach to Scripture. The horizons of the Old and the New Testaments, the contextual horizon of the communicators, and the cultural arenas of the contemporary recipients are integral components of this process. We have here the beginning of a theological model that calls for our encountering the four hermeneutical horizons and applying them to the communication process in relation to our receptors. We must also continue to be concerned about the impact that a communicator's bias has on the content of the communication. Will the communicator's horizon enhance or impede God's agenda in building a new relationship with the receptors? Put another way, will the receptors be able to know God by means of the communication? This is the bottom-line theological question emerging from the application of the four-horizon approach to contextualized Gospel communication.

EFFECTIVE COMMUNICATION
LEADS TO THEOLOGICAL DEVELOPMENT

The entire process of Gospel communication based on cultural and biblical input leads to the development of theology within new cultural contexts. Gilliland's key questions make this clear.

> True theology is the attempt on the part of the church to explain and interpret the meaning of the Gospel for its own life and to answer questions raised by the Christian faith, using the thought, values, and categories of truth that are authentic within that place and time (Gilliland, 1989a: 10–11).

Such recognition of the relationship between (a) a particular context, (b) Scripture, and (c) the church enables the theology that develops to serve the new Christian community. Such local theology is not, then, a set of foreign concepts interjected into the consciousness of a people as a systematized set of propositions for understanding God. Rather, it constitutes a means of recognizing the dynamic impact that God has on the people of the receptors' culture caught up in rapid change in today's world. Without local logic and reason generated from the receptors' worldview, theology will make no sense to them, and the people will correctly question their need to pay any attention to it. Such irrelevance, in turn, can seriously damage the reputation of Christians in that context whose ideas and practices have little or no impact on the values and perspectives of the receptor culture.

With all of this in mind we can say that communication (based on principles of contextualization) is both a product (what people should understand about the message of the Gospel as understood in the deep-level structure of their context) and a process (an interaction of the truths of a culture with the truths of Scripture such that new expressions of Christianity come into being). These new ways of being church will include the development of what Schreiter calls "local theologies" (1985) and will present the significance of the Gospel in new and exciting ways within the receptors' context.

This model of local relevance recognizes the need for communicators to understand the contexts in which they minister. It also encourages monocultural communicators who are external to the receptor context to relate their own culture to biblical perspectives that deal with surface-level practices and deep-level beliefs and values in the receptor context that may be similar to those in the communicators' contexts. In God's infinite wisdom, God has provided a plan for people in each time and place. This plan has been made available throughout revelation history. At times it can be used to justify cultural practices in a particular context. At other times it may provide a means of advocating change among those who do not live out the way of life God desires for them. Without critique both affirmation and transformation of the receptors' culture are inadequate and may lead to syncretism and heresy. Theological development must be a matter of clarifying the Christian message "in a continuing effort to understand the faith and to demonstrate obedience to Jesus Christ in all dimensions of life" (Gilliland, 1989: 12). It is to this matter of theological tradition influenced by the development of a hermeneutical community that we present the following biblical case study.

A BIBLICAL CASE STUDY OF EFFECTIVE COMMUNICATION

The book of Hebrews provides a wonderful example of a hermeneutical community in the New Testament horizon that struggled through this process of theologically relevant communication. The author of the letter to the Hebrews is attempting to help the audience understand who they are in light of their ancestry and the rituals and ceremonies associated with the temple as presented in the Old Testament horizon. Here was a community of converted Messianic Jews who understood their historical context and their tradition, but struggled with their identity as a people in light of Christ's life, death, and resurrection. Here are all of the elements related to appropriate communication that seeks relevance. Applying the principles presented in part II of this book in combination with Gilliland's key questions, we develop this case study by attempting to understand the cultural contexts and then relate that information to the development of a relevant communication that, in turn, demonstrates theological development.

The Hebrew Cultural Issues

A quick look at the discourse structure of the book of Hebrews shows that the key themes running through the book are the identity of Christ; the place of the Hebrew ancestors tracing back to Abraham, Isaac, and Jacob; and the present status of Hebrew Christians as they struggle with their faith and cultural identity—particularly represented in the rituals and ceremonies surrounding sacrifices and temple concerns. These include the nature of the priesthood. Hebrews is heavily oriented toward the Old Testament. It employs Martin Noth's (1960) concept of "re-presentation" of past cultural and theological history in the present. It collapses time and makes the past relevant for the present context. So, for example, Abraham is presented as saying to the new Hebrew Christian audience, "Here is my witness. I left home without knowing where I was going. . . . I lived in the promised land like a stranger in a foreign country." Through this device, Abraham became a witness to the audience. They heard him speak, they saw him in their minds' eye, their ancestor testified to them through the creativity of the author. Abraham tells the Hebrew Christians what he saw and experienced. This becomes a testimony of Abraham's faith—re-presentation takes place. The focus is on the event and time is inconsequential. In a sense (and we must be careful here) the horizons collapse upon each other. But remember, horizon I and IV may represent similar societies separated by time. The author to the Hebrews collapses the time frame so the contemporary audience can experience Abraham as a witness to their situation. Bediako understood this but his audience at a North American seminary did not.

The writer to the Hebrews then comes to his argument in chapter 12 where he begins, "Therefore being surrounded by so great a cloud of witnesses . . ." The opening, *toigarouv,* is one of the strongest conjunctions in Greek, clearly joining chapters 11 and 12. It is generally translated "therefore" or "wherefore." The verse continues: "We are surrounded by a cloud of witnesses *(nephos marturon)."* To whom does this refer and what is the content of their witness? The verse goes on in English: "let us throw off everything that hinders, the sin that so easily entangles, and let us run with perseverance the race . . . looking to Jesus who is the author and perfector of our faith." What did the audience receiving this manuscript first infer about this text? What would have been their reception given an understanding of all that precedes this statement? It is in light of the issues already presented by the Hebrew writer and through the concept of re-presentation that they understand this portion of the text. The Hebrew Christians, in light of their conceptual (or cognitive) text, would probably have heard something like this:

> The cloud of witnesses from the past is now surrounding them in the present. Being surrounded by those who have expressed faith, Hebrew Christians can also join in the race that others have run. In fact, their ancestors who did not originally receive the promise will now be perfected because of their faith in Jesus. Jesus the Messiah is the promise. And now that the Hebrew Christians know that, they, together with their faithful ancestors, may receive the promise that is completed in Jesus the Christ, the one true High Priest.

In order to appreciate how the Hebrew Christians could come to this conclusion, we must take the second step in the process and evaluate the cultural issues involved in the biblical context.

Cultural Issues in the Text

The biblical text available to the Hebrew Christians was in large measure what we now call the Old Testament. This provides information relating to Gilliland's first, general background question. The focus was probably on the Torah, but the whole of the writings was undoubtedly taken into consideration, especially the historical books that placed them as a people with a specific time and place. The Hebrew receptors were called upon by the author of this letter to consider the issues pertaining to their ancestors, those who ran the race before them, those who are so clearly depicted in Hebrews chapter 11. This cloud of witnesses extended from Abel to Daniel and the post-exilic and intertestamental periods down to Christ. All witnessed to their faith and, therefore, pleased God. In the process others took note of their acts of faith and either struck out against them, or were brought to acknowledge the source of that faith. We want to follow the development of the "witness" idea here. How does the author of Hebrews develop the use of the word *marturon?* The word has a wide collocation drawing on the richness of the Hebrew language, which here is translated into Greek.[4] The author builds a semantic constellation centered around the concept of "witness."

In Hebrews 7:17, *martupeitai* expresses the sense of a declared statement. The Scriptures "say" (they give witness) that the referent is a priest forever in the order of Melchizedek. In Hebrews 10:15, the Holy Spirit "testifies" to us about this. Again the word is *marturei* and the Holy Spirit bears witness to the veracity of Scripture: "This is the covenant I will make with them." Through the writer to the Hebrews, the Holy Spirit uses the Old Testament words to speak (give testimony) to the converted Jewish Christians, applying covenantal language to signify a relationship between the horizontal and the vertical—human beings in relation to each other and to their creator.

Using the same linguistic forms, the author then dramatically changes the meaning. Just a few verses further in 10:28 the author notes, "Anyone who rejected the law of Moses died without mercy on the 'testimony' of two or three witnesses." Now the author is using legal language. In 11:2 the author introduces the list of those who expressed their faith by noting "this is what the ancients were commended for." And the key word? *Emarturethesan,* how they were "witnessed" or "testified" about. In 11:4, Abel, "by faith, offered to God a better sacrifice than Cain. By faith he was commended (*emarturethe*), he was witnessed about, he was declared to be a righteous man. In 11:39, the author reaches the grand finale; all these in the recitation were "commended" (*marturethentes*) for their faith. It should be translated, "these all witnessed about their faith." Then the clincher: "yet none of them received what had been promised to them because God had planned something better for us [the receptors of the letter to the Hebrews] so that only together with us they [all the witnesses] would be made perfect."

Comparison of Text and Issues of Context

With the cultural and biblical context of horizons I and II as background, and with reference to the original audience, we now ask, "Who are these witnesses?" Or, more accurately, "Who did the author's Hebrew audience think these witnesses were?" Applying the concept of re-presentation, and considering the expanded collocation of the Greek word *marturon,* the original receptors of the book of Hebrews drew certain hermeneutical conclusions that fit the text to their context. It deals with Gilliland's second question: What are the presenting problems? In this text there is an activity of testifying to the veracity of the witnesses. They, in effect, give a character witness of their faith and of God's faithfulness. There is also a semantic constellation here that includes ocular witnesses: They testify to what they saw; it was an experiential witness.[5] What did the Old Testament witnesses of Hebrews chapter 11 do? How did they express their faith? They verbally retold what they saw. What is the content? It is their experience. And what was the result of their witnesses? Verse 39 says they were all witnesses yet none of them received what had been promised. They all died without realizing God's promise to them.

With this as background the audience is ready to answer how this understanding will meet their needs. The author of Hebrews sets up the argument of the book through a narrative theology so that the audience can understand who the witnesses are. For the readers of Hebrews, it is clear that the witnesses of chapter 11 are the ancestors, their literal, consanguineal kin, descendants of Abraham, Isaac, and Jacob. They surround the audience, they identify with them, they watch them. And as they are there together, they are all together in the race of life, running with their eyes on the goal that was promised, a goal that is fulfilled in Jesus Christ. These ancestors were all commended (witnessed about) for their faith by the Holy Spirit. They gave witness to their own faith through their experience, which is clearly part of the biblical and historical record of their nation. Yet despite their apparent success none of them received what had been promised. God had planned something better for all of them (collectively) so that in concert they would all be made perfect through recognition of the promised One, the Messiah, the Holy One of Israel. Through re-presentation the author joins the ancestors together with the receptor audience. At that moment in the text, contextualization takes place for them—they experience a huge "ahh haa" that enables them to appreciate the revealed Jesus, the Christ, as their promised Messiah. So they run the race with their eyes fixed on Jesus the author and perfector of their faith. They understand this because he is a part of the context. It makes sense to them and thereby allows the author of Hebrews to move on with the application. "Set aside any encumbrances so you will be able to run in such a way that you will perfect the faith of those who went before. Jesus is the model and he is the one who will keep you from sin" (12:2,3). This Promised One for whom the Jews waited so patiently is also their Lord (*kurios*). And their ancestors too may be perfected through the present action of the Hebrew Christian receptors. This creates a new responsibility to act as the author admonishes them. It also connects them to a special relationship they have with their ancestors. They are in a symbiotic relationship, depending on each other and together depending on Jesus the Christ, the perfector of true faith.

COMMUNICATION ISSUES

In working through this process of ensuring relevance in communication we have exemplified the use of the horizons model and its application to principles of relevant communication. How this portion of Scripture, with its connection to the whole of the Bible and the identity and activity of women and men of faith, gets communicated in our day is further impacted by horizons III and IV. We must consider both the communicator's worldview and that of the contemporary receptors. The illustration from Hebrews chapter 11 above gives us a good example of the process as we watch a biblical author link ancient text and context with contemporary issues that impact a particular audience. We must do no less in our day. First, we must consider the presenter's bias.

Communicator's Bias

In his commentary on Hebrews, F. F. Bruce discusses the "witness" issue quite differently than what we have just presented. Bruce writes:

[O]ur author has said repeatedly that they were well attested by virtue of their faith; to them all, as to Abel, God himself bore witness. This is from the earlier references. But now they in turn are called witnesses. A "cloud" of witnesses. . . . But in what sense are they "witnesses"? Not, probably, in the sense of spectators, watching their successors as they in turn run the race for which they have entered; but rather in the sense that by their loyalty and endurance they have borne witness to the possibilities of the life of faith. (1990: 333)

Bruce's perspective from his horizon is a very different argument than we believe the original audience understood. Clearly he had not listened to Bediako. Notice his western and even Enlightenment-based bias. He is saying these witnesses were not spectators watching their successors. Rather it is their loyalty and endurance that provides the witness to the possibilities of the life of faith. His focus is not on people, not on relationships, but rather on what they do. His focus is task-oriented rather than person-oriented as we saw in the basic values profile in chapter 6.

While Bruce's commentary reflects his culture, which we applaud, we can find no support for his application of "witness" in the text of Hebrews. How would the Hebrews have understood the text? Bruce forgets, even as a commentator, how much his horizon tends to impact what he sees in the text. He does not understand the issue of ancestors (in large measure because of his culture) and, therefore, despite his skill as a theologian, he misses both the historical and textual perspective of the passage. This provides an important lesson for those who cross cultural barriers to bring a biblical message to people who may be quite similar culturally to the biblical contexts being examined.

Application to Contemporary Contexts

With what we believe to be a clearer perspective of the text of Hebrews, we can now ask Gilliland's third key question in an attempt to appreciate theological issues. We can now gain insight by reading Hebrews from an African, or Latin American, or Asian perspective, where ancestors are understood.[6] The text says the ancestors are perfected together with us, the new recipients, as together we run the race. In Jesus we are all perfected. Christ is the perfector, the one who makes faith complete. This, then, guards against any tendency to worship those ancestors. We are not to worship them; they are not saints.[7] Rather they are runners like us, striving to reach the same goal—to experience the promise in Jesus Christ. Bediako clearly makes the point when he says that "the place and significance of ancestors in the African primal worldview actually offers opportunities for 'filling out' some dimensions of spiritual experience and historical consciousness which are inherent in the Christian religion" (Bediako, 1995: 212).

The metaphor is a bit like a circular track, and each time we run past, the ancestors check up on us. This changes the western perspective of linear time. It shifts the focus from time-orientation to event-orientation. So for all of us in the race together, someday it will be over and we will all be perfected in Christ. The image is incredible. The ancestors should not be the objects of adoration. Rather they are "witnesses" to us of what they know so we can press on toward the prize God has given to all because of what Jesus has done (Phil. 3:14). Note again the importance of re-presentation and the hermeneutical spiraling that results. As a contemporary audience of horizon IV, we too can listen afresh to the text through a new appreciation of the original receptors' understanding (this was what Bediako was trying to get the audience at Fuller Seminary to do). When non-Jews, down through the ages, understand this revelation, they are illuminated with new appreciation, not only for the Hebrew perspective, but also of their own human condition. Like the Jews, they also are witnesses of Jesus the Christ who is their Lord (*kurios*). And their ancestors too may be perfected through the present action of the new receptors. This is very good news, indeed.

The reality of the cloud of witnesses must be acknowledged. The western view often ignores that reality. If we really believe in the continuing existence of the soul, and if we negate what the Enlightenment has taught us about death as the ultimate end, we should not have trouble believing the biblical record that the ancestors are really there. Now we are able to hear the author's call to lay aside those weights and entanglements and join in the race with our eyes fixed, not on the witnesses (the runners don't watch the crowd in the stands) but on Jesus, the goal, the Promised One. However we communicate this, we must ensure that the focus is on Christ, not any human element. Human beings, along with the rest of creation, are the witnesses. Jesus Christ is the one of whom we witness, the Word who sustains the foundation of the earth and who will sit on the throne in the New Jerusalem.

THEOLOGICAL DEVELOPMENT

We are now ready to consider the theological development that results from relevant communication—Gilliland's fourth key question. The original audience of this text is a group of converted Jews, Hebrew Christians who were looking for a sign, a promised one, a child born to a virgin. All Jews through history looked for the same manifestation. They sought through their spiritual experience, as God's covenantal people, to build a relationship with God, to keep God's commandments (the old covenant, Heb. 8:8, 9), and to seek the promise (the new covenant, Heb. 8:10–11; 12:2). In such a context, the author does not develop an anti-Gnostic argument.[8] Rather, the author speaks within a Jewish mindset that includes an elasticity of time. So he says, "I want to encourage you to run this race. As you run, you join a race that started a long, long time ago and finds its conclusion in a faith experience with the promise, with Jesus Christ himself, with a new covenant" (Heb. 8:10–12). Having established this as a basis, the author goes on to castigate them for wanting to turn away or succumb to false teaching. In short, the author of Hebrews contextualizes the message for the audience and encourages them to put the argument to the test by acknowledging and experiencing the promise made to the ancestors. When this audience connected with what the author was really saying and experienced it vicariously through the host of ancestors extending back to Abraham, they could acknowledge their pilgrimage with God who continually pursued them regardless of their disinterest.

Furthermore, the Hebrew relationship with God was possible through Jesus Christ, who entered into the holy place, not to die like the high priest but to give true life because he himself was the temple curtain (Heb. 10:19). This refers to another key revelational metaphor that was central to Jewish religion: the relationship of the high priest to the holy of holies and vicariously to God himself. It is a deep-level metaphor that has been a stumbling block throughout the history of the temple, from the wilderness tabernacle to the incredible beauty of the second temple destroyed in 70 A.D. By weaving these symbols throughout the text of Hebrews, the author is further saying that this is not just a religion for Jews. It is a matter of belief in the incarnational revelation of Jesus as the second Adam (recapturing what the first Adam lost) and accepting the access that Jesus Christ gives to all who believe regardless of religious background (Rom. 5:12–17). Thus Jesus Christ who rent the veil and exposed the holy of holies becomes the true high priest about whom the author attested in Hebrews 4. That access is more than a physical connection like someone's presence in a room. It is a relationship with God who made all humans, who knows God's creation, and who wants to have fellowship with everyone (Gen. 1:26). Thus Jews and Gentiles alike receive significant information from this text. On the one hand, it reconnects Jews to their heritage. On the other, it reestablishes relationships for all peoples with God. Only in the company of all who are yet to come will people be made perfect (Heb. 11:40). The text has now gone beyond sectarian religious practices of a particular people seeking after God. Rather, it reflects God seeking out all human beings for the purpose of reconciling them to God's self. It also reflects a special relationship with all humankind based on principles spelled out in God's communication.

Theology is based on God's revelation through the text of Scripture. As representatives of the human condition, we must affirm that all theology is context-conditioned and people's inferences are made on the basis of their understanding of God's intent. All theology, then, is local theology and reflects the worldview of those who hold to it. It is a composite collectivity that reflects the way all humans may relate to the God who seeks them out in both their individual and their collective identity. All are one in Christ who fulfills human history and draws all people to God, as God intended at creation (Col. 1:20).

In this case study from the book of Hebrews, we see an application of the hermeneutical spiral and the four horizons from a biblical perspective. This process is evident throughout Scripture. It also pertains to effective communication in our day. The message of Scripture is made relevant in whatever context it finds itself. Each context, however, brings its own strengths to bear on an understanding of the text, just as weaknesses are also exposed. By appreciating these respective strengths and weaknesses (which often relate to worldview) we can more deeply appreciate the truth of God's revelation throughout the biblical story and bring that understanding to bear in a clearer communication of what God intends to say to any given people.

SCRIPTURE PRESENTS GOD'S COMMUNICATIONAL INTENT

In the theoretical development of this book, we saw the need to reflect on the way God, through the biblical authors, has ensured that God's intended message be faithfully communicated in all contexts. The hermeneutical spiraling process has impacted how we go about doing research in order to ensure effective understanding of the original context and communicate that understanding in contemporary contexts. Bringing the biblical horizons to bear upon the present-day horizons results in theologizing that, in turn, discovers new deep-level structures of meaning in new receptor cultures. Theologizing in the midst of a people is an ongoing process. In this way God's truth will be upheld and hocus pocus will be avoided.

Several years ago coauthor Shaw received a letter from a well-meaning mission leader seeking a commentary he could use with church leaders in an Asian context. He requested suggestions for a general commentary that would meet the needs of all of his pastors who came from many different languages. Dan responded by noting that there was no such thing as a generalized commentary. Commentaries are always written with specific theological and cultural biases. To correct the problem for his group of pastors, Dan suggested the mission leader teach biblical concepts and then encourage the pastors to write their own commentaries as a result of their having interpreted the passages they had preached. Unfortunately, Dan failed to give him the hermeneutical principles that would make that process possible. This book is a way of making amends.

While at Fuller Seminary, Kwame Bediado was preaching a similar message, which also forms the crux of Gilliland's process of contextualization. The implications of this process are far-reaching and complex. They point to the need for effective Gospel communication both within a faith community and by that faith community who themselves become God's missionary people and reach out to others. This points the way to the next two chapters.

NOTES

1. Edited by Dean Gilliland, this book was contributed to by each member of the School of World Mission faculty at the time. It represented application of contextualization theory to each faculty member's specialty. Gilliland's thinking stimulated a creative new approach to, and an understanding of, contextualization.

2. We will assume readers have a degree of familiarity with the development of the contextualization concept. Together with others, we have written extensively on this and it is not our purpose here to reiterate that literature. For further reference note Taber, 1978; Hesselgrave, 1978 and 1989; Gilliland, 1989a, and numerous relevant articles by this book's authors in *Missiology, Evangelical Missions Quarterly, The Bible Translator,* and *Notes on Scripture in Use*.

3. In the first edition of *Christianity Confronts Culture,* Mayers develops a rather elaborate series of questions designed to help missionaries reduce their own cultural biases when interacting with people of another society. These questions were designed to be answered in sequence and help expatriates interact more effectively in a crosscultural situation. Mayers called this progression of questions the "Prior Question of Trust," or more simply, "PQT." The questions are:

1. What are the cultural norms?
2. Are the people living within those norms?
3. Do the norms need changing?
4. Who is responsible for changing the cultural norms?

Taken together, these form the basis of appreciating a cultural context and recognizing the roles of the respective participants in building cross-cultural relationships (Mayers, 1987: 5–15).

4. Notice the author's theology of translation here. The author knows the ancient texts well and quotes the people of Scripture freely in Greek, not Hebrew. The author is translating, communicating, making the message relevant to a new context.

5. Recall the criteria for canonicity presented in chapter 2. Here we see that in practice. The author is saying, "if you don't believe me, believe these others who through their faith have been witnesses of that which God has done." But the focus is on human behavior not divine activity.

6. Notice that we have shifted horizons now. When looking at the Hebrews case study we were in horizon II (the New Testament). Now we shift to horizon IV (the receptors) and look to see how the text informs the receptors' context.

7. In Latin America translators should never translate the "witnesses" with the word *santos*. Those saints are all the images to be worshipped and often serve as intermediaries. If *santos* is used, it destroys the whole imagery the Hebrews author sets up and negates the message of the entire book.

8. Notice that Paul does not even touch this cloud of witness concept in his presentation to the Colossians. That is because the Gnostic concept of emanation is so close that it would be terribly confusing and could easily tend to syncretism.

· 8 ·

Enabling Relevant Communication

Audiences need to be able to hear God speak in acceptable and meaningful ways in their own language spoken in the context of their culture.

*W*hen translating for the Samo, coauthor Dan Shaw ran into a major transla-tion and theological problem when translating John 3:16. The Samo language has no word for "God." Neither are there words for "love," "world," or "believe." Without these concepts this critical verse loses much of its content. What was he to do? He explains.

As I learned in Sunday school, John 3:16 is what the Bible is all about—the Gospel in a nutshell. But how was I to communicate this verse without these key words? Like any other language, Samo is not deficient. I knew Nida and Taber's famous dictum, "If it can be said in one language, it can be said in another" (1982: 4). I quickly realized I had to get beyond the horizontal and surface plane. This was not just about how to translate John 3:16. That would have been simply a matter of applying translation principles to a particular language prob-lem—a transposition of human ideas. Rather, I wanted to help them deal with the theological issue of who God is: God's power, God's relationship with human beings, and the far-reaching implications of that relationship for dealing with is-sues of life, death, and eternal life. I needed to get beyond the immediate text to the whole of Scripture and allow the Samo to stand in awe at this incredible God who included them in his plan for humanity. What could this mean for them in-dividually and as a group of former cannibals living in the dense rain forest on the Island of New Guinea?

As a translator I knew how to solve the lexical and semantic problems. As an an-thropologist I knew the importance of considering both the cultural setting of those who first received John's Gospel, as well as the need to understand the Samo culture. I knew the value of analyzing collocational ranges. I appreciated the value of text/communication styles and how these are used for effective presentation of a mes-sage. I also knew the Samo were aware of a "guy in the sky" who was always ready

177

to zap them when they did wrong (mothers would caution playing children not to make too much noise lest they attract his attention). But this was not the concept of God characterized in John 3:16 by the apostle.

Eventually I discovered the concept of the ayo, of the oldest among a group of brothers who lived in a longhouse. This was a benevolent, caring man who was never in charge but always in control—a traffic director for the entire household. They spoke of him as "the authority person." When combined with an all-inclusive possessive pronoun this term eventually became the term we used for God— oye ayo, "our authority person." When extended to all the people who "sleep in all the places of the earth" (a way to communicate "the world") the Samo began to appreciate God in a whole new way, in relationship to themselves and to their enemies.

The relationship between the ayo and those in a longhouse reflected a strong, caring concern for everyone in the household—"love." For the Samo, a very practical, down to earth people surviving in a hostile environment, belief was a matter of experience. How do they know something is true? They see it, hear it, feel it! In short, they experience truth. This has profound implications far beyond trying to translate John 3:16. It relates to the broader context of all of John chapter 3, including Nicodemus's awe of Christ and Israel's experience with the brass serpent in the desert, particular experiences tied to the history of a specific people in a particular time and place. More broadly, it is about how humans experience God.

As a Bible translator I was, in fact, communicating through this verse in its place within a text, an entire semantic constellation tied to the very purpose of Scripture. Suddenly the Samo found themselves in the flow of human involvement with a caring God who knew them and wanted to have an intimate, family-type relationship with them—not merely sit in judgment and zap them without warning. As a result of understanding John 3:16, the Samo also found themselves in relationship with people beyond their recognized circle of alliance, with the whole of humanity beyond their borders, including people they normally considered enemies. That the "one in control" of their feared enemies, the Bedamoni, also had authority over them was not only revelatory, it was transforming. This new understanding—experienced through relationship—had eternal implications for a "life that would not end" and gave insight to a spirit world populated by evil beings, but also included the pool of ancestors who constantly reentered the world to energize a newborn baby and move through the cycle of life once again to join the ancestors and assist the living in their struggle. These new and far-reaching theological insights relating to the Samo also challenged my understanding of the text, forced me to reevaluate my own assumptions, and made me appreciate more deeply the Samo from whom I learned so much about God.

When translating John 3:16 into the Samo language the focus was on the need to understand theological, linguistic, and cultural relationships. This remains the missional focus that will extend well beyond this book, as contemporary communicators of God's Word process the message.

MODELS OF THEOLOGICAL
DEVELOPMENT FOR EFFECTIVE COMMUNICATION

What theological questions arise out of the context in which Gospel presentation has taken place? Obviously this relates back to questions of culture type, cultural subsystems, worldview issues, and the impact of these models on how the society interfaces with the world around it vis-à-vis culture change (issues discussed in chapter 6). At the same time, the nature of the ministry context is central for dealing with theological questions. How we encourage and enable people to study God's Word and apply it to their lives is crucial. How does God reveal his intention through the biblical record? How is this made relevant for the people of a particular context? To help answer these questions, we turn now to some models suggested by those who have struggled with these issues. They reflect an application of anthropology to missiological thinking and help us reflect on how to encourage effective communication in contemporary cultures. We will use a case study to demonstrate the application of theoretical models to real life situations.

The Encounter Model

Charles Kraft has developed a model of three encounters as a process for indigenous theological development (1992). This encounter model is particularly significant when truth encounter, power encounter, and allegiance encounter are matched with different levels of worldview, as presented in figure 8.1. Truth encounter, then, is at the cognitive level—it is cerebral with a focus on understanding. This level is closer to the surface and anything that goes against it is worked out in terms of behavior that is positively or negatively reinforced. Kraft sees power encounter as developing freedom from bondage, which involves what Hiebert called the "affective" or feeling realm, the so-called middle zone in the framework for analysis of religious systems (Hiebert et al., 1999). Here error is viewed as something that is fundamentally wrong and society must face the challenge. The third encounter in Kraft's model deals with the area of allegiance. Here the emphasis is on issues of relationship on the one hand, and basic assumptions about the nature of being on the other. This is the deep structure where everything is evaluated in terms of cultural assumptions. Error is viewed as sin. This is where God ultimately interacts with people. God strives for their allegiance because relationship with people is God's passion. God wants them to turn from what they consider to be sin toward him in order to reduce their bondage (middle level) and behave in ways that are both biblically and culturally appropriate (surface level).

Notice the ripple effect into the context, and the impact of what Kraft calls a "paradigm shift" at the deep level. Unless all of this makes sense to the

Truth Encounter (Focus on Understanding)	**Cognitive, explicit behavior** (Surface Structures)
Power Encounter (Focus on Freedom)	**Affective/Emotive feelings** (Middle Zone)
Allegiance Encounter (Focus on Relationship)	**Evaluative/Value-based implicit expectations— paradigms** (Deep Structures)

Figure 8.1.   Kraft's Encounter Model Applied to Levels of Worldview

people of a culture, they will not consider changing allegiance (which, because this is at the worldview level, is the primary encounter in the model) from what they know to something new and unknown. This provides a rationale for keeping the communicator out of the equation as much as possible in order to avoid what we have called the "filter effect." The Holy Spirit must be allowed to communicate as directly as possible with the people of the receptor culture, with their deepest human concerns, discovering how God can meet them at the deepest levels of their culture.

Faith, Tradition, Behavior Model

Robert Schreiter (1985: 113–117) related Chomsky's linguistic model of deep and surface structure with its assumptions about competence and performance to the whole idea of faith and tradition. Chomsky maintained that people generate a whole variety of linguistic structures based on panhuman concepts, and that grammar provides the means whereby speech forms are structured. Schreiter developed the idea of grammar as a critique of a person's competence with respect to the way they act on their beliefs and values. He related this to Christianity by viewing the deep structure in terms of faith issues that filter through the "grammar" of church tradition to help people build a theology. He moved from faith issues to their manifestations as they developed over two thousand years of church history. While his Roman Catholic heritage is obvious, Schreiter made an important point. As they pertain to practice, matters of faith always filter through the tradition of the church—the historical development of dogma. Thus, faith is impacted by tradition that, in turn, affects the development of theology, including praxis. Schreiter concludes, "The [model] . . . tries to respect the variety within the Christian tradition as well as its constant concern for orthodoxy" (1985: 117). As Evangelicals, we would wish that Schreiter's model had a clearer place for the role of Scripture in the construction of local theologies. Figure 8.2 is an attempt to diagram this process.

How do we make this model work for us? Schreiter's model is an extension of a worldview model. At the deep level, dealing with beliefs and values, we have matters of faith, or what Chomsky calls "competence." This is

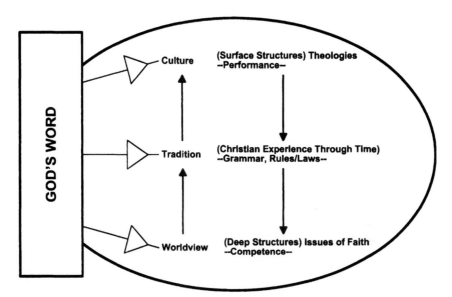

Figure 8.2.   A Cultural Structure Critiqued by Scripture

from where we human beings draw our understanding of reality (written with a small "r"). When we get to the surface structure, we have all of the cultural manifestations, the myriad of cultural expressions that human beings experience every day. This is where people perform in accordance with their cultural assumptions. From these emerge what Schreiter called "local theologies." These are surface manifestations that express how a particular worldview relates to the context of life into which God has entered through his Word. The deep structure impacts the surface manifestations, which, in turn, feed information back to the worldview and eventually contribute to cultural/theological change.

In between the deep structure and the surface manifestations is the "grammar," the developed tradition of the church reflecting the councils and creeds. These enable each new church to remain within orthodoxy as it relates to their particular orthopraxy. This middle segment based on Christian experience through time connects the deep and surface levels and ensures that what people know of the struggles of the church theologians can be instructive in developing a new receptor culture's own theology. Important as an historical perspective is, Protestants do not place the same emphasis on church tradition as Schreiter does. While he maintains that tradition is the critique that enables the contemporary church to appreciate its position, we would say Scripture provides the critique for both the tradition and the current manifestations of faith communities. In figure 8.2, then, the focus is not on the developing church and its theology but rather on utilizing the place of Scripture, God's Word, in the midst of God's people as a means for interpreting faith and integrating it at every level.

Missiologically, it is important to watch what happens when God incarnates, when God enters into the human context. God does this through his Word, the Bible. This is more than a rationale for Bible translation (though Sanneh, 1989, argues that point well). It also has theological implications, as God's Word interacts with the different components of a culture. This is not linear. Rather the focus is on how the components relate to each other as together they express a new understanding of God in the new context.

Cultural Models

As Scripture critiques worldview, it too interacts with every level pictured in figure 8.1. It critiques the surface structure patterns as well as a people's beliefs and values. Furthermore, Scripture has a much greater depth than the mere two thousand years of Christian tradition. Scripture rests upon the whole of the Old Testament, a tradition going back to the very foundation of the earth. This is what Paul alluded to when he reiterated the Jewish genealogy going back to Abraham, Isaac, and Jacob. Whenever he spoke in a synagogue, he told the story of God's revelation over time. He reinforced the tradition, received from the ancestors. As we demonstrated in chapter 7, the writer to the Hebrews expanded on that understanding and developed a powerful rationale for Hebrew believers to maintain their faith. At issue here is the need to not only look at the tradition of the church but also account for local tradition. We are looking at the mythology of a culture. We are looking at a people's understanding of what in fact provided a critique for them before Scripture came. This is very important. It is the crux of Paul's discussion in Romans chapters 1, 2, and 3.

Relevant Gospel communication seeks to take these models and apply them to the actual process of assisting people in the development of a local theology that is their theology. At the same time, we must be mindful of the dangers of inappropriate contextualization that could result in syncretism and heresy (Hiebert et al., 1999: 22ff). Schreiter's answer was to focus on what has gone before, on theological development elsewhere. He was not willing to let go of tradition. Ecclesiastical creeds and dogma, for him, are at the center. That is why the Roman Catholics have been very good at what they earlier called "adaptation" and more recently "inculturation" (Shorter, 1989). This approach reflects on God's Word from below by focusing on cultural issues as the basis for biblical understanding—hearing God speak out of the pain and need of people who need liberating. Schreiter suggests that in order to contextualize, a faith community must understand itself within a particular culture from which it interacts with the traditions of the church at large. However, when Schreiter's model is taken to its logical conclusion, it may produce syncretism as a theology almost purely from below.

Our position, in contrast, is to avoid having a local theology introduce heresy into church orthodoxy in the name of local viability. The hermeneutical spiral must keep spiraling and continually drawing its impetus from above, not only from below: Scripture, not culture, drives the spiral. (See figure 8.2.) At the same time, in order to maintain relevance in a specific society, all that we have discussed regarding the entire communication process, including the development of local theologies, must be taken into consideration. This is a complex balancing act in which relevant communication results in theological development within a particular time, place, and culture. One such case from the Samo may serve as an example of how theologizing works in light of the theological, communicational, and cultural models presented in part II.

DEVELOPING A LOCAL
THEOLOGY: A SAMO CASE STUDY

When the Samo become Christians, like all other believers, they put their faith in Christ. When Jesus came as the incarnation, the Samo assumed that his spirit energized a newborn baby and followed through the expected series of life cycle events (nose piercing, initiation, and building relationships in keeping with his societal roles).[1] This reflects Samo worldview expectations. Putting his death in the Samo frame of reference, Jesus died in a violent manner at a juncture the Samo would call the "prime of life." When he died, Scripture says that he was laid to rest. In other words, in the Samo view, he returned to the *kogwa*, "the ancestors." But then God's power was used to resurrect Jesus from the dead. This is crucial. It was not Jesus' power. He was dead. It was the power of God or, we can say here, the power of the Holy Spirit. So the risen Christ has two spirits:

his own *fini,* "life force or spirit," and the Holy Spirit bestowed on him by God the father. In the Samo view of things, the only people with a plurality of spirits are shaman, individuals who serve the people as mediums between the world of the ancestors and those who are alive upon this earth. So, the question is, can the Samo talk about Christ as the shaman who is a medium between themselves and God that in fact replaces all other mediums? Does their allegiance to Christ remove the need for Samo mediums? Can the Samo view Christ as the ultimate medium? Romans 8:34, Hebrews 7:25, and I John 2:1 all deal with this idea of Christ interceding for earthbound humans in the heavenlies. When the Samo hear that, they hear "mediumship" and their conceptual text flashes "shaman." Christ is able to do particularly well in this capacity because of his incarnation. He lived on earth and is well acquainted with the human condition (including the Samo). At the same time he also lives with God and knows the heavenly world in which he now sits at the right hand of his father. This sets up a potential theology for the Samo. But first we need to understand the worldview assumptions the Samo bring to their theological development.

The Nature of Samo Mediumship

In the stream of Samo identities, mediums are men or women who have been singled out by the ancestors to assist in their interaction with human beings. These shaman are endowed by the ancestors with a special spirit of mediation. This spirit is able to leave the shaman's body and by means of astral travel arrive at the ancestral abode where it ascertains information on behalf of human concern and takes it back to benefit ordinary human beings. Samo mediums utilize spiritual power on behalf of the people. They are in contrast to sorcerers who work against the best interests of human beings, often in association with evil spirits. Sorcerers, like shaman, have an extra spirit given by the "evil one." Similarly this spirit is in touch with the evil forces who would do harm to human beings. Sorcerers take advantage of weakness, broken relationships, and other human frailties to be destructive, to pull things apart. In contrast, Shaman seek to hold things together. The source of their extra spirit causes shaman and sorcerers to operate very differently. Mediums serve as channels for the ancestors who are assumed to be good for the welfare of the Samo. Sorcerers, in contrast, are manipulators of evil, bringing hardship, sickness, and even death—often on request, sometimes by an enemy (Shaw, 1990b: 129ff). For the Samo, this contrast between shaman who represent the good ancestors and sorcerers who represent evil is reflective of a cosmological battle in which good and evil are locked in deadly conflict and mere humans are but pawns in the framework of life upon the earth—caught in the middle (Shaw, 1986).

When in need of cosmic assistance, the Samo call upon a shaman to come to ascertain the will of the ancestors. Such an event takes the form of an all-night *kogowa foniyo,* "ancestor song fest," where the shaman contacts the ancestors through the medium role. Upon arriving at the ancestral abode "beyond the tree tops," the medium spirit communes with the ancestors, a conversation that is confirmed to those listening by glossolalia, an ancestral language that often includes bird calls and other animal-like sounds. When the information has been gathered, the mediating spirit returns to "translate" the received message so ordinary people can understand the cosmic word from the ancestors. Once reunited with the shaman's body, the spirit begins to sing the message it received from the ancestors. Those who hear repeat the refrain, and soon the longhouse is filled with an antiphonal song—the shaman singing a phrase and the audience repeating it. The ancestral message is thereby repeated for all to understand and act upon. In the morning people take action on what they have heard, restoring human relationship, correcting wrongs, seeking out and destroying the sorcerer's evil, or whatever is necessary to make amends and restore wholeness to the community. For the Samo, shaman do things openly and bring a spiritual message to the people so they can make a correction and restore unity. In contrast, sorcerers do things in secret and use their power against human well-being. While shaman strive for the benefit of the community in the midst of the people, sorcerers work against the community in secret. This contrast turned out to be crucial in understanding Christ's role and had strong implications for leadership roles within the church.

There is one further worldview insight that will help make this case study applicable to the theological discussion that follows. The Samo view humans as being pretty much on their own. In the cosmic struggle, they have to work things out for themselves. It is only when all of their efforts through ritual and ceremony have failed that they call in a shaman and seek spiritual guidance. In other words, seeking direction from the ancestors is a last resort. In the anthropological sense then, each Samo is, in fact, a shaman and as such knows how to ward off evil power through the use of herbal remedies, charms and amulets, and rituals and ceremonies by which they confront spiritual forces both individually and as a group (Shaw, 1981).

Theological Implications of Samo Mediumship

With this background of the Samo "cognitive environment" relating to shamanism and mediumship, we can now pose a theological question: How will the Samo understand I Timothy 2:5 (and other passages) that refer to Christ as the "mediator" between God and human beings? It is a theological question that must be answered on the basis of the Samo worldview but must also be informed by biblical perspective and church tradition. We will explore how the models we have presented may assist us in order to appreciate the development of a local Samo theology.

If the Samo receive Scripture and understand Christ to be like their shaman, then they must determine what makes Jesus different. It appears that Jesus, like all other shaman, had an added spirit, a special "holy spirit" that he utilized to communicate with spiritual beings. He worked on behalf of the people, and like all other human beings, he died. However, the timing of his death is significant for the Samo because it came when he was reaching full productivity—in the prime of life. He died at the point when he could be the most help to the community. While the similarity between Christ and Samo shaman is clear, what is the point of contrast that makes Jesus different from any human medium? The real difference that Scripture repeatedly points out is the resurrection.

That is exactly what Paul was saying to the Colossians, which many say was addressed to Gnostics. The Gnostic worldview was similar to that of the Samo, with their understanding of the spirit world. Colossians is about the superiority of Jesus over the Gnostic emanations, and it is precisely the resurrection that provides the answer. Jesus's entire life cycle capped by the resurrection and his return to the right hand of God, enables him to mediate on behalf of all human beings. His death is not the focus; his resurrection by God's power is the point of Paul's message. For the Samo, it is the resurrection that takes Jesus out of the constant cycle of death and rebirth to energize another infant. Without resurrection he would be like any other ancestral spirit, expected to cycle back. But because of the resurrection he now becomes the "ancestor" who has led the captives free, the one who sits at the right hand of the father to intercede on behalf of human beings, including the Samo. What this means, then, is that Samo Christians no longer need a human shaman. Rather, they can relate directly to God through Christ, the medium between God and all humans (I Tim. 2:5).

The change of identity at death also fits Samo expectations. Because of a change in the person's location (with the ancestors), the terminology used to identify and discuss them changes as well. Death moves people into a different relationship with the living and names and relational interaction all change accordingly. Similarly, Jesus lived among us but now, through the process of death and resurrection, is in a different relationship that can be recognized with the new name *Kurios,* Christ the Lord. Therefore, Jesus is now the died-but-alive medium, which is very different than the normal concept of Samo shaman.

Nor does Christ fit the usual conception of the ancestors who constantly cycle back to life. Yes, Christ will return, but it will not be to live this life over again, starting by energizing a newborn baby and cycling through life. Rather he will create a new life in a new place for all who give allegiance to him.

The power of the Holy Spirit in this process is also important. It is God's spirit who activated Jesus and raised him from the dead. This same Spirit of God quickens human beings, including Samo. This power makes us believers.

John 3:16 tells the Samo they become believers by virtue of accepting Christ's experience on their behalf. So faith and belief must be defined through participation in Jesus's experience by virtue of the power of the Holy Spirit. This is not just personal experience, nor is it merely giving assent to a proposition as in the Enlightenment traditions of the west. The Samo must experience this power—it becomes an encounter that corresponds with what Jesus was telling Nicodemus.

In all of this, cultural symbolism is also important. In John chapter 3, Jesus utilized a symbol that was familiar to the Jews: the snake. But for the Samo, the snake is not perceived the same way, especially since they do not understand sacrifice. For them, the symbol is no longer the snake but rather their concept of mediumship and the involvement with the shaman on behalf of human need. For Jews who understood sacrifice, holding up the serpent made sense, since they remembered Moses lifting the brass serpent in the wilderness (Num. 21: 8, 9). For the Samo, a different symbolism is needed. The root metaphor here is human need. It is crucial for Jews and Samo alike. In order to help the Samo understand Jesus' human experience, we must bring Jesus into the Samo context and focus on their needs: sickness, survival in a hostile world, having enough to eat, and battling with evil forces. These are the very issues Jesus talked so much about and helped people deal with—issues that embody all of life. Jesus healed the sick, cast out demons, fed hungry people, and even raised the dead in order to relieve human suffering and point people to a relationship with God. The symbols come out of life experiences that transcend the Jews and the Samo to impact all human beings. Jesus' encounter with human experience becomes the focus. Can he do what he said he would do? The Scriptures say yes, and much of the narrative unfolds to communicate how Jesus answered those panhuman questions.

What does the Samo experience with Jesus say? Dan Shaw found out one day when joining a group of Samo men walking through the forest for several hours to reach another village. He tells the story this way:

> Before we departed I suggested we pray for God's protection as we walked through the forest. No one argued, I prayed a simple prayer and we began our journey. Soon, most of the men were busy putting leaves into their hair, and stuffing grass into arm and leg bands—all to camouflage themselves from the *hogai*, "evil forest spirits." They called and whistled to each other as they walked, hoping to frighten any unsuspecting spirit away. In the midst of all this, I was in a conversation with Milo.
>
> About an hour into the journey, I suddenly realized that Milo had no camouflage; he was unprotected. When I pointed this out he smiled, looked at me, and said, "You have no camouflage either. Besides, didn't you pray for God's protection? If God is protecting us, why do we need mere camouflage?" I was totally amazed by this demonstration of faith. This man who

had lived in fear of bush spirits all of his life and would do anything to protect himself forfeited the camouflage to see if God would adequately protect him without the traditional covering. When we arrived at the edge of the village clearing that marked our destination, I suggested we stop and thank God for protecting us on our journey. Here we were, having traversed the territory of spiritual enemies, and through God's protection we had arrived unscathed. What a testimony of Samo faith and pragmatism.

Application of Theological Development

What the Samo did in terms of their worldview was to equate Christ with the good side, with the mediums who assist human beings on behalf of the ancestors. On the other side they associated evil with the work of the devil and his hosts in the earthly realm. In other words, the Samo maintain the struggle established at the fall of Adam and Eve between Satan and the promised one. But for them this is not a result of understanding Scripture. Rather it comes out of their pragmatism, out of living and trying to survive in their jungle environment. The Samo use shaman to help them survive. Christ in his heavenly position can do the same thing. Following Chomsky and Schreiter after him, the deep structure is maintained as it relates to survival. In Hiebert's terms, and recognizing Kraft's encounter model, the transempirical connects with the empirical, working themselves out in the "middle zone" where cultural symbols prevail in a "power encounter."

When we apply critical contextualization to this Samo example, it creates a whole new perspective within the cultural context. Christian Samo no longer think of mediumship in the same way as non-Christian Samo. It is a radically transformed mediumship that it is now focused on a relationship with a nonresident shaman who can be brought into any situation at any time. The focus is on the believer's relationship with Christ, calling upon God (the source of all things who goes back to a time before there were ancestors) for assistance in living life. A new understanding of I Timothy 2:5 emerges. It reflects traditional Samo values and concerns without violating the intent of the biblical text. They are not on their own; they can work within Christian traditions that are themselves informed by Scripture. By appropriating these models to understand the Samo perspective, we can see they need to avoid heresy by ensuring that Christ is unique, though he is understood through the concept of mediumship. Because of the resurrection, Jesus is different, more than a supershaman. Had they put him on top of the crowd of shaman, they would have moved toward heresy. If that were the case, all of the other shaman would be able to manipulate God on behalf of human beings, which would compound the problem theologically. But for the Samo, the focus is on their relationship with God through Christ, who can perform his duties because of the incarnation and the resurrection. This Samo application of biblical truth gives new insight into the rest of the body of Christ. God's Word supports the Samo view, but westerners never saw it that way before. The biblical horizon and the Samo horizon interface to create new understanding for all Christians.

Application to the Life of the Church

There are some interesting ramifications of this theologizing process as the Samo apply it to what Christians do in church. Traditionally, the Samo knew the medium spirit was communicating with the ancestors when they heard the glossolalia. Speaking in tongues was the manifestation of the spirit's presence. Sorcerers, in contrast, did not do that. And what was really important about mediumship was the action that took place after the message was communicated. It was interpreted not only through song but also into action necessitated by the revelation. Now look at a Samo church service.

Similar to spiritual activity in the context of communal living in a Samo household, a church service is a microcosm of Samo life; it reflects their social structure.[2] It is not a formal performance by leaders but rather is very participatory. There are no actual Samo pastors. Their leadership style comes out of their social structure with a focus on siblingship. During a worship service people often give their testimony and connect their experience to a Scripture passage, or someone will preach a sermonette based on something they learned as they studied Scripture or from an experience in their life. Someone else will introduce a song, singing it for the congregation and then helping them learn it through repetition.[3] Someone else may have a problem with another person and, following their understanding of Scripture in the context of their traditional culture, bring these differences to the community for resolution. Prayer is a constant part of Samo services that often go on for hours as people move in and out of the experience as their interests and needs dictate. This is an event that involves the whole community (including nonbelievers). It is not a performance of the few. An excerpt from Dan Shaw's journal demonstrates the church's response to speaking in tongues.

> While visiting the Samo I went to church on Sunday morning.[4] In the course of things, Toyo, who was in front at the time, invited the congregation to pray. Everybody began to pray in unison, and as I listened I began to hear some very un-Samo sounds. My first reaction was, "What Pentecostal missionary came through here?" At the end of the service I talked with Toyo [who is also one of my co-initiate brothers].[5]
>
> "Where did this idea of speaking in tongues come from?" I asked.
>
> "Oh," he said, "We've always done this."
>
> "What are you talking about?" I responded. "I lived here for twelve years and, except for the shaman, I never heard glossolalia."

Toyo then explained, "Well, you're right, our shaman used to do it all the time. Now, as we pray, our spirits connect to Christ our mediator, who speaks to us through the power of the Holy Spirit. This is what you heard as we prayed. With this knowledge from God we can act as God wants us to. Knowing what is right, we go out and behave properly."

Here was a direct application of Samo cultural knowledge to their interpretation of Scripture and appropriate living. Their cognitive environment interfaced with biblical truth to create a whole new approach to prayer, both public and private. Dan would not have led the Samo down that path, but their experience and their reading of Scripture did. Fortunately for the Samo, Dan's theological biases did not filter out God's message for them. It did not get in the way of their understanding and application of Scripture. And the follow-through was important. Having communicated with God through Christ, they needed to act on the information for the good of their lives and community.

So in effect, every Samo Christian can be a shaman. Because of Jesus' death and resurrection, all believers have new life that will not end. Because of Christ the Holy Spirit possesses them. Therefore, they now have two spirits (just like a shaman) and can interact directly with Christ, who intercedes for them and guides them into truth that makes sense and upon which they can take appropriate action. The Samo approach to shamanism impacts their approach to God. We find nothing in Scripture that gives a reason to tell the Samo they should do otherwise. In fact, given their worldview, there should be no surprise either from the Samo or the biblical perspective. Here is a wonderful manifestation of the saints communicating with God and yet serving one another as a "priesthood of believers" (I Pet. 2:9).

The Samo figured all of this out themselves, with no missionary around.[6] Now their spirits are in tune with their understanding of mediumship and, in that context, their recognition of Jesus' life, teachings, death, resurrection, and glorification all relate to their experience—both traditionally and in light of their understanding of Scripture. Christ serves as their spiritual medium, communicating with God on their behalf. The Holy Spirit provides the means of making that power available to the Samo in the context of living their lives. It is no wonder that over 60 percent of the Samo have turned their allegiance from human shaman and communication with the ancestors to a focus on Christ and their relationship with God through him as both medium and older brother—the resurrected ancestor.

Of course, the Samo experience with Christ grows as they receive more Scripture. In keeping with models of change, they will continue to adjust their understanding and further develop their theology. Hopefully they will maintain a balance between their worldview and the traditions of the church. The way to protect against this process going awry is to revise their translation of Scripture in keeping with the rapid changes that encroach upon them both from the outside world and biblically as the Holy Spirit changes their minds about those issues that work against God's calling on their lives. Scripture must be seen as relevant, a reflection of the current worldview as well as the process of change. Failure to do so will guarantee a nominal church in two or three generations. The response to that nominality in the Samo context could well be super-mediums who place themselves with Christ, similar to what is happening in some African independent churches.

SCRIPTURE IS THE DIVINE
SOURCE FOR HUMAN INTERACTION

Reflecting back on Schreiter's reading of Chomsky with respect to issues of faith and practice (deep and surface structures), let us suppose Scripture acts much like grammar. In this capacity it does several things. It sometimes critiques, sometimes shapes, and sometimes serves as a vehicle of formation (and change). Scripture impacts all aspects of people trying to understand God. It is not linear in terms of a filtering from bottom to top. Rather, Scripture permeates the whole shape, color, and nuances of a culture's understanding of God. In this respect, then, it is too simplistic to take Kraft's three-encounter model and relate each type of encounter to only one level of worldview (nor would he expect us to do so). The model is useful as a starting point but must be adapted interactively to impact all aspects of human involvement. The human brain integrates all levels of the model and makes it much more complex. There is a case for saying that truth encounter, power encounter, and allegiance encounter each operate at all three levels. There is a sense in which this entire model works like a kaleidoscope. It is nearly impossible to predict where it will emerge or at what level.

In the application of his model, Kraft suggests that there is often a progression from a manifestation of power to a greater understanding of truth, which then precipitates a change of allegiance. How this is manifest in any particular context, however, will vary considerably. For Koreans, relational issues and emotional ties among generations are most deeply transformational. For westerners, in contrast, family relationships are not as important as dealing with values and cultural assumptions. In the Samo case study of mediumship, Christ as a special medium symbolizes allegiance to God in the surface structure. Truth encounter comes as the implications of Christ in this position between heaven and earth reverberate, enabling the Samo to understand deep-level issues of life and death. The Holy Spirit enters into the power encounter realm as the Samo test their new faith by appealing to God's protection rather than the power of magical camouflage.

When translating for the Samo, Dan Shaw needed a term for God. The Samo concept of a "zapper in the sky guy" did not fit well with the biblical intent. Their understanding of an all-pervading spiritual force was not specific enough. When he combined already familiar ideas about relationship and identity, the Samo altered their perception of the words, *oye* and *ayo;* they gained new understanding. The composite term filled out their awareness of One who exists and whose nature is not determined by language. By using this contrived but relevant term for God the Samo were able to apply it to further theological understanding. A relationship-oriented term for Jesus, who was God's son and therefore, by extension, culturally and biblically an older brother, made perfect sense. The Holy Spirit as God's breath became the essence of strength and life for new believers. Using the term *oye ayo* for God had a ripple effect that fit with the Samo "conceptual text." This semantic constellation provided a way for the Samo to understand the Trinity. It also gave them a new understanding of the ancestors who based their mythology on what went before— the Bible told that story; it was God's truth. In the stream of things, Dan and the group of translators also gained totally new insight.

Theologizing in the local context, demands an understanding of both biblical and sociolinguistic contexts in which the message takes shape. This is the stuff of worldview and how it impacts Christian experience within a particular hermeneutical community. This brings us to chapter 9, pursuing relevant communication.

NOTES

1. For the Samo, life is a finite manifestation of an infinite connection with the ancestors. Their cosmology provides an incarnational structure in which ancestors periodically recycle through life to energize a newborn baby, live and die to once again assist those who live upon the earth in their constant struggle with evil (Shaw, 1996: 97). Christ breaks this cycle. For the Samo, he becomes the link between the creation, and eternity with resurrection as the liberating power for eternal life.

2. There is an important connection between social structure and the way human beings worship and/or think about God. Religion is the human effort to understand God; it is in fact a search for salvation. In contrast, Christianity affirms that God seeks to relate with and responds to human beings. God desires to establish a relationship with them and that relationship takes shape within people's cultural experience. That is why incarnation is so important. The Christian faith is not about religion but about relationship. We say this because the Christian message addresses each society and enables people uniquely to process divine information, God's Word, through a people's unique worldview perspective.

3. In this way the Samo have written over three hundred songs. Many, as in their traditional life, reflect personal experience and tell the story of what happened to them and how God helped them out. Today guitars, imported from beyond their forest, are often used to accompany these songs.

4. Church can be any time for the Samo, but the influence of outside pastors and missionaries still prevails with the traditional 11:00 A.M. Sunday service. The Samo have no problem with this as it provides a respite in the cycle of daily affairs required to procure food and maintain their livelihood.

5. In 1973 the Samo decided to include coauthor Shaw in an initiation ceremony in order to fully incorporate him into the kinship structure of the society. Nearly all of the men, and several of the women with whom he was initiated, eventually assumed leadership roles in the Samo church.

6. In 1981 the Shaws left their home among the Samo and took up residence in Pasadena where Dr. Shaw joined the SWM faculty. Following their departure and using Scripture as their source of understanding, the Samo began to apply "God's talk" to their lives in new and exciting ways. The result was a people movement (Tippett, 1971: 198ff) that spread throughout the area. Periodic visits over the years have enabled Dan to document the impact of this cultural transformation, not influence it (Shaw, 1996: cf. chapter 7 entitled, "From Shaman to Pastor").

· 9 ·

Pursuing Relevant Communication

God's message is understood in the midst of the deep-level meanings that receptors bring to the text. This process is at once spiritual, technical and relational.

*Life is a constant juxtaposition of responsibilities, opportunities, and relationships
that impact daily decision making and quality of life. Adding the complexities of cross-
cultural living with the potential for clashing values and interests makes for a very exciting life, so long as one is not inclined to be concerned about what may appear to be
interruptions. The difference between communicating and being a communicator (doing versus being) is often a fine line, as coauthor Dan Shaw discovered one afternoon.*

I was sitting in my study when there was a commotion and Milo ran in obviously
distraught. "They have come to take Woiduwo because Seloli has run away again.
You must do something!" Milo and Woiduwo had been happily married for about
two years, but such was not the case for Milo's sister who had been exchanged to
Sodiyobi village to be married to a man named Daba.[1] Theirs had been a rocky relationship punctuated by open fighting and obvious ill will. Now Daba's brothers had
come to take Woiduwo back so they could exchange her again and find a better wife
for Daba. Milo informed me that as his older brother, it was my responsibility to tell
Seloli to return to Daba so he and Woiduwo could continue their happy marriage.
What a responsibility! A marriage counselor I was not. I prayed a quick prayer as
the unhappy couple were escorted into the office where I was working on a first draft
of the book of Titus.

   Building on my understanding of Samo relationships and drawing from the translation of Titus chapter 2 in front of me, I began to probe how this couple had failed
to measure up to cultural expectations as well as God's. So I read verse five and
asked Seloli if she was a good wife who submitted to her husband "so that no one
could speak evil of the message that comes from God." She quietly mumbled a negative response. I turned to Daba and read verse six. Did he live a self-controlled
lifestyle? This young man had a violent temper and the verse grabbed his attention.

I then encouraged both of them to act in a manner that would not allow others to criticize their behavior, prayed with them, and extracted a promise to return to their village and work on their relationship. They did, and Milo thanked me profusely. For my part, I was pleased that Daba and Seloli had responded to God's prompting. God's Word had impacted their lives as well as all the inhabitants of Kwobi and Sodiyobi villages who considered themselves allies because of the respective marriages. God had been honored.

Presenters of the Gospel who effectively communicate God's Word in today's world are very much part of the interface of the horizons. They are involved in the flowing development of truth through time and space. In fact, communicators are key players in this movement. We all become "translators" as we communicate. If we are to be faithful, we must understand several things. We must understand the original intent of any biblical passage, be it a verse, a book, or the whole of the canon. What was the passage saying to people in its original time and place? What was the message? We must then understand the shape the passage has taken throughout revelational history and the history of the People of God. We must understand what shape it takes related to our own spirituality. And then, as agents of transformation, we must understand how it will shape a new appreciation for God as the message is introduced into new, contemporary contexts. In so doing, we have the pleasure of watching people in today's world infer God's message to humanity. As we have noted throughout this book, this gives old theology new insight. Theology, like culture, is always changing to keep pace with the changes in the church, which in turn speaks to the surrounding community. Though the Scripture on which theology builds does not change, over time we may become aware of semantic constellations of meaning that are quite unexpected, surprises that God can use to convey new truth.

A TRI-DIMENSIONAL
APPROACH TO COMMUNICATION

In her dissertation on communicative translation in India, Christeena Alaichamy developed a model that reflects the key elements of communication. These elements correspond very closely with the chapters in this part of our book. She calls these elements "spiritual," "technical," and "relational." She maintains that every translation must include these three elements for effective communication to take place (1997: 141ff). This insight (see figure 9.1) represents the process of making Scripture available to people. However, it also relates well to four horizons and the hermeneutical issues we have raised. Each element contains an entire set of assumptions unique to itself that at the same time interacts with each other to form a whole. In each phase there is connection between communicators and receptors. We presented the "technical" aspect in chapter 5 as part of appropriate communication theory (cf. figure 5.1). In figure 9.1 we put it to work in pursuing relevant communication.

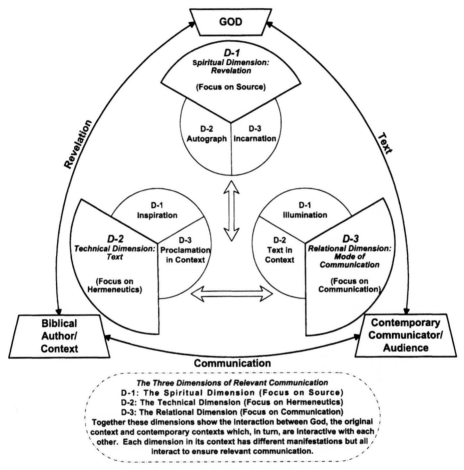

Figure 9.1.   A Tri-Dimensional Approach to Communication

The process begins with God's spiritual intent to communicate with human beings. Following the principle of incarnation, God came into the human context and interacted with people using language and expressing issues of importance within their experience. In the discussion of the horizons, this communication between God and human beings is reflected in the revelatory acts encased horizons I and II. This implies direct (or divine) revelation and establishes the authority of the Communicator (God) who comes with intentionality. In this dimension, God was the original communicator, ensuring that God's intended message was clear to a particular audience. However, God rarely communicated directly with people. The process usually included a human author who received the word and passed it on, which leads to the technical dimension.

As biblical authors received an inspired message, they sought to present it in a medium that their immediate receptors (God's target audience) could understand. As communicators, these biblical authors re-created what God had said into the language and culture of their respective audiences (this is still relative to horizons I and II). Each progressive audience through time received new ideas commensurate with what they already knew about God and their own circumstances. Theologically this is called "progressive revelation," and it is important to understand that where people already knew God, he expected them to apply that understanding to the interpretation of the message. This technical dimension is designed to ensure effective communication. Here author-communicators passed on God's message as they understood it. Theologically this has been called the "autograph" and forms a text that can be analyzed. While the focus at this level traditionally has been on exegesis, there is also a strong hermeneutical element for that particular context, language, and situation. God specifically spoke to Moses and he took the message to Pharaoh, to Aaron, and to the people of Israel as God intended. The particularity of the context, in some measure, dictated the means of communication. Much more than words were used—the signs and wonders associated with the Exodus impacted the communication and its interpretation. These extratextual activities, in turn, served to reinforce the words. God and Moses worked together as a team to ensure that their receptors understood the message God communicated.

How is all of this transferred to people who were not part of the context of the autograph? That is the province of the relational element of Alaichamy's approach. Communicators (horizon III) must be in close relationship with the people to whom they seek to present the Gospel (in horizon IV). Understanding the particular context enables them to utilize comparable themes (root metaphors) from Scripture in order to allow Jesus to incarnate in the new context. People need to see that the word has come to dwell among them. Often the presenter embodies that word in a way that enables others to see Jesus. The experiences of the various parties in this relationship communicates important information about God's intent to interact with humanity. The message is no longer direct revelation or inspiration, but rather illumination as proclaimers and receptors interact to ensure that the message is properly understood.

Throughout this approach, each element has a spiritual, technical, and relational aspect, and each is part of the whole process at each step: God entering the human context, biblical authors re-creating what they understood God to say, and communicators presenting the vital message. Through all of this, the focus is on God interacting with those whom God has created. God knows what God wants to say to human beings and appropriates incarnation to do that. Biblical authors and communicators must discern through the power of the Holy Spirit what God intends to communicate and ensure that is what people receive. This is more an emphasis on ensuring the spirit of the communication (on proclaiming the intent) rather than on the words themselves. The text, then, becomes the medium (however it is presented) through which people are able to know God. Proclamation must always be in community. It must also focus on relationship with God, not on the Hebrew or Greek words and how they can be transferred into another context. In concert, the spiritual, technical, and relational elements of the communication task work together to create the environment in which God can be known. In what follows we draw on Alaichamy's approach by examining these three major aspects of communication: the spiritual, technical, and relational.

Spiritual Aspects of Communication

Lamin Sanneh reinforced Alaichamy's viewpoint when speaking of Samuel Ajayi Crowther, the first African Bishop of the Anglican Church in Nigeria. The beloved Bishop was a man well ahead of his time in the mid-nineteenth century. He recognized that mission and communication through translation formed an alliance between cultural symbols and living faith.

> Crowther recognized that translation was more than a mechanical exercise, and that something of the genius of the people was involved. Language was not merely a tool fashioned to achieve limited and temporary goals. It was a dynamic cultural resource reflecting the spirit of the people and illuminating their sense of values.... The translator should be prepared to dig underneath the layers of half-conscious notions and dim familiarities to reclaim the accumulated treasure.... Christian material did not, therefore, so much infringe the earlier sense of [traditional] religious propriety as deepen it. New converts would now possess a richer repertoire of religious feeling. (Sanneh, 1989: 165, 171)

Today, we must take Crowther's understanding to the next level and ensure that God's Word deepens people's spiritual understanding of who God is. This is an important point for us. Sanneh continues:

> When . . . [an] indigenous equivalent is adopted as the God of the scriptures, then those worshipping in God's name have necessarily brought within range all the familiar associations of the term.... This does not deny the possibility of change. On the contrary, it helps to legitimize change and resolve . . . potential difficulties. (1989: 177)

Nida and Taber anticipated this hermeneutical explosiveness with their concept of dynamic equivalence as applied to Bible translation (Nida and Taber, 1981). Later Charles Kraft expanded the concept to the whole of the missionary enterprise (Kraft, 1979). Gilliland further notes:

> The central truths are absolute, while communication and application fit local needs and questions. This does not mean that we make Jesus over to fit every situation or need as it arises. It does mean, however, that while firmly anchored to the Christ of apostolic witness, there must be an immediacy about the Gospel. (Gilliland, 1989c: 53)

How, then, in the new receptor culture can we say, "I will be your God, you will be my people and I will dwell in your midst?" How do people say that? How can it be understood? Clearly the answer is not simply to provide a literal "translation" of these words or phrases. No! Rather, we seek to create an understanding in the new context of the essence of relationship. Don Richardson's "peace child" concept derives from this kind of hermeneutic. God was not so interested in the words Richardson used. Rather, God was interested in the relationship the Richardson's had with the Sawi people and the understanding of God they derived because of the Sawi impact on them.

As an illustration of the communicability principle, we quote again from Gilliland who recounts a clear rationale for the apostle Paul's use of the image of "reconciliation" when speaking to a primarily Greek audience.

> Paul constantly searched for language that best suited the questions raised in each place. He found expressions that conveyed truth with the highest degree of local impact. He had no quarrel with Jewish terms when he was addressing issues that related to Jews. . . . But his loyalty to traditional expression was never the final guide. . . . Ralph Martin has made a strong case for *katallasso* (reconcile) and *katallage* (reconciliation) as . . . a word that fits the gentile world. The Greek worldview called for a resolution of tensions between people and their gods. But the term would have related poorly to the Jews. The more acceptable way to speak of the mediating work of Christ for the Jews would be the use of *hilaskesthai* (propitiate, make expiation for). . . . The surprising thing about *katallasso* is that it was always used in secular ways, never in a theological way. For example in diplomatic exchanges it translates as "exchange of hostility for friendship." Paul seizes on this "worldly" term and makes it into a beautiful picture of the way Jews and Gentiles come to God. (Gilliland, 1989: 55–56)

Sanneh takes us deeper into this process as he warns:

> Attention is drawn to the deceptive power of seeking to translate in a straightforward manner, and then finding that more (or less) is being said by the translator than was intended . . . (bringing) the translator into the quicksand of indigenous cultural nuances. (Sanneh, 1989: 195)

So this hermeneutical flow is the theological rationale for rejecting what may be the worst possible question: How do I translate the text? The real question should be: What did God intend when God communicated the text? In other words, how would God have said it using the language of the people in the particular context in which we now seek to present the same ideas? Put another way, given the flow of meaningful development from the point of original communication, what is now the best possible way to present the same concepts God used to build relationships with human beings in the first place?

God's Word, then, provides the narrative of countless human experiences as God interacted with human beings. Perhaps this is why narrative (telling the story) and the theology that emerges from it has become so important today. Wherever we pick up the story, the message is basically the same. Kraft likens the Bible to a book of fascinating "case studies," all of which are about God in relationship with human beings whom God desires to draw close to himself (1979: 198ff). This is the same story reiterated throughout the mythology and oral history of people everywhere.

The Kilibob stories along the north coast of the island of New Guinea resonate with these panhuman themes: a world being created perfect, defiled by human desire, resulting in one of two brothers departing with the promise to return with a solution while the other does his best to survive. The so-called cargo cults in this same region of New Guinea have often been placed in the context of the long-lost brother returning with the promised redemption. John Strelan has documented these religious manifestations and characterized them as the insatiable human "search for salvation" (Stralen, 1977). The "cargo" aspect that accompanies the story is a reflection of perceived need for restoration of a quality of life that was lost. The stories are rich with human recognition of restored relationships and the inability of mere humans to do it by themselves. There is a source of atonement beyond human circumstance that, when realized, results in utopia.

The same story is retold in countless ways across the ages and in all parts of the world. It is the story of the human search for truth that Satan has hidden or at best twisted ever so slightly. The result is human sin, missing the mark set by God who alone can correct the problem that began with Adam and Eve. Scripture contains a resolution to the human story, and we must tell it wherever we go, in whatever way will communicate so people can see themselves and recognize Jesus when they experience his messengers.

Technical Aspects of Communication

The second aspect of communication in Alaichamy's approach challenges us to know what it is we are communicating. This goes back to the discussion of truth, and the nature of the text in chapter 1. Irrespective of prevailing questions regarding the source-text, we are nevertheless convinced that Gospel communicators must be committed to understanding the author's intent as far as that is possible. In the final analysis we say: This is what we have, this is what we seek to communicate. This takes exegesis into account and treats authorial intent seriously. What did the author intend to communicate through the source-text? What were the words and phrases that were actually used? However, this analysis also involves the hermeneutical spiral. Into what other contexts has this text permeated and how was it perceived there? Such questions are important as we seek to communicate God's intended meaning in a new context while anticipating how the message may be formulated to create relevance in accordance with the contextual grid of yet another set of circumstances.

To do this, however, we also need a broad view of Scripture as a whole and its impact upon the world at large. We have to appreciate how the whole Bible and the whole of historical theology have influenced the text we are working on. This is where the concept of Scripture as a tapestry (presented in chapter 3) serves us well. Seeing Scripture as a tapestry of God's action takes seriously both the multiplicity of historical contexts (the cultures in which biblical revelation occurred) and the horizontal continuity of God's self-disclosure in history (cf. figure 3.1). We must also take seriously the narrative structure of a large part of the Bible, a fact that has been recognized throughout the church's history and manifests itself today in a growing interest in narrative theology. This approach recognizes that the biblical narratives contain both history and theology and are brought together via a story format. These themes in the narrative then interact with the themes of local communities to create new truth that enlightens other communities as they too seek to know God. Narrative theology is an attempt to build bridges both between the various horizons in Scripture and from Scripture to our day (Van Engen, 1996b: 45).

To some extent, this reflection on the text is a continuity issue. Effective communication requires that we remain faithful to that which has gone before, and yet it is incredibly diversified in its manifestations in order to ensure a dynamic reshaping in new contexts. In the new structure, it may appear so different that some people say it doesn't look anything like Scripture, or what went before in other contexts (recall the application of Samo shamanism to an understanding of Christ mediating for the Samo in chapter 8). However, as we have shown through the application of the four-horizon model, reshaping the message to be relevant in the context is exactly what God does. The Pharisees had the Torah and the Prophets. To this they added the Targums to help interpret Scripture. And they were convinced they had it all figured out. Then God introduced their Messiah as a babe in a manger. No one was looking for the Messiah there—but the shepherds found him, the angels announced his arrival, the wise men worshipped him, and Mary and Joseph cared for him.

In Acts chapter 15 a new insight developed out of another surprise. Based on the coming of the Holy Spirit to Cornelius and his household in Acts chapter 10, it became evident that God loved the Gentiles as well. This caused the apostles to begin to see the Gentiles and their own Jewish heritage in a new light. Moving through the history of the church, Martin Luther further illustrates the same process. Luther was a monk who hated God because he could not possibly love a God who was only a judge. Then one day he read Romans 1:17, "the just shall live by faith." It leapt off the page for Luther and came to mean something new to him. He discovered a reinterpretation of almost everything he knew up to that point. For Martin Luther the issue was not only law and grace but also German nationalism and the German language. There is a theological reason why Luther translated Scripture. He saw this phrase and recognized what Paul was doing in relation to God's grace in both Old and New Testaments. He immediately began to translate the Scriptures into the vernacular so other Germans could receive the same insight he had just come to understand. As the people of Germany began to understand more fully the grace of God received by faith, the Protestant Reformation took form, a veritable revolution in the Christian church.

As presenters of the Gospel, we must always look first to what the text says, and ultimately to what God intended in the text. The church has always had a tendency to add something to the text: the text and tradition; the text and words of knowledge; the text and experience; the text and creed. In Roman Catholic tradition it was Scripture and tradition. In the Enlightenment, especially in the nineteenth century and before Karl Barth, it was Scripture and reason à la Emanuel Kant. In our generation it may be Scripture and experience. But every time we add to the text, the text is undermined. The text itself no longer speaks because it is clouded by the additions. And so there have been well-intentioned Christians who have used the text of Scripture to defend the Crusades, to defend the Salem witch hunts, to defend Hitler, to defend racism, to defend Apartheid, and the list goes on. It is amazing how over the years people have found ways of using cultural issues to defend unbiblical ideas as "Christian." And yet, despite the incidents, we continue to want to use God to defend our own agendas rather than allow God to critique us.

Throughout the history of the Christian church, whenever something is added to the text, problems of comprehensibility quickly develop and the translation is no longer faithful to God's intended communication. That is another reason why "how do I translate the text?" is a bad question. Inevitably communicators end up superimposing their own understanding, theology, and creeds on the text rather than allowing a dynamic hermeneutic to shine through the canonical semantic flow of the text to impact a new people with new insight so they, in turn, develop new theology. The point for our focus here is that the Bible must become real; it must be relevant to the culture. When it is, it will be relational and critical (in terms of God's critique of culture), affirming and transforming both communicators and receptors.

Relational Aspects of Communication

The third aspect of Alaichamy's approach to relevant communication has to do with how proclaimers participate in the process of Gospel presentation. How they view themselves is important, not only in terms of self-image, but also as communicators of truth from one context to another, to paraphrase deWaard and Nida (1986). Typically, communicators have been viewed as the bridge between the source-text and the receptors. As human beings, they bring their own ideas that impact everything they do, including textual analysis. But communicators should, to the extent they are able, make a conscious effort to avoid being the filter through which a message is transferred. As communicators interact within a particular context, they must take into account the entire communication context that includes all four horizons we examined in chapter 4. An appreciation of the commonality of the human condition can greatly reduce the complexity of handling diverse horizons. Through it all God is desirous of a relationship with God's creation. As God's creatures, we all have much in common physiologically, emotionally, and relationally. How these aspects of our being are manifested in a particular sociocultural milieu is what makes the Gospel communicator's task exciting and full of surprises.

So, for example, Shaw was in for a big surprise when he got to Genesis 9 in the translation of Samo Scriptures. This is the passage in which God tells Noah that human life is special and no animal or other human being should take a human life. If this happens the murderer should be put to death. Dan recorded the Samo response in his journal.

> On hearing Genesis 9 Hogwanobiayo blurted out, "You mean to say that God doesn't want us going on cannibal raids?" Not being a cannibal, I had never considered this passage from that perspective. However, since God told Noah that . . . [human beings were special], the application of the passage to cannibalism was, indeed, relevant. My older brother went on to indicate how they had not understood the government's concern with cannibalism, and why national pastors had told them that raiding was bad. He told me I was the first to make sense concerning this issue. I quickly responded that it was not my words that made sense, but God's—the power of the Holy Spirit communicating to the Samo that their culture was contrary to God's desire for them. God cares about human life and they can appropriate that concern to their daily living. What a powerful message this was for the Samo. (Shaw, 1988: 67)

To appropriately communicate the Gospel we must know the entire spectrum of interaction involved in our task: knowledge of the text, understanding and intentionality about ourselves, and an appreciation of the perspectives, interests, attitudes, awareness, and conceptual grid of our receptors. Only in this way can we anticipate difficulties in the process and attempt to deal with them so the message comes through. Despite Dan's theological understanding of Genesis 9 on the one hand or the Samo view of cannibalism in the context of their culture on the other, he needed to ask: What is God's message? To the Hebrews God said, "What I have created should be treated with respect." Over time this took many forms including the creation of cities of refuge for those who had committed a crime. For the Samo, deep in their rain forest with an elaborate alliance system designed to protect them against enemy raids, it meant recognizing God as the one in authority over themselves as well as over their enemies. This provided a rationale for the cessation of raiding and the cannibalism that inevitably accompanied raids. God's message to the Samo was that God was in control, not the Samo. He would be their protector. God would be their alliance partner.

By adding the relational element to her approach to communication, Alaichamy ensures that interaction with the community is itself communicating the message. This extends the incarnation principle to the relationships people have with each other. This element is what Tom and Betty Sue Brewster called bonding (Brewster and Brewster, 1982). The Gospel communicator's goal is not only to understand and be able to minister within a receptor language and culture, but to manifest Jesus in their midst. If we begin to see the interaction of the text with the context and recognize the power of the Holy Spirit to energize the entire process, then communicators of the Gospel can move beyond their own agenda and see more clearly what God desires for people everywhere as well as for a particular people. This then allows people to place themselves in the narrative of Scripture in order to extend its meaning to themselves.

CONNECTING WITH THE FOURTH HORIZON

In this chapter we have looked at the cultural nature of contexts around the world where Christians seek to present the Gospel. By using Alaichamy's tridimensional approach to effective communication, we have presented the spiritual, technical, and relational elements of relevant Gospel proclamation. Effective communication relates both to the context within which communication takes place and the perspectives of the Gospel communicator. The interface of these parameters creates a greater awareness of the issues central to communicating and calls for communicators to be more intentional about the strategies they use to present their understanding of God's intended message. Communicators will want to apply the standards of communication and the regulative principles discussed in chapter 5 so that the message may be perceived as relevant. In code model terms, we want to eliminate as much "noise" as possible, obstructions that would detract from hearing the message appropriately. We seek to generate a positive response. In the process, however, we must constantly stay in tune with the vertical dimension of God's intention as communicated to humankind through the biblical text. All of this requires that we approach the communication task with a view of the total context represented by the four horizons: God, the original receptors who wrote it down and produced a text, the communicators who now pass on the message, and those who hear today whose circumstances are often very different from those who heard the original message. At issue is bringing God's Word and contemporary peoples together while minimizing the bias of mediating communicators. The role is not to interpret for a particular people, but rather to provide the text for people in a new context to deal with in terms of their language and culture. Thus the new audience connects with a long line of historical and spiritual influence that incorporates both biblical and church traditions.

SUMMARY

We began our discussion in part III by considering Gilliland's view of the interaction of truth as revealed in Scripture with the truth within a culture to establish new, Christian truth for each context. Each element of truth impacts the next, thereby giving integrity to the whole and helping believers understand the Gospel message in their circumstances. Thus a new theology arises from the receptors' traditions as they are impacted by a sense of relevance of God's word to them. But theology is based on Scripture, the text of what God said. God's Word is powerful. Ultimately, fidelity in Gospel communication must involve consistency with God's intended meaning as expressed in the text of Scripture.

This is Sanneh's point about the communicability of Scripture. Translation and its accompanying communication make what God intended available to everyone in the particularity of their contexts. This communication must then apply to people's felt needs, in the midst of which they work out their own salvation. This is the essence of the theologizing process. People usually begin from their point of need and that, in turn, becomes their location for theologizing. As receptors understand God through their worldview with respect to their basic cultural values and biases, their theology is going to be meaningful to them because it connects God's Word as text to their context. As Scripture is proclaimed, people receive it and do exactly what the original receptors did: apply it to their experience, to what they already understand. Therefore, we need to communicate what God intended people to understand about God in such a way that makes sense to an audience in its situation.

If Scripture is the final rule of faith and practice, Scripture itself is the final critique of Gospel communication. We have to convert the receptor's worldview into that which touches the biblical world so that we can start interfacing these cultural realms, personally and experientially as well as philosophically. The translator does not create a name for God, but rather finds the remnant that is still there: eternity in their hearts (Eccles. 3:11).

As communicators we need to see ourselves not as the experts, nor as technicians, nor as religiously or theologically astute scholars. Rather, we need to cultivate the ability to interact as fellow travelers in this global context and allow the message to come out of that interaction. Our focus, then, becomes relational and enabling. Such was Dan's experience with Milo's rather recalcitrant sister and her strong-willed husband. His journal fills in the details:

> Daba and Seloli were not measuring up to their own cultural standards, let alone God's expectations. When asked to mediate in a difficult situation, I felt constrained by cultural standards which were not my own. Yet as a Christian and a Bible translator, I also felt constrained by values and principles God applied to all people. In that situation, I was able, by the grace of God, to bring his panhuman expectations to bear upon Samo particularity and watch the Holy Spirit work. As it turned out, I had used Scripture in the same way the Samo traditionally used their mythology, as a repository for explaining truth. Scripture, like their myths, could be relied upon to solve life's problems.

As it turned out, this was a valuable and relational experience for the Samo church as it learned to apply God's message to the reality of the way the Samo live. It also changed Dan's perspective of doing versus being. The way the Samo "do" church is reflective of their cultural interests and their discovery that God cares about those issues as much as they do. Thereon hangs the point of this final section of the book. In order to avoid people misunderstanding what God has communicated through God's Word, audiences must receive it in a manner that communicates fully in their context. For that to happen, all four horizons must interact and inform each other so that people can reinterpret it, "represent" it in ways that make a difference in their lives. When understood, God's message has spiritual, technical, and relational implications that bring together God's vertical interaction with the horizontal dimension of life as God would want people to live it.

For our purposes we have appropriated theological and social science models in order to develop our theses and arguments. We have sought to relate God's truth in theologically, communicationally, and culturally relevant ways. The models we have used throughout this book break down at some point—analogies always do. But their value is in providing a general overview of ways to synthesize and apply God's intentions to all human contexts. Once a communicator interacts in a particular place, the application of the models quickly gives way to specifics that are unique to that community. This affects interpreting the biblical text that, in turn, adjusts our understanding of the issues in focus as we attempt to understand what God is doing through all of the horizons. Thus, in our theoretical development we also see the hermeneutical spiraling process impacting how we go about researching in order to enable relevant communication of the Gospel. Bringing the biblical horizons to bear upon the present-day horizons results in theologizing that, in turn, sheds new light on the way Christians have traditionally understood the Gospel. Theologizing in the midst of a people is an ongoing process. In this way God's truth will be upheld and hocus pocus will be avoided.

NOTE

1. Samo marriage emphasizes the need for alliances between communities, not love and belonging. Men determine the best alliance for their community's needs and which of their sisters will best suit the desired arrangement. Woiduwa and Milo had developed a very close relationship that was somewhat unusual in Samo culture. Seloli and Daba had not been so fortunate.

Conclusion

Communicating God's
Word in a Complex World

As people around the world hear God's Word proclaimed and accept it as their own they develop a new awareness of the dynamic interaction between the God who speaks, the text that records God's message, the communicator who brings the word, and the audience that attaches new understanding to the communication. As people begin to know God in their context, they themselves become communicators of the Gospel—continuing the missional intent of Scripture.

Twenty-four hours with a humble Mexican peasant who understood the power of God in the midst of his people demonstrated the importance of the receptor's place in effective communication. This is how coauthor Charles Van Engen tells the story.

Pedro was one of my students in the extension seminary in Tapachula, Chiapas, Mexico. Pedro was a new Christian when he began taking courses. Because of poor health he was constantly on medication that made him drowsy. So he slept through most of my classes. He did his work at home, but slept through classes and, in fact, the seminary director and I were thinking of asking him to stop coming.

One morning I was up early to face a full day of tasks for the Kingdom. A knock drew me to the front door only to see Pedro.

"Pedro!" I exclaimed, "What a surprise to see you! Classes don't start again for another month!" (I thought he had slept through the previously announced dates for the next set of classes.)

"Hermano Carlos, I'm not here for class. I came to get you. Over a year ago, you agreed to go with me and speak to the people of my town about the Gospel. I have come to take you there, today!"

Well, I had my long list of important things to do that day—and Pedro wasn't on it. Somehow, though, the Holy Spirit enabled me to recognize that I needed to follow Jesus' mission—not my long list of tasks. Mission, after all is of the way. It belongs to Jesus our Lord. It is Jesus' mission.

"OK," I mumbled, "But the old Jeep isn't running, I'll have to fix it first." As I worked on the old Jeep, Pedro sat on my front porch, fast asleep. By ten that morning the Jeep was ready, and we set out.

Here began my odyssey in theology of communication, a journey of mission in the way. We had to drive that old tin box of a Jeep down a blacktop road in 110-degree heat for two hours. Then we began a four-hour climb up a mountainous, two-track road, over huge boulders—like going up stairs. And Pedro? He was sound asleep beside me!

When we finally arrived, Pedro awoke, looked around at the empty settlement and said, "Oh, hermano Carlos, you rest now. Everyone is out in the coffee trees right now. I'll call you later." And Pedro disappeared. It was now my turn to take a nap after glancing at my wet and soggy list of jobs for the day that was still in my shirt pocket.

About seven that evening Pedro called me to eat in the traditional Mexican kitchen around the comal, over an open fire, and enjoy the black beans, chicken, tortillas, and thick coffee. Delicious! Upon completing the meal Pedro said, "It's time now, come with me."

We went to the largest house in town. We entered the living room where all the furniture had been removed. There standing wall-to-wall, were about two hundred people. They had all become Christians in the last two years through the witness of Pedro Odilón. "They want to know about the Bible, and more about Jesus Christ," Pedro said. For the next several hours, I had the privilege of teaching the Bible to these new believers. This was mission on the way.

By the time I finished answering questions, it was after midnight. Everyone went home and Pedro and I gingerly made our way back down the mountain road, out onto the highway and arrived home early the next morning. My wife, Jean, greeted us and asked, "How was it?" I could only shake my head and exclaim, "Unbelievable!" In those twenty-four hours, because of Pedro Odilón, I had experienced what communicating the Gospel is all about. It is mission of, in, and on the way.

The impact on me of that day was much greater than it was on Pedro and his little mountain church. Over the next several years Pedro went on to plant four more churches up in those mountains. But I learned a lesson that has stayed with me and which forms the foundation of this book. And the lesson is this. The knowledge we learn and pass on in seminaries and formal research and analysis must have an impact on those with whom we interact or it is useless. Studying about Jesus is not the same as personally encountering Jesus. [1]

FAITH IN COMMUNITY

What, then, happens to God's Word in the hands of receptors? How will they use it? What will they do with this sacred trust? If people consider what God has communicated and use that to reflect on their circumstances, they gain an appreciation for what God is saying to them. At a recent conference on hermeneutics, Mark Kinser made the point that "the Bible emerges as a communal composition drawing upon a communal tradition" (Kinser, 2001: 1).[2] Thus Scripture flows not only from God's mouth expressed through inspired writers, but also through a "community that transmits an inspired tradition. . . . [B]iblical authors draw upon communal, oral tradition and existing written sources" (Kinzer, 2001: 2). He concludes, "hermeneutics must take account of the inescapable bond between Scripture and community" (2001: 21). This is also Thomas Cahill's thesis in his best-selling book on "how a tribe of desert nomads changed the way everyone thinks and feels" (Cahill, 1998). The same is true as God's Word impacts people in our day. Pedro Odilón certainly understood that. He took what God said seriously and exposed Mayan peasants to the reality of God in their midst.

Scripture brings people together as a faith community in the context of their culture as well as in the broader interaction with Christians everywhere. Within the society, non-Christians will not consider them crazy, but rather wonder how they can seemingly live up to cultural expectations and respond as they do—as Jesus would, were he there. In the broader Christian community, they can interact with others based on principles of understanding God's Word and sharing their faith experience. By so doing they both share their experience with others and learn from others—they contribute to the global hermeneutical spiral.

As Robert Schrieter (1986) pointed out, a new community of faith is not isolated and on its own, especially in our increasingly networked world. Groups of isolated people like Pedro's collection of churches or the Samo surviving in the rain forest are increasingly rare and will no longer be the primary focus of missiological development and understanding. Increasingly, urban communities with their complexity and pluralism must be considered the primary context for mission. In tandem with knowledgeable outsiders who understand the four horizons, local leaders can work through many issues together and, in so doing, learn from one another. However, theology is never developed in a vacuum. Nor is it ever permanent. In fact, theology is always temporary, relevant to one generation who passes on what they know to the next who, in their changing world, develop new theologies to maintain relevancy to the issues they must handle. This could be viewed as an adaptation of the hermeneutical spiral within a community of believers. This process takes a community toward the high calling Jesus gives them. Together communicators and believing community members strive to understand and localize the Gospel. This involves the believers themselves, wherever they are or whatever may be their cultural context, coming to know God in the midst of their circumstances.

If God's Word benefited the original receptors, it can certainly benefit people in our contemporary world, as well. Theology is simply the articulation of all of the horizons working together to enable people to enter into relationship with God. Remember, the source is not the text. The source is God and relationship with God is the objective of creation. The goal of the canon is the re-creation of a new heaven and a new earth in a new Jerusalem where we will enjoy God forever (Rev. 21: 3, 4). The community of believers, then, can be used by God to reveal God's intended meaning to the rest of Christianity as well as to the world at large.

CONTEXT AND THEOLOGY
ENSURE COMMUNICABILITY

The four-horizon hermeneutic we have espoused integrates the total communication context. Rather than being boxed in within one particular philosophical or theological perspective or one particular tradition, the model frees all of the participants in the communication process to interact, thereby emphasizing responsible, critiqued, ongoing theological development. Bringing the biblical horizons into the here-and-now results in theologizing that in turn sheds new light on the old stories. Theologizing in the midst of a people is an ongoing process. It is a way of ensuring that God's truth will be upheld.

This approach moves beyond contextualization. While contextualization has become a catchword for "localization" or "inculturation," our four-horizons approach strives to take the whole of human experience into account in order to develop insight for future generations of believers. The process is based on following the example of New Testament authors as they applied Old Testament concerns to their circumstances. Contextualization emphasizes the dynamic relationship, in a particular time and place, between what we have called horizon III and horizon IV. We have sought to add to the equation the truths communicated in the biblical horizons in order to have greater insight into how receptors everywhere may know God in their contexts. Our objective has been to seek ways whereby God's intentions regarding all people are clearly and sensibly processed to enable people to grasp God's message for them and apply it to their circumstances with as little outside influence as possible. In this way, while the manifestations of God's presence and concern may vary greatly today (even as they did throughout the development of the canon), an understanding of a people's need for relationship with God is appreciated and developed in ways that ensure people can, in fact, know God. Contextualization emphasizes the action of the communicator. We have sought to emphasize the value of understanding God's intended meaning on the part of audiences everywhere. Unless adapted to local understanding via an application of linguistic and cultural standards of communicability, the message will be considered irrelevant and people will not make the effort to understand it on their own.

Communicators must follow through on the process and ensure that a message is perceived as relevant and encourages people to match their understanding with the author's (and ultimately God's) expectations. Without this influential understanding we force contemporary receptors to apply their issues (concerns from their context) upon the text, rather than the communication having its intended impact. If a message has been presented without regard for context and authorial intent, the result will most assuredly be syncretism and heresy. To avoid this, communicators must, to the extent possible, deconstruct the author's intent and represent the message to ensure relevance for a new audience. An appreciation for authorial assumptions, discourse type, and the language and culture of the original communication will assist communicators in making decisions central to a new presentation that matters to a new audience. Without this background receptors will assume their own conceptual text is correct and, therefore, may not "hear" what the text said. Communicators, then, must use every device possible to ensure that the intended message is, in fact, understood. In a word, make sure it is *relevant*. Only then will God's Word penetrate new worlds and transform lives. And each response will be different, impacted by assumptions, context-specific expectations, and individual experience—in short, response is the result of a collective, as well as individual, cognitive environment.

It is essential, then, that communicators of the Gospel learn to listen to biblical texts as well as pay attention to the people around them. It often happens that communicators discover things in the Bible by being willing to listen to the people with whom they work. Ruth Lienhard recently completed a dissertation studying the rationale behind large numbers of people leaving the church among the Daba and Bana of Chad. Her study began by trying to understand issues of shame and guilt in the context of Daba and Bana life. To her surprise, what her research revealed was the importance of honor and the restoration of harmony. The Daba and the Bana had mechanisms in their culture for restoring members to the community after harmony had been disrupted. Unfortunately the church, based on western perspectives brought by outsiders with a "justice orientation," did not have a restorative mechanism, despite all of the evidence for it in Scripture. Through her research Lienhard discovered a new appreciation for the honor orientation of Scripture and in so doing came to appreciate God in a light quite different from her Swiss cultural background. Through her research Ruth enabled the Daba and Bana, in their turn, to gain a new appreciation of God who clearly cared for them and their needs:

> They have come to understand that the Bible addresses their need for harmony. They have been struggling with shame and isolation, both in their cul-

ture and in church. Now the Bible has answers to these, its message makes a difference in their lives and even transforms their culture. In fact, where culture brings shame and disharmony, God brings honor and harmony. A church which takes this seriously will not only live in harmony and peace, but also incorporate God's will as revealed in his book. As people read God's Word, translated into their language, they will understand what their culture has already taught them: that sin is a destructive force and relationships with both God and human beings need to be restored. . . . Finally, the [Daba and Bana] now need to use the message of the Bible to make their own theology of restoration biblically based and at the same time addressing their needs. They can do this because they have access to the Bible in the language they speak and understand. Scripture in the hand of the people enables them to reflect on their culture and on the Bible. The result then is a church that has harmonious interactions in the community of believers. . . . This study has also shown me how much my culture and my faith are [intertwined], and how easily I read the Bible through my cultural glasses. At the same time it revealed how great our God is: he can reach every culture. (Lienhard, 2001: 241–243)

In appreciating such insight we must be willing to learn and not be boxed in by the understanding of one particular horizon. God is bigger than that. God seeks to move us beyond contextualization to a broader awareness of God's communication in the human condition. The local and the contextualized are important, but an appreciation for God in relationship with believers everywhere is a crucial component of the process of Gospel communication.

Throughout this book we have paid attention to textual and theological issues that are closely related to a context: both to the cultural concerns of the original author and audience as well as contemporary peoples. Our purpose has been to connect all we have said in order to enable people to think theologically in local contexts, yet allow the local church to be informed by two thousand years of history. We attempt to break out of traditional molds and give people the freedom, within the bounds of the hermeneutical process we espouse, to express themselves and the perspective they bring to our increasingly greater appreciation of what it means to know God. For this reason we conclude the book with some ground rules for communication that are faithful to the source, appropriate for the context, and relevant to the hearts and minds of receptors. These ground rules serve both as summary of all that has gone before, and as a means to actively encourage ongoing proclamation in our complex world.

GROUND RULES FOR
COMMUNICATING THE GOSPEL

With the information we presented in this book as background to understanding the issues pertinent to communicating God's Word in our world, we can now present some ground rules for relevant Gospel communication. These serve as general principles that can be applied in any context.

Communication is Based on Biblical Truth

The first ground rule for Gospel communication ensures the biblical focus necessary for building a hermeneutical community and a biblical critique of the cultural manifestations in that community. Effective communication comes out of biblical critique. Such critique may, in fact, come from the traditions of the church as people have struggled through two millennia with the realities of conflict between faith and culture. Christian tradition registers the developing fullness of the church as it has expanded throughout the whole earth. The resulting dialogue provides an exchange of ideas about biblical truth as it pertains to pancultural, or human, issues that are informed by what God has already communicated to others. Therefore, a new catholicity provides an enhanced "theological framework out of which the Church might understand itself and its mission under changed circumstances" (Schreiter, 1997: 127).

God's Word, however, both affirms and critiques. So much within culture is mundane. Merely living that is amoral, redundant, and reflective. It is surviving in contexts impacted by economic, social, political, and religious structures that are constantly changing. God affirms humans in the midst of their survival. Occasionally people become aware of the similarity of their lives with what takes place in Scripture. They get excited about God affirming the way they live. This affirmation brings them in touch with God's truth, as well as with others who subscribe to the same truth. The global interaction that results both affirms much of human relationship and the need to critique human error as the Gospel transforms human lives. This is Lingenfelter's objective as he seeks ways to escape the impact of Adam's fall and bring transformation to people living in any culture (Lingenfelter, 1998). God's truth is central to effective communication that sets people free from cultural biases that do not reflect God's intent. This awareness, in turn, allows Gospel receptors to express truth in their context and make appropriate adjustments so that the Holy Spirit may transform their lives to more closely reflect what God expects from them. This is theology at work and it must always be tied to biblical text—Scripture is the source-text for all Christian traditions upon which future generations can build.

Communication is an Ongoing Process, Not a Product

A second ground rule for effective Gospel communication involves the recognition of communication as a process. Too many people think of communication as the end result—what the Gospel should look like in a particular place. Faithful, appropriate, and relevant communicators dare not fall into this trap. We are dealing with a process that starts by understanding what it is that God intends human beings to be in the first place. We use the present tense here to highlight the fact that the message is cast in the text of a closed canon we have called horizons I and II, yet continues to impact all receptors in the present. When that text enters horizon IV something new takes place. We seek to discover the key metaphors or worldview themes and discern a connection between the text and the new context. To do this, the communicator's perspective (horizon III) must also be considered and understood with respect to worldview and the assumptions of that view as they can be brought to bear on the relevance of biblical texts to contemporary contexts.

The theological, communicational, and cultural issues in focus throughout this book represent a process of appropriate communication of the Gospel. The final product is not a great sermon, nor a translation of Scripture, nor even the birth of a church. It is believers in relationship with God, people being conformed to Christ's image. This involves taking biblical themes, values, and insights and matching them with themes, values, and insights of the receptors, thereby seeking to facilitate a communication of God's agenda in their circumstances. This is the process that enables an ongoing dialogue between God's truth and cultural truth, and addresses the need for relevance as well as recognition of cultural change and intercultural relationships of people in a complex world.

Communication is Based on the Principle of Relevance

The third ground rule for Gospel communication recognizes that linguistic and cultural relevance is crucial to the development of theological relevance. The Gospel must make sense for a church to grow within a particular context. Relevance implies the need to make sense. When people receive God's Word they will be motivated to understand it and relate it to what they already know. God's truth will combine with the truths of their community. Their knowledge provides the grid through which they will filter all new information and come to an understanding that reveals truth, not hocus pocus.

Gospel presentation is not about forms and meanings based on Shannon and Weaver's code model. Rather, it is about enabling people to appreciate what they already know as a result of being created in the image of God. With their "common" knowledge they make inferences about the intent of God's communication with the whole of creation. As the Bible is an enscripturated document, it is infinitely communicable. And that communication is a result of interfacing God's intent with human assumptions. The frustration in times past was that this interfacing too often resulted in different interpretations. Based on exegetical principles and code model theory, these interpretations focused on the words, not the ideas behind the words. Based on hermeneutical principles and an awareness of the hermeneutical spiral, our point throughout this book is that different interpretations emerge from specific contexts to give human beings everywhere new insight into God's message. The focus is on what God wants humankind to understand and how a relationship with God impacts that understanding for a specific people. This implies that to be relevant in any context the Word must become a new incarnation. It must connect with what is known so people can relate it to what is unknown. New receptor worlds provide the rest of us with new glasses, new perspectives, through which to read what was always there but had never been seen before.

Communication Impacts Cultural Change

A fourth ground rule has to do with change. The people of a society never stop changing. Pressures from within and without constantly bombard a community, resulting in near constant adjustment to underlying beliefs and values as well as cultural manifestations of behavior. Faithful, appropriate, and relevant Gospel communication is not a quick fix for the age-old questions of indigeneity. Communicators must take seriously both the local contexts and the global theological themes that Christians face everywhere. In so doing, they will focus on equipping and enabling people to make decisions about their relationship to God. By appreciating what receptors already know about God, communicators can point people to God by reiterating God's intent as presented through what God has said. This allows God to step into their circumstances and call for a faith response through the power of the Holy Spirit. Such a response encourages a change of attitude about Jesus. This, in turn, impacts the way people in that context live out their lives.

As believers interact with their surrounding culture and the world at large, the church provides a nurturing sanctuary. The community of believers in a particular context may form a buffer as the faith community and the surrounding society undergo change. Many churches have served to preserve cultural traditions while maintaining the integrity of the Gospel. The Orthodox Church in the Confederation of Russian States is a case in point. As that society underwent radical change in the early 1990s, people turned to the church for a sense of stability and preservation of tradition. As already noted, the other side of the issue of change relates to biblical critique as the church holds society accountable as understood by Christian truth. The greater the impact a faith community has on its context, the more it needs to share its understanding of God's intended meaning. This calls for the whole church to be involved in the hermeneutical spiral, which leads us to the missional nature of communication.

Communication is Mission

The final ground rule for Gospel communication relates to the missionary nature of the church. With a fundamental understanding of the Gospel and the resulting theological development among a particular people, the process can be replicated in ever-widening circles of influence on people in other cultural contexts and culture types. Furthermore, the blessings are immeasurable for the sending community of believers as they not only impact others but also are impacted by new a understanding that forces a reevaluation of Scripture and adjustments in their own theology. Local congregations need to be intentional about proclaiming the Gospel beyond their borders (however defined by culture, language, or distance) in order to be missionary churches. This is Van Engen's point in his book *God's Missionary People* (1991).

GOD'S TRUTH OR HOCUS POCUS?

As human beings, we have a tendency to deal with theological questions with respect to our own cultural biases. Without even realizing it, we tend to factor out the original context, the circumstances into which God spoke in the first place. On the other hand, globalization, with its reduction of time and distance and reliance on technology, forces us to hold an increasing awareness of things beyond our borders

If, as a result of effective communication, we expect Gospel receptors to both contextualize and theologize the Gospel message for their own context, the communicated message must provide the necessary background (biblically, historically, and theologically) and information for the receptors to make sense of it. A team approach joins relevant biblical expertise (details concerning the source-text provided by a theologically trained outsider) with the receptors' understanding of issues central to their needs and interests (the receptors represented by trained insiders who can apply communication principles to their circumstances). To the extent possible, outsiders can encourage and enable the process. However, they must never engineer the results.

As communicators we can never rid ourselves of our presuppositions, nor should we want to. Culture-free communication is impossible. The hermeneutical process that informs the entire argument of this book forces us to be aware of biases that emerge from a particular understanding of the Gospel. We must, however, make a conscious effort to see that those biases do not unduly influence the process of theologizing, either locally or globally. Sensitivity to the four horizons as they interact and the consciousness of the nature of ongoing theological reflection will draw believers deeper into God's Word. This movement is central to the process. As people reach out to others, they in turn are impacted by them and so learn more about God's intentions for all human beings. Each horizon in turn reflects incarnation of God's expectations in a particular time and place. God's Word is never done; it just keeps communicating in new and effective ways relevant to the circumstances in which it finds itself. It reflects God, the creator, enabler, and sustainer of the universe.

Chuck Van Engen gained new insight from Pedro Odilón and his peasant communities in the highlands of Chiapas. While Van Engen expounded God's Word to these people, he gained new understanding of personal well-being and interest in being in relationship with God. The questions his audience asked provided a perspective that forced him to reflect upon the biblical horizons in new ways. This prompted responses he had never thought of before. This process impacted Chuck's thinking and theologizing, as well. It enabled him to develop a new appreciation of "theology and mission in, of, and on the way." This is a theology of relevance that communicates in ways unimaginable until the horizons find a new interface in the circumstances of immediacy. New understanding emerges to further inform and instruct believers and bring on a new relationship with God.

We conclude with the doxology from the writer to the Hebrews. It represents a summation of our purpose in writing this book. We have sought to avoid hocus-pocus. We have sought ways whereby what is presented about God is the truth God wanted all human beings to understand and apply to living fulfilling lives. The result of this understanding should be a desire to relate to God by living out God's communicational intent for all people everywhere. Living a life informed by God will take on a myriad of manifestations, some simple, some more complex, but the collective message for our human condition is as follows: "God will make [us] ready to obey him and [we] will always be eager to do right. May Jesus help [us] do what pleases God. To Jesus Christ be glory forever and ever! Amen." (Heb. 13:21)

NOTES

1. Adapted from Charles Van Engen's inaugural lecture in the Arthur F. Glasser Chair of Biblical Theology of Mission, 1996.
2. Hashivenu Forum III, February 4–6, 2001, Pasadena, California.

Appendix A

A Biblical Example of Hermeneutics: Jesus, the "Lamb of God"

*W*hen we read the Bible, we do not receive it apart from its contexts. It comes as content-in-context. It does not come as if it had been dropped to earth from heaven, unattached to human life. Rather, God's revelation is always conveyed through the medium of persons (both authors and audience) and their cultures. Thus the biblical text has dual authorship: divine and human. Every time the New Testament uses the Old, what was written originally and intended by the Old Testament authors is both continuous and discontinuous with the way it was understood and used by the New Testament interpreters, who in their turn also became authors. This continuity/discontinuity dialectic provides us with us a degree of elasticity that we can legitimately use in our own interpretation of Scripture through the operation of the Holy Spirit, without thereby opening the canon.

When we come to the history of revelation, we return to the canonicity issue discussed in chapter 2. We are the people of God and we are, therefore in continuity with historical revelation, while at the same time tied to our own context. There must be a hermeneutical thread that binds us to the Scriptures while allowing freedom and breadth of relevant interpretation. Our understanding does not add to the canon, but is a deeper discovery of new meaning that makes the Bible relevant in the present: same revelation, new meaning. "I will be your God, you will be my people and I will dwell in your midst" is the same "old" truth throughout all human history, yet it is always encased in "new" forms. The New Testament authors in one sense never add to the Old. They add something "new," but they do not add more to the "old."[1] Our calling is to add a "new" understanding to that of Christians before us, but we do not add to the revelation enscripturated in the New Testament.

We can see this process at work when we examine the Gospel of John. When reading this Gospel, communicators seek to understand it for appropriate proclamation at every level. Communicators need to demonstrate careful exegesis, thoughtful biblical hermeneutics, and conscious awareness of the historical development of dogma, leading to a new appropriation of the same Gospel. The surface-level meanings of individual Greek words may be found in a theological dictionary of the New Testament. Yet their deep-level meanings will be understood only through a discourse-level analysis of the whole text, examining how those words were juxtaposed with the other elements of the discourse. Put another way, words must be taken in context.[2]

For example, we can illustrate the hermeneutical process espoused in this book by examining a central metaphor that John applies to Jesus, the "Lamb of God." John the Baptist probably did not know fully what he was saying when he saw Jesus and, moved by the Holy Spirit, proclaimed, "Behold the Lamb of God" (John 1:29). He did not understand the cross and resurrection at that point. What did John the Baptist think? And what did John the Evangelist as the author of the Gospel think that John the Baptist meant? And what did those who heard John the Baptist's words understand him to say? And what of the Christians among whom John wrote his Gospel?

BIBLICAL HERMENEUTICAL CONTEXTS

A search for answers begins by going back to the root metaphor in the Old Testament. The focus is on sacrifice, and we go back to Abraham and the near-sacrifice of Isaac (Gen. 12:6), then to the Passover (Exod. 12–13), and then to Moses in the desert. What did Moses do with the root metaphor? He set up the tabernacle complete with a priestly structure, rituals, and ceremonies centered on sacrifice. Where did he get the idea of sacrifice? Was Moses aware of the stories of Abraham raising altars in worship to God under the trees of Mamre, a special holy place for Abraham? As we follow this process of re-presentation, we begin to see that to understand John the Baptist we must go back through the root metaphors and see them through the lenses of the various contexts where sacrifice and worship appear in Scripture. The New Testament writers were well aware of the root metaphors of the Old Testament.

This process provides a clearer picture of why the lamb as a sacrificial symbol is so central to appreciating who God is and what Christ did on the cross. What was understood by John the Baptist, John the Evangelist, and their faith communities in the time-space of their contexts provides the theological and biblical background necessary to give meaning to the discourse we read today.

Then there is the context of Hellenized Judaism that followed the time of Jesus and influenced the thought forms of the Apostolic writings, which, in turn, impacted the whole of church history in a variety of different contexts (c.f. Walls, 1996). After the resurrection, the ascension and the coming of the

Holy Spirit, the followers of Jesus began to see what "Behold the Lamb of God" meant, based on placing Jesus in continuity with salvation history, and adding their new (*kainos*) understanding to what had been revealed before to them. Those who came after the Pentecost event could look back to John the Baptist and place his words in the full discourse of the canon. And in such a case, the whole is greater than the sum of its parts. The Old Testament, then, is the foundation on which the Messiah can, indeed must, be understood. Together, the two testaments reflect God's revealed hiddenness that becomes the foundation for the church's theology.

CONTEMPORARY
HERMENEUTICAL CONTEXTS

How can we communicate "Lamb of God" for a contemporary audience? We must begin with a comparable study of the metaphor in the context into which we wish to present what God did through Christ. The "translation" of "Lamb of God" requires the interpretation of an entire semantic constellation—all of the meanings reflected through time and space brought together in a new context. In so doing we preserve the special revelation in Jesus, but that special revelation is related to all that went before. As followers of Christ we accept his sacrifice that draws its meaning from previous eras of understanding emanating from both the Hebrew and Hellenist perspectives. In a sense, what is happening in our world today is no different than what took place in the shift from Abraham to Moses or from John the Baptist to the Apostle Paul.

Contemporary communicators may follow this hermeneutical process in order to appropriately proclaim the intended meaning of Scripture for new receptors engaged in yet another sociocultural shift. That meaning makes clear the intention of the text as well as the relation of the text to a new context in which it now communicates God's truth. People may use the same propositions and words, but the way they do this, and the meaning they attach, may differ according to their context-dependent understanding. Meaning is always context sensitive.

Early Bible translators, and Gospel communicators in general, tended to present the exegetical stuff of words rather than the context-dependent, discourse-level semantic constellations of intended meaning. Lamin Sanneh (1989) pointed out the difference between Christianity and Islam. He emphasized that the Bible is infinitely translatable. Translatability is communicability. While Sanneh writes as a historian, he is really doing theology. The Bible is infinitely translatable because what is translated is a long series of history and context-specific signs, root metaphors, and meanings that point to Jesus Christ.

Contemporary audiences may find sacrifice and an appreciation of "Lamb of God" difficult (as the Samo did). However, by seeing how the biblical authors present this concept, we can come to a new understanding of such strategic biblical metaphors with all that went before to enrich the meaning. And by noting how each contemporary context enables receptors to understand the meaning in new ways, we gain nuances from the new context that provide an understanding we never knew before. Therefore, we must grasp in some detail the hermeneutical spiral, which, in turn, leads to an adequate development and application of the four horizons.

This is how biblical theology is developed. But it starts with seeing the text in its particular context. As we follow a concept step-by-step through its development (at the level of the word, the theme, a whole book, or the Bible as a collection of books making up a whole), we can note its impact on each audience it touches. The hermeneutical process requires each of the four horizons: the Old Testament writers and receptors, the New Testament apostles and their respective audiences represented by the churches they founded, the twenty centuries of the Church's reflection, the missionary churches, and the contemporary Gospel communicators presenting God's truth in the new, postmodern churches arising from the needs of relativist, pluralist audiences. An awesome history, an awesome communication task!

NOTES

1. See the difference in the New Testament use of *neos* and *kainos* as developed in Van Engen, 1996b: 71–89 and presented in chapter 1 of this book.

2. We prefer to avoid labeling this a form/meaning distinction because those linguistic labels ignore the macro-level issues central to understanding the text. Rather we are getting at something that is much more a matter of wisdom and understanding. It is in fact a deeper appreciation of God's intention that the original authors could not anticipate from their position in history. Looking back, we can understand this in a new way. The New Testament writers did it with the Old Testament, applying it to their perspective and context. The same thing happens when the Gospel takes root in new soil among a new people: They may see things that communicators from another context could not appreciate. This applies the hermeneutical spiral to the task of appreciating what God intended through an examination of what God said. Thus we gain new understanding because God is revealed in a new context and people respond in new and exciting ways.

Discourse Analysis for Appropriate Communication

> Broadly speaking, discourse analysis is a process of handling the text from the top down for the purpose of ascertaining its thematic structure. Communicators of a message organize their presentation in order to ensure, to the extent possible, that their intent comes across—that there is logic to their communication. Those who receive that message make inferences based on the structure of the presentation. Thus an analysis of a discourse provides the big picture, the overall structure of a text (biblical or otherwise, oral or written) in order to present its parts, and show how they are organized in order to best communicate a particular message. (Culy, 1989)

$\mathscr{T}$here is a wide range of definitions ascribed to "discourse analysis," either emphasizing the level of a communicative unit in a larger text, generally viewed as the sentence level or above (Callow, 1974: 11), or focusing on the overall nature of a text and how it fits into the broader cultural and linguistic context in which it was communicated (Longacre, 1977: 18).[1] In short, the concept of a discourse is rather "ambiguous" (Stubbs, 1983:1), and open to considerable variation depending on the subdiscipline in focus: philosophical (Grice, 1975; Wittgenstein, 1953), structural linguistics (Halliday, 1978, 1989), text linguistics (deBeaugrande and Dressler, 1981), or the ethnography of speech (Tyler, 1978)—to name but a few of the applications of discourse. Regardless of the focus, at issue is the fact that communicators shape their message in a variety of styles or genre. Kathleen Callow notes:

> Thus, a translator, faced with alternative ways of saying the same thing, has four different criteria, or rather sets of criteria, which he can apply to determine which is the most suitable.[2] These four categories of appropriateness are *grouping* (how the utterance concerned fits into some larger group,

which itself functions as a unit in the discourse as a whole); *cohesion* (how participants and events mentioned in the utterance relate to other participants and events already mentioned in the discourse); *information structure* (how much information the utterance conveys, and of what kind); and *prominence* (how important the utterance is compared to other utterances in the same discourse) (Callow, 1974: 11).

Callow uses these categories of appropriateness to organize the chapters of her book on discourse. Every communication is divided into units that can be grouped in various ways to signal communicators' intent. The units of the discourse, then, enable communicators to develop the ideas essential to the text and the relationships necessary to demonstrate the connectivity and coherence of a communication. Subsumed throughout this discussion is a need to appreciate the context into which the discourse was originally communicated as well as the nature of the cultural circumstances into which it will need to be "translated" in order to make sense. In short, communication must account for the context of the text (Shaw, 1989). In this limited space we will not present a definitive discussion of all of the ramifications of discourse analysis. Rather we enable readers to appreciate the importance of understanding key principles that, in turn, inform them of the value these considerations have in the organization of text for effective communication of the message embedded within them.

DISCOURSE GENRE

[G]enre [is] constitutive of meaning [that] conditions our expectations as readers and permits understanding to take place. . . . The genre provides the literary context for a given [text] and therefore, partly determines what the [text] means and how it should be taken. . . . Genre thus enables the reader to interpret meaning and to recognize what kinds of truth claims are being made in and by a text. (Vanhoozer, 1986: 80)

All communicators have an objective in communicating. In an early draft of her book, *Man and Message*, Callow followed Halliday (1970: 322ff) by noting that every communication has three basic functions: "ideational" or content-oriented, "interpersonal" or social interaction, and "textual" or discourse-oriented. Later (1998) she reorganized this to emphasize the "import" of an author in communicating to affect ideas, impact emotions, or change behavior. Furthermore, Larson notes that communicators "will choose the discourse type which best communicates [their] purpose" (Larson, 1984: 365). Thus, if a communicator is interested in telling a story, time line is important and the units are organized in a time frame to communicate the sequencing of events subsumed in the discourse. Communicating how to bake a cake, on the other hand, while also accounting for the need of chronological sequence, prescribes appropriate actions designed to affect behavior that will result in a presentable desert. Beekman et al. demonstrate how the juxtaposition of chronological sequencing and "prescription" (designed to affect behavior) form a matrix that reflects communicational intent (Beekman et al., 1981: 38). In figure B.1 we present the primary genre reflected in this matrix followed by a brief explanation of each major type. While there are many subtypes, these four broad discourse genre subsume human communication and apply in almost any sociolinguistic context. We use Larson's purpose for communicating to define each genre.

	NON-PRESCRIPTIVE	**PRESCRIPTIVE**
CHRONOLOGICAL	**Narrative** (recount events)	**Procedural** (prescribe how to do something)
NON-CHRONOLOGICAL	**Expository** (explain or argue a case/thesis)	**Hortatory** (urge a course of action)

Based on Beekman, et al., 1981: 38.

Figure B.1.   Four Primary Types of Discourse Genre

Narrative Discourse

Chronological, nonprescriptive discourse is narrative in nature, recounting a series of events with or without a plot.

Expository Discourse

In using nonchronological, nonprescriptive discourse, a communicator organizes the message in order to explain, define, interpret, or provide information. Such exposition develops the author's thesis and usually sums up in order to anticipate and counteract a rebuttal.

Procedural Discourse

Chronological, prescriptive discourse gives instruction designed to achieve a goal. By so doing, an author hopes that those who receive the message will follow through and accomplish the objectives of the particular procedure.

Hortatory Discourse

Nonchronological, prescriptive discourse attempts to influence people's conduct by prescribing a course of action—get people to follow through on the author's intent to ensure action that will bring about a change of behavior.

SCHEMA: SEGMENTING DISCOURSE

Each genre, because it represents a different authorial intent, organizes communication differently, thereby resulting in a different segmentation of the units that comprise each discourse. John Tuggy calls this "schema" (1992), or "paragraph patterning" (2003). He uses this to show how an author structures information to communicate a particular intent. Each schema breaks discourse into three broad parts or categories: an introduction, a body, and a conclusion. The introduction serves to establish the author's ostentation (intent to communicate) and develop rapport with the audience while ensuring they understand the basic content of a topic and/or theme of a discourse. The body of a discourse communicates the message, utilizing a variety of communication markers, styles, and structures to ensure the content is understood. Finally, the conclusion brings closure to the discourse. Inasmuch as presenting ideas in different genre requires different structures, the primary focus of schema is on the body of the discourse. The body of the text includes certain obligatory and optional elements used to group material according to a particular communicative purpose in order to present ideas, affect emotions, and change behavior. These elements, then, are considered central to presenting the content of a discourse and ensuring that an audience can make inferences that match the author's intentions. Narrative, for example, is presented as a series of episodes designed to bring resolution to the rationale for recounting the story, while hortatory discourse is structured to incite receptors to action. We will look at these parts of discourse for the body of each genre.

Central to this process of segmenting discourse is the contrastive rationale for marking those segments within each genre. Thus narrative text is segmented on the basis of actors and their activities, time line, spatial shifts, and other context-specific criteria that often mark changes in episode. Expository text, on the other hand, is segmented for the purpose of showing the logic of an argument and presenting evidence to support a line of reasoning presented in the theme. It stands to reason, then, that the relationships between the various parts of a text will reflect the schema and work to reinforce an author's intent in using a particular genre.

Narrative Discourse

Narrative discourse recounts a series of events organized chronologically in a nonprescriptive manner. The focus is on telling a story (narration with plot development) or distributing information (descriptive narration with no plot) by recounting what happened, who was involved, when it happened, and where and how the action took place, all in a typically time- and place-specific context. Texts are typically first person and experientially oriented to the narrator or recount the activities of others in the third person. The body of the text includes certain obligatory elements considered central to narrating information: orientation, a series of episodes, and a finale that summarizes or brings the information together in a relevant way. Each of these obligatory elements, in turn, contains segments that, while optional, enable narrators to develop ideas with a considerable amount of creativity. Storytellers in most societies around the world maximize these elements to grab people's attention and weave their story—they bring their audience into the story and often make them part of the process by including audience participation, graphics, and sound effects that rival the best cinematography. A generalized schema for narrative discourse based on Tuggy follows:

+ Orientation
  ± Introduction
  ± Setting
  ± Contraction of theme
+ Episode (indefinite number)
  ± Setting
  ± Problem
  ± Resolution
  ± Outcome
+ Finale
  ± Theme/moral/effect

Each element represents a different segment of the text and each segment draws on the importance of stimulus-response semantic relationships to other segments of the text. Narrative genre often includes considerable dialogue (or repartee) between characters, thereby enabling narrators to convey information through the characters in the story (cf. the book of Ruth).

Expository Discourse

In using expository genre, proclaimers attempt to explain, define, interpret, or provide information through a logical presentation that is both nonchronological and nonprescriptive—often a thesis or hypothesis to prove or disprove. Communicators use this genre to emphasize their theses through statements structured to present a rationale and ensure understanding of their viewpoint. They focus on why they consider something is so, or provide an explanation that is in line with a particular argumentation. A generalized schema for the body of expository genre includes:

+ Thesis
+ Evidence
± Inference/recapitulation

The relationships that serve to hold these segments of expository text together emphasize logic and clarification: generic-specific, reason-result, and grounds-conclusion. Textbooks, editorials, essays, and arguments of all kinds are included in this type of discourse (cf. the book of Romans).

Procedural Discourse

Procedural texts enable communicators to give instruction designed to achieve a particular goal or result. The genre presents information in a chronological, step-by-step order necessary to prescribe action that realizes a goal. A generalized schema for the body of procedural discourse includes the basic outline:

+ Orientation
+ Steps in procedure
+ Accomplishment/goal

Dominant relationships between these segments of the text emphasize commands to ensure a proper procedure, means-purpose, which provides the rationale, and means-result, which seeks to guarantee the correct outcomes (cf. Luke 10:1–10).

Hortatory Discourse

Finally hortatory discourse enables authors to present information logically structured around second-person commands designed to prescribe an appropriate presentation of a theme, often presented in the introduction or early in the text. Like exposition, the strength of the presentation is based on a logical flow of information (rather than a chronological sequencing) that seeks a particular response. It tells receptors what needs to be done and why based on the generalized schema that leads receptors to respond to an appeal:

+ Basis/theme
± Diffusion of tension
± Enablement
+ Appeal
± Evaluation

The primary relationships in focus revolve around grounds–exhortation (cf. the book of Philemon).

While each genre may stand alone, in the normal flow of communication within a discourse, there is also often a considerable amount of embedding of different genres within a broader text. Any given text may include a multiplicity of intent with a variety of approaches incorporated into the communication. So a story, for example, may be entertaining while at the same time communicating a particular moral or purpose. Many of the parables are like this, thereby incorporating hortatory genre into a narrative mode. Thus, within any given text there may be a wide variety of semantic relationships that go far beyond what may be expected simply by identifying the genre. These relationships are necessary to communicate the variation that signals to an audience that something beyond a mere story, for example, is being communicated. They must understand the content of a message in order to make inferences that match what the author intended.

We present figure B.2 (following page) as a summation, patterned on Larson (1984: 366), to demonstrate the characteristics of the main discourse genre. This highlights the need for further detail if the analysis of biblical texts in their context is the readers' goal. Our objective is simply to alert readers to the importance of taking discourse seriously and utilizing these principles to structure their message for appropriate proclamation.

This overview, with a top-down, macro perspective of a text, should be complimented with a bottom-up, micro perspective that utilizes propositional analysis to appreciate the relationship between the smaller elements of a text. Both discourse and propositional analysis are essential to understanding any given discourse. In this way people using languages and finding themselves in contexts unfamiliar to the original communicators can appreciate what those people said and intended others to understand.

Genre	Person Orientation	Time (Illocutionary force)	"Backbone"	Relational Structure
NARRATIVE	First/Third	Past (Statements)	Main-line Events	Story/Information line (Stimulus-Response)
EXPOSITORY	Third	(Statements)	Themes	Logic/Reason (Cause-Effect)
PROCEDURAL	Second/Third	Present (Commands)	Procedures	Process (Steps-Goal)
HORTATORY	Second	(Commands)	Injunctions	Action (Grounds-Exhortation)

Adapted from Larson 1984: 366.

Figure B.2.   Characteristics of The Four Primary Genres

By way of overview, then, discourse analysis involves making choices regarding the general nature of text. What genre did an author use to get a particular message across and what does that choice tell us about the intent of the communication? What units within a discourse does an author use to organize the message and convey information subsumed by the choice of genre? How does an author organize the information to reflect a sense of cohesion? What segments of the text are more prominent than others and thereby carry the primary content load supported by further text that fills out the message and makes it interesting? The answers to these questions provide an understanding of the discourse and its information flow (either oral or written), which can then be restructured for presentation using the styles and structures appropriate in a different context for the purpose of effective and/or relevant communication. These macro elements of the text are complimented by a comparable organization of information from the bottom up so that the entire communication may be presented in a manner deemed comprehensible in a different sociolinguistic time and place (cf. the elaborate and detailed *Semantic Structural Analysis* series for each New Testament book made available by Wycliffe Bible Translators).

"RE-COMMUNICATION":
ONE DISCOURSE OR TWO?

Anthony Pym (1992: 2) asks a practical question that demands a hermeneutical response:, "should a source text and its corresponding target text form or conform to one or two discourses?" (29). The answer is important for the communication enterprise because it forces an understanding of the limits of transfer that are implied in disparate cultures and languages. Should discourse as a concept be limited to only the source side of communication, or is it a notion that transcends the respective structures of different times and places and focuses on ensuring the "recommunication" of ideas that concern all human beings?[3] While philosophical in nature, the pragmatics of communication are such that we must look to the nature of text and its structure as well as to the context that structures it to answer the question.

We must go beyond linguistic structures and anticipate an appreciation of the cultural context in which a discourse is shaped. Each culture type is different, organizing the world around it differently because, in some measure, the rationale for organization is different (cf. chapter 6). Discourse, then, is a reflection of an author's attempt to categorize the world within a particular communication and transfer information to demonstrate a particular intent. The message is structured in order to highlight that intent. If the receptors do not share that structure, or the structures they use do not communicate that objective, the author will not be understood and, like culture shock, there will be misunderstanding that results in miscommunication. Pym's own response demonstrates the dilemma created by his question:

> If a source text and a target text are equivalent because [they are] within the same discourse, translation is a banal phenomenon. And if they are different discourses because in different tongues, then translation would appear to be an unthinkable phenomenon.
>
> The only way to cut across this dilemma is to regard translation as the active movement by which discourse may be extended from one cultural setting to another. What translation theory would then want to know about discourses is the relative degree of difficulty and success involved in their extension and the degree to which they may undergo transformation through translation. It is here that translation could become a discovery procedure of some importance to intercultural discourse analysis. (Pym, 1992: 35)

Fortunately the general nature of the four primary discourse types presented by Beekman et al. reflect a high degree of human commonality. The fine points of organizing the segmented structure within each type are where we expect to find difference and the need for adjustment. We could expect translation across cultures within a culture type to be more communicative than translation across culture types. However, the question remains, is a translation of a text the same discourse or another? The answer, in part, comes from our hermeneutical development of the distance or discontinuity between horizons (see figure 4.10). When that gap represents large amounts of time, space, linguistic, and cultural expectations that were not anticipated when the communication was instigated, people in the contemporary context are unable to fathom the source context. In that case, two discourses are extant and the skill of the communicator in bridging the gap will be severely tested. Neither translation theory nor cultural theory taken alone can readily resolve the dilemma. However taken together, in light of an appreciation of human commonality and an application of our four-horizon hermeneutic, we can move to resolution.

The corporate nature of humankind who, created in the image of God, desire to know God is central to answering the question. Enlightened by the Holy Spirit, God draws all people to himself (John 12:32) and through the power of the Word (both the text and the incarnation) enables them to appreciate the value of that word in a context that is relevant for them. A communicator analyzes the text, appreciating the intent and meaning for the context of communication, and then seeks to deliver that understanding to the new audience. That audience, in turn, must undergo the same hermeneutical process of analysis, deconstruction of meaning, and application to their own context to enable understanding to be complete (this is the essence of relevance theory). The text is the same: it is God's Word enscripturated. But the particular understanding and application of that text in a different context deepens and broadens the understanding of God's intent for people in that context and for the rest of humankind. The hermeneutical spiral ensures that there is ongoing and increasing awareness within a specific communication situation. Across linguistic and cultural barriers, however, new insight gained from the Word in a new context enables greater appreciation of God's intent, both in the process and the product of a communication.

Therefore, the issue is not the number of discourses involved, but how people who receive the content of a message understand it in light of what was originally intended, and how that intent impacts their context. The genre chosen to communicate a message will reflect an author's intent as well as the expectations of an audience: communicating information, arguing a case for a particular thesis or idea, prescribing a procedure in order to create new insight, or urging a particular course of action. Scripture contains all of this and more. How the content of biblical text (God's Word) is organized within the bounds of linguistic and cultural structures both constrains communication to the particularities of a time and place while at the same time, through recommunication, liberates it to expand within the bounds of human understanding. Now the text of the discourse has the potential to take people to new heights of knowing God. Being in relationship with the ultimate author of the text enables people to rise above being human and truly makes them human beings—in what they say and in what they do (Col. 3:17).

NOTES

1. There is a large literature on this subject that we will not touch on here. Rather our purpose is to present a basic awareness of the importance of taking discourse into account and relating it to the hermeneutical process. In this way it becomes a valuable tool for understanding an author's intent on the one hand and communicating that same message into a new and unrelated context. For key overviews of this subject see Nida and Taber (1981), who set in motion the application of discourse to translation principles in the 1970s and 1980s; John Beekman et al. (1981 in its many editions); Kathleen Callow's (1974) ground-breaking effort in her complementary supplement to John Beekman and John Callow's strategic work, *Translating the Word of God;* Katherine Barnwell's (1980) important work written for non-English speakers; Mildred Larson's often referenced *Meaning Based Translation* (1984), Joseph Grimes' insightful *The Thread of Discourse* (1976); and Robert Longacre's (1983) major contribution to the field, which in turn gave rise to the *Journal of Translation and Textlinguistics* that continues to produce valuable literature. Other strategic authors in the field include Tyler (1978, who handles text from a sociolinguistic perspective), Stubbs (1983), Brown and Yule (1984), and Brown's anticipated *Analyzing Discourse* (2003), and Pym (1992).

2. Callow uses the term "translator," but because our purpose throughout this book is broader, we encourage readers to think "communicator." The objectives and process is essentially the same.

3. We appreciate Glenn Rogers' (2002) insight on the concept of "recommunication." Though similar to "translation" this idea conveys the concept of communication we have utilized throughout this book. Communication can take place in any context and may reflect on ensuring a message is understood in a particular time and place in order to enable people to appreciate the context of a discourse initially communicated in a different time and place.

References

Addai, W. 1999. Metaphor, Values, and Ethno-Leadership: A Missiological Study with Implications for Christian Leadership in Ghana. Ph.D. Dissertation. Fuller Theological Seminary.

Alaichamy, Christeena. 1997. Communicative Translation: Theory and Principles for Application to Cross Cultural Translation in India. Ph.D. Dissertation. Fuller Theological Seminary.

Alaichamy, Paul. 1997. Intermediate Language Translation Aids: An Experiment in the Indian Context. Ph.D. Dissertation. Fuller Theological Seminary.

Bailey, K. E. 1983. *Poet and Peasant and Through Peasant Eyes: A Literary-Cultural Approach to the Parables in Luke.* Grand Rapids, Mich.: Eerdmans.

Bailey, S. 2002. Communication Strategies for Christian Witness among the Lowland Lao Informed by Worldview Themes in Khwan Rituals. Ph.D. Dissertation. Fuller Theological Seminary.

Barbour, I. G. 1974. *Myths, Models, and Paradigms: A Comparative Study in Science and Religion.* New York: Harper & Row.

Barnett, H. G. 1953. *Innovation: The Basis of Cultural Change.* New York: McGraw-Hill.

Barnwell, K. 1980. *Introduction to Semantics and Translation.* Horsley's Green, Eng.: Summer Institute of Linguistics.

Barth, Christoph. 1991. *God with Us: A Theological Introduction to the Old Testament.* Grand Rapids, Mich.: Eerdmans.

Barth, Karl. 1958. *Church Dogmatics.* 13 volumes. Edinburgh, Eng.: T and T Clark.

Bediako, K. 1995. *Christianity in Africa: The Renewal of a Non-Western Religion.* Maryknoll, N.Y.: Orbis Books.

Beekman, J., and J. Callow. 1974. *Translating the Word of God.* Grand Rapids, Mich.: Zondervan.

Beekman, J., J. Callow, and M. Kopesec. 1981. *The Semantic Structure of Written Communication.* Dallas, Tex.: Summer Institute of Linguistics.

Benedict, R. 1934. *Patterns of Culture.* Boston: Houghton Mifflin.

Berger, P. L. 1969. *The Sacred Canopy: Elements of a Sociological Theory of Religion.* Garden City, N.Y.: Doubleday.

Berger, P. L., B. Berger, and H. Kellner. 1973. *The Homeless Mind: Modernization and Consciousness.* New York: Random House.

Berkhof, H. 1979. *Christian Faith: An Introduction to the Study of the Faith.* Grand Rapids, Mich.: Eerdmans.

———. 1985. *Introduction to the Study of Dogmatics.* Grand Rapids, Mich.: Eerdmans.

Berkhof, Hendrikus, and P. A. Potter. 1964. *Key Words of the Gospel: Biblical Studies Delivered at the Mexico Meeting of the World Council of Churches Commission on World Mission and Evangelism.* London: SCM Press.

Berkhof, Louis. 1932. *Reformed Dogmatic.* Grand Rapids, Mich.: Eerdmans.

Berkouwer, G. C. 1956. *General Revelation.* Grand Rapids, Mich.: Eerdmans.

———. 1965. *The Second Vatical Council and the New Catholicism.* L. B. Smedes, trans. Grand Rapids, Mich.: Eerdmans.

———. 1975. *Holy Scripture.* Grand Rapids, Mich.: Eerdmans.

Berlo, D. K. 1960. *Process of Communication.* New York: Holt, Rinehart and Winston.

Blass, R. 1990. *Relevance Relations in Discourse: A Study with Special Reference to Sissala.* Cambridge, Eng.: Cambridge University Press.

Bleicher, Josef. 1980. *Contemporary Hermeneutics: Hermeneutics as Method, Philosophy, and Critique.* London: Routledge & Kegan Paul.

Boff, C. 1987. *Theology and Praxis: Epistemological Foundations.* Maryknoll, N.Y.: Orbis Books.

Boff, L., and C. Boff. 1987. *Introducting Liberation Theology.* Maryknoll, N.Y.: Orbis Books.

Bosch, D. J. 1991. *Transforming Mission: Paradigm Shifts in Theology of Mission.* Maryknoll, N.Y.: Orbis Books.

Brewster, E. T., and E. S. Brewster. 1982. *Bonding and the Missionary Task.* Pasadena, Calif.: Lingua House.

Brown, F. 2000. *Enhanced Brown-Driver-Briggs Hebrew and English Lexicon.* Bellingham, Wash.: Logos Research Systems.

Brown, G., and G. Yule *Discourse Analysis.* Cambridge, Eng.: Cambridge University Press.

Bruce, F. F. 1990. *The Epistle to the Hebrews.* Revised edition. The New International Commentary on the New Testament. Grand Rapids, Mich.: Eerdmans. (Originally published in 1964.)

Brunner, Emil. 1950. *The Christian Doctrine of God.* Philadelphia: Westminster.

Burling, R. 1964. "Cognition and Componential Analysis: God's Truth or Hocus-Pocus." *American Anthropologist* 66: 20–28.

Bush, F. 1992. "Images of Israel: The People of God in the Torah." In *Studies in Old Testament Theology,* R. L. Hubbard, Jr. et al., eds. Waco, Tex.: Word. Pp. 99–115.

Bush, F. W. 1996. *Ruth, Esther.* Word Biblical Commentary, vol. 9. Dallas, Tex.: Word Books.

Cahill, T. 1998. *The Gifts of the Jews: How a Tribe of Desert Nomads Changed the Way Everyone Thinks and Feels.* New York: Nan A. Talese.

Caird, G. G. 1980. *The Language and Imagery of the Bible.* Philadelphia: Westminster.

Callow, K. 1974. *Discourse Considerations in Translating the Word of God.* Grand Rapids, Mich.: Zondervan.

———. 1998. *Man and Message: A Guide to Meaning-Based Text Analysis.* Lanham, Md.: University Press of America.

Calvin, J. 1960. *Institutes of the Christian Religion.* Vol. I. F. L. Battles, trans. Philadelphia: Westminster. Pp. 78–81.

Carson, D. A. 1984. *Biblical Interpretation and the Church: The Problem of Contextualization.* Nashville, Tenn.: Thomas Nelson.

Chiles, B. S. 1979. *Introduction to the Old Testament as Scripture.* Philadelphia: Fortress Press.

———. 1984. *The New Testament as Canon.* Valley Forge, Penn.: Trinity Press.

Chomsky, N. 1957. *Syntactic Structures.* The Hague: Mouton.

Clinton, J. R. 1977. *Interpreting the Scriptures: Figures and Idioms.* Pasadena, Calif.: Barnabas Resources.

Cook, Guillermo. 1985. *The Expectation of the Poor: Latin American Basic Ecclesial Communities in Protestant Perspective.* Maryknoll, N.Y.: Orbis Books.

Costas, O. 1976. *Theology of the Crossroads in Contemporary Latin America.* Amsterdam: Rodopi.

Croatto, J. S. 1973. *Liberación y Libertad: Pautas Hermenéuticas.* Buenos Aires: Ediciones Mundo Nuevo.

———. 1987. *Biblical Hermeneutics: Toward A Theory of Reading as the Production of Meaning.* Maryknoll, N.Y.: Orbis Books. (Originally published as *Hermenéutica bíblica: Para una teoría de la lectura como producción sentido.* Buenos Aires: Asociación Ediciones la Aurora, 1984.)

Cross, F. M. 1973. *Canaanite Myth and Hebrew Epic Essays in the History of the Religion of Israel.* Cambridge, Mass.: Harvard University Press.

Culy, M. M. 1989. "The Top Down Approach to Translation." *Notes on Translation* 7: 28–51.

deBeaugrande, R., and W. Dressler. 1981. *Introduction to Text Linguistics.* London: Longman.

Deibler, E., ed. *Semantic and Structural Analyses.* A series of analytical commentaries on the Greek text of New Testament books. Dallas, Tex.: Summer Institute of Linguistics Publications.

Dilley, R. 1999. *The Problem of Context.* Oxford, Eng.: Berghahn Books.

Dye, T. W. 1980. *The Bible Translation Strategy.* Dallas, Tex.: Wycliffe Bible Translators.

Elà, J. M. 1988. *My Faith as an African.* J. Pairman-Brown and S. Perry, trans. Maryknoll, N.Y.: Orbis Books.

Engle, J. F., and W. A. Dyrness. 2000. *Changing the Mind of Missions: Where Have We Gone Wrong?* Downers Grove, Ill.: InterVarsity Press.

Escobar, S. E. 1987. *La Fe Evangélica y las Teologías de la Liberación.* El Paso, Tex.: Casa Bautista.

Fee, G. 1993. *New Testament Exegesis: A Handbook for Students and Pastors.* Louisville, Ky.: Westminster/John Knox.

Ferm, D. 1986. *Third World Liberation Theologies: An Introductory Survey.* Maryknoll, N.Y.: Orbis Books.

Fernando, A. 1986. "Missionaries Still Needed—But of a Special Kind." *Evangelical Missions Quarterly* 24:18–25.

Flannery, A. P. 1975. *Vatican Council (2nd: 1972–1965).* Grand Rapids, Mich.: Eerdmans.

Gadamer, H. G. 1975. *Truth and Method.* New York: Seabury Press.

———. 1976. *Philosophical Hermeneutics.* David Linge, trans. Berkeley: University of California Press.

García, I. 1987. *Justice in Latin American Theology of Liberation.* Atlanta, Ga.: John Knox.

Gibbs, E. 2000. *Church Next: Quantum Changes in How We Do Ministry.* Downers Grove, Ill.: InterVarsity Press.

Gibellini, R., ed. 1979. *Frontiers of Theology in Latin America.*. Maryknoll, N.Y.: Orbis Books.

Gilliland, D. S., ed. 1989a. *The Word Among Us: Contextualizing Theology for Mission Today.* Dallas, Tex.: Word.

———. 1989b. "Contextual Theology as Incarnational Mission." In *The Word Among Us.* D. S. Gilliland, ed. Dallas, Tex.: Word. Pp. 9–31.

———. 1989c. "New Testament Contextualization: Continuity and Particularity in Paul's Theology." In *The Word Among Us.* D. S. Gilliland, ed. Dallas, Tex.: Word. Pp. 52–73.

Glasser, A. F. 1989. "Old Testament Contextualization: Revelation and Its Environment." In *The Word Among Us.* D. S. Gilliland, ed. Dallas, Tex.: Word. Pp. 32–51.

———. 1992. Kingdom and Mission: A Biblical Study of the Kingdom of God and the World Mission of His People. Course Syllabus. Pasadena, Calif.: Fuller Theological Seminary. (This has been rewritten and republished as Arthur Glasser, with Charles Van Engen, Dean Gilliland and Shawn Redford, *Announcing the Kingdom: The Story of God's Mission in the Bible.* Grand Rapids, Mich.: Baker Book House, 2002.)

Goodenough, W. H. 1957. "Cultural Anthropology and Linguistics." *Report of the Seventh Annual Round Table Meeting on Linguistics and Language Study.* Monograph Series on Languages and Linguistics, no. 9. Paul Garvin, ed. Washington, D.C.: Georgetown University Press. Pp. 167–173.

———. 1965. "Rethinking 'Status' and 'Role'." In *The Relevance of Models for Social Anthropology.* Association of Social Anthropology, Monograph 1. London: Tavistock. Pp. 1–24.

Gottwald, N. K. 1979. *The Tribes of Yahweh: A Sociology of the Religion of Liberated Israel, 1250–1050 B.C.* Maryknoll, N.Y.: Orbis Books.

Green, G. L. 2001. *Context and Communication.* Unpublished ms. Wheaton, Ill.: Wheaton College.

Grenz, S. J. 1996. *A Primer on Postmodernism.* Grand Rapids, Mich.: Eerdmans.

Grice, H. P. 1975. "Logic and Conversation." In P. Cole and J. C. Morgan, eds. *Syntax and Semantics.* Vol. 3. Speech Acts. New York: Academic Press. Pp. 43–58.

———. 1989. *Studies in the Way of Words.* Cambridge, Mass.: Harvard University Press.

Grimes, J. E. 1976. *The Thread of Discourse.* The Hague: Mouton.

Grudem, W. 1994. *Systematic Theology: An Introduction to Biblical Doctrine.* Grand Rapids, Mich.: Zondervan.

Guder, D., ed. 1998. *Missional Church: A Vision for the Sending of the Church in North America.* Grand Rapids, Mich.: Eerdmans.

Gutierrez, G. 1974. *A Theology of Liberation.* Maryknoll, N.Y.: Orbis Books.

Gutt, E. A. 1991. *Translation and Relevance: Cognition and Context.* Oxford, Eng.: Basil Blackwell.

———. 1992. *Relevance Theory: A Guide to Successful Communication in Translation.* Dallas, Tex.: Summer Institute of Linguistics.

Haight, R. 1985. *An Alternative Vision: An Interpretation of Liberation Theology.* New York: Paulist.

Hall, E. T. 1959. *The Silent Language.* New York: Doubleday.

Halliday, M. A. K. 1970. "Language Structure and Language Function." In *New Horizons in Linguistics.* J. Lyons, ed. Harmondsworth, Eng.: Penguin Books.

———. 1978. *Language as Social Semiotic: The Social Interpretation of Language and Meaning.* London: Arnold.

————. 1989. *Spoken and Written Language.* Oxford: Oxford University Press.

Hays, Richard B. 1989. *Echoes of Scripture in the Writings of Paul.* New Haven, Conn.: Yale University Press.

Hesselgrave, D. J., ed. 1978. *Theology and Mission.* Grand Rapids, Mich.: Baker Book House.

Hesselgrave, D. J., and E. Rommen. 1989. *Contextualization: Meanings, Methods, and Models.* Grand Rapids, Mich: Baker Book House.

Hiebert, P. G. 1982. "The Bicultural Bridge." *Mission Focus* 10: 1–6.

————. 1982b. "The Flaw of the Excluded Middle." *Missiology* 10, no. 1: 35–47.

————. 1983. *Cultural Anthropology.* 2nd edition. Grand Rapids, Mich.: Baker Book House.

————. 1985. *Anthropological Insights for Missionaries.* Grand Rapids, Mich.: Baker Book House.

————. 1987. "Critical Contextualization." *International Bulletin of Missionary Research* 11, no. 3: 104–112.

————. 1989a. "Metatheology: The Step Beyond Contextualization." *Reflection and Projection: Missiology at the Threshold of 2001.* H. Kasdorf and K. Müller, eds. Bad Liebenzell, Ger.: Verlag der Liebenzeller Mission.

————. 1989b. "Form and Meaning in Contextualization of the Gospel." In *The Word Among Us.* D.S. Gilliland, ed. Dallas, Tex.: Word. Pp. 101–120.

————. 1994. *Anthropological Reflections on Missiological Issues.* Grand Rapids, Mich.: Baker Book House.

Hiebert, P. G., and R. D. Shaw. 1995. "Contextualizing the Power and the Glory." *International Journal of Frontier Missions* 12: 155–160.

Hiebert, P. G., R. D. Shaw, and T. Tiénou. 1999. *Understanding Folk Religion: A Christian Response to Popular Beliefs and Practices.* Grand Rapids, Mich.: Baker Book House.

Hill, H. 2003. Communicating Context in the Adioukrou Bible Translation in Côte d'Ivoire: Enlarging the Mutual Cognitive Environment. Ph.D. Dissertation, Fuller Theological Seminary.

Hirsch, E. D. 1967. *Validity in Interpretation.* New Haven, Conn.: Yale University Press.

Hoekendijk, J. C. 1952. "The Church in Missionary Thinking." *International Review of Missions* 41, no. 163 (April): 324–336.

Howard, R. J. 1982. *Three Faces of Hermeneutics.* Berkeley: University of California Press

Hubbard, D. A. 1989. *Hosea: An Introduction and Commentary.* Old Testament. Tyndale Commentary Series, vol. 229. Downers Grove, Ill.: InterVarsity Press.

Hubbard, R. L, Jr., R. K. Johnston, and R. Meye. 1992. *Studies in Old Testament Theology: Historical and Contemporary Images of God and God's People.* Dallas, Tex.: Word.

Humboldt, W. von. 2000. *On Language: On the Diversity of Human Language Construction and Its Influence on the Mental Development of the Human Species.* Peter Heath, trans. Cambridge: Cambridge University Press. (Originally published in German, 1836.)

Kaiser, W., and M. Silva. 1994. *An Introduction to Biblical Hermeneutics: The Search for Meaning.* Grand Rapids, Mich.: Zondervan.

Kearney, M. 1984. *World View.* Novato, Calif.: Chandler and Sharp.

Keesing, R. M. 1989. "Exotic Readings of Cultural Texts." *Current Anthropology* 30: 459–479.

Kim, S. Y. 1982. *The Origin of Paul's Gospel*. Grand Rapids, Mich.: Eerdmans.

———. 2001. *Paul and the New Perspective: Second Thoughts on the Origin of Paul's Gospel*. Grand Rapids, Mich.: Eerdmans.

Kinser, M. 2001. "Scripture As Inspired, Canonical Tradition." Hashivenu Forum III. February 4–6, 2001. Pasadena, Calif.

Kraft, C. H. 1979. *Christianity in Culture: A Study in Dynamic Biblical Theologizing in Cross-Cultural Perspective*. Maryknoll, N.Y.: Orbis Books.

———. 1989. *Christianity with Power: Your Worldview and Your Experience with the Supernatural*. Ann Arbor, Mich.: Servant.

———. 1991. *Communication Theory for Christian Witness*. Revised edition. Maryknoll, N.Y.: Orbis Books. (Originally published in 1983).

———. 1990. "Allegiance, Truth, and Power Encounter in Christian Witness." In *Pentecost, Mission, and Ecumenism's Essays on Intercultural Theology*. J. A. B. Jongeneel, ed. New York: Peter Lang. Pp. 215–30.

———. 1996. *Anthropology for Christian Witness*. Maryknoll: Orbis Books.

Kuhn, T. S. 1962. *The Structure of Scientific Revolutions*. Chicago: University of Chicago Press.

———. 1977. *The Essential Tension: Selected Studies in Scientific Tradition and Change*. Chicago: University of Chicago Press.

Küng, H., and D. Tracy, eds. 1989. *Paradigm Change in Theology: A Symposium for the Future*. New York: Crossroad.

LaHaye, T., and J. B. Jenkins. 2000. *Left Behind*. A book series based on the Book of Revelation. Wheaton, Ill.: Tyndale House.

Lakatos, I. 1978. *Methodology of Scientific Research Programmes*. Cambridge, Mass.: Cambridge University Press.

Lakoff, G., and M. Johnson. 1979. *Metaphors We Live By*. Chicago: University of Chicago Press.

———. 1999. *Philosophy of the Flesh: The Embodied Mind and Its Challenge to Western Thought*. New York: Basic Books.

Larson, M. L. 1984. *Meaning Based Translation: A Guide to Cross-Language Equivalence*. Lanham, Md.: University Press of America.

La Sor, W. S., D. A. Hubbard, and F. W. Bush. 1983. *Old Testament Survey*. Grand Rapids, Mich.: Eerdmans.

Lienhard, R. 2001. Deeply Shamed and Restored: Biblical Guidelines for Re-Establishing Harmony among the Daba and Bana. Ph.D. Dissertation. Fuller Theological Seminary.

Lingenfelter, S. 1992. *Transforming Culture*. Grand Rapids, Mich.: Baker Book House.

———. 1998. *Agents of Transformation*. Grand Rapids, Mich.: Baker Book House.

Lingenfelter, S., and M. Mayers, 1986. *Ministering Cross-Culturally: An Incarnational Model for Personal Relationships*. Grand Rapids, Mich.: Baker Book House.

Longacre, R. E. 1977. "A Discourse Manifesto." *Notes on Linguistics* 4: 17–29.

———. 1983. *The Grammar of Discourse: Topics in Language and Linguistics*. New York: Plenum Press.

Lundin, R., A. C. Thiselton, and C. Walhout. 1985. *The Responsibility of Hermeneutics*. Grand Rapids, Mich.: Eerdmans.

———. 1999. *The Promise of Hermeneutics*. Grand Rapids, Mich.: Eerdmans.

Malinowski, B. 1922. *Argonauts of the Western Pacific*. New York: Dutton.

Malphurs, A. 1999. *Doing Church: A Biblical Guide for Leading Ministries Through Change*. Grand Rapids, Mich.: Kregel.

Martin, R. P. 1977. "Approaches to New Testament Exegesis." In *New Testament Interpretation: Essays on Principles and Methods*. I. H. Marshall, ed. Grand Rapids, Mich.: Eerdmans. Pp. 220–251.

Maslow, A. 1954. *Motivation and Personality*. New York: Harper & Row.

Mayers, M. K. 1982. *The Basic Values: A Model of Cognitive Styles for Analyzing Human Behavior*. La Mirada, Calif.: Biola University.

———. 1987. Christianity Confronts Culture: A Strategy for Cross-Cultural Evangelism. Grand Rapids, Mich.: Zondervan. (originally published in 1974.)

McCallum, D., ed. 1996. *The Death of Truth*. Minneapolis: Bethany House.

McCluhan, H. M. and Q. Fiore. 1967. *The Medium is the Message*. New York: Bantam Books.

McElhanon, K. A. 2000. "Symbols, Symbolism." In *Evangelical Dictionary of World Missions*. A. S. Moreau, ed. Grand Rapids, Mich.: Baker Book House. Pp. 923–924.

Meeks, W. A. 1983. *The First Urban Christians: The Social World of the Apostle Paul*. New Haven, Conn.: Yale University Press.

Middleton, J. R., and B. J. Walsh. 1995. *Truth Is Stranger Than It Used to Be: Biblical Faith in a Postmodern Age*. Downers Grove, Ill.: InterVarsity Press.

Miguez Bonino, J. 1975. *Revolutionary Theology Comes of Age*. London: SPCK.

Mueller-Vollmer, K., ed. 1985. *The Hermeneutics Reader*. New York: Continuum.

Muller, R. A. 1991. *The Study of Theology: From Biblical Interpretation to Contemporary Formulation*. Grand Rapids, Mich.: Zondervan.

Murphy, N. 1990. *Theology in the Age of Scientific Reasoning*. Ithaca, N.Y.: Cornell University Press.

———. 1997. *Anglo-American Postmodernity: Philosophical Perspectives on Science, Religion, and Ethics*. Boulder, Colo.: Westview Press.

Newbigin, L. 1979. "Context and Conversion." *International Review of Mission* 68, no. 271: 301–312.

———. 1989. *The Gospel in a Pluralist Society*. Grand Rapids, Mich.: Eerdmans.

Nida, E. A. 1952. *God's Word in Man's Language*. New York: Harper & Brothers.

———. 1964. *Toward a Science of Translation*. London: Tavistock.

Nida, E. A., and C. R. Taber. 1981. *The Theory and Practice of Translation*. 2nd edition. Leiden, Ger.: E. J. Brill. (Originally published in 1969.)

Nishioka, Y. 1995. Rice and Bread: Metaphorical Construction of Reality—Toward a New Approach to World View. Ph.D. Dissertation. Fuller Theological Seminary.

———. 1998. "Worldview Methodology in Mission Theology: A Comparison between Kraft's and Hiebert's Approaches. *Missiology* 26: 457–476.

Niyang, S. J. 1997. Vernacular Scripture Evangelism in the Multi-Lingual Context of Northern Nigeria: Application of Sociolinguistic Theory to Scripture Promotion. Ph.D. Dissertation. Fuller Theological Seminary.

Noth, M. 1960. "The 'Re-Presentation' of the Old Testament Proclamation." In *Essays on Old Testament Hermeneutics*. C. Westermann, ed. Richmond, Va.: John Knox. Pp. 76–88.

Olson, B. 1978. *Bruchko*. Carol Stream, Ill.: Creation House.

Osborne, G. R. 1991. *The Hermeneutical Spiral: A Comprehensive Introduction to Biblical Interpretation*. Downers Grove, Ill.: InterVarsity Press.

———. 1995. *Crucial Questions about the Bible*. Grand Rapids, Mich.: Baker Book House.

Osborne, K. B. 1970. "A Christian Graveyard Cult in the New Guinea Highlands." *Practical Anthropology*. 17: 10–15.

Padilla, C. R. 1985. *Mission Between the Times: Essays on the Kingdom*. Grand Rapids, Mich.: Eerdmans.

Peterson, E. H., ed. 1994. *Stories For the Christian Year*. By the Chrysostom Society. New York: Collier Books.

Phillips, J. B. 1953. *Your God Is Too Small*. New York: McMillan.

Pierce, C. S. 1955. *Philosophical Writings of Pierce*. J. Buchler, ed. New York: Dover. (Originally published in 1940.)

Pike, K. L. 1967. *Language in Relation to a Unified Theory of the Structure of Human Behavior*. The Hague: Mouton.

Poythress, Vern S. 1988. *Science and Hermeneutics*. Grand Rapids, Mich.: Zondervan.

Pym, A. 1991. *Translation and Text Transfer: An Essay on the Principles of Intercultural Communication*. Frankfurt, New York: Peter Lang.

———. 1992. "Limits and Frustrations of Discourse Analysis in Translation Theory." *Fremdsprachen* 2/3 (1991): 27–35.

Redfield, R. 1953. *The Primitive World and Its Transformation*. Ithaca, N.Y.: Cornell University Press.

Richardson, D. 1974. *Peace Child*. Glendale, Calif.: G. L. Regal Books.

Ricoeur, P. 1976. *Interpretation Theory: Discourse and the Surplus of Meaning*. Fort Worth: Texas Christian University Press.

———. 1979. "What is Text?" In P. Ricoeur, *Hermeneutics and the Human Sciences*. J. B. Thompson, trans. New York: Cambridge University Press. Pp. 145–164.

———. 1991. "Imagination in Discourse and in Action " In P. Ricoeur, *From Text to Action: Essays in Hermeneutics II*. K. Blamey and J. B. Thompson, trans. Evanston, Ill.: Northwestern University Press. Pp. 168–187.

Rogers, G. 2002. Communicating the Meta-Theme of God's Relationship to all Human Beings. Ph.D. Dissertation. Fuller Theological Seminary.

Rountree, S. 2001. Testing Scripture Translation for Comprehension Testing. Ph. D. Dissertation. Fuller Theological Seminary.

Rumph, J. 1996. *Stories from the Front Lines: Power Evangelism in Today's World*. Grand Rapids, Mich.: Chosen Books.

Ryan, D. 1969. "Christianity, Cargo Cults, and Politics among the Toaripi of Papua," *Oceania* 40: 114ff.

Sanders, A. 1988. Learning Styles in Melanesia: Toward the Use and Implications of Kolb's Model for National Translator Training. Ph.D. Dissertation. Fuller Theological Seminary.

Sanneh, L. 1989. *Translating the Message: The Missionary Impact on Culture*. Maryknoll, N.Y.: Orbis Books.

Saussure, F. de. 1959. *Course in General Linguistics*. Wade Baskin, trans. New York: Philosophical Library. (Originally published in French, 1915.)

Schreiter, R. J. 1985. *Constructing Local Theologies*. Maryknoll, N.Y.: Orbis Books.

———. 1997. *The New Catholicity: Theology between the Global and the Local*. Maryknoll, N.Y.: Orbis Books.

Searle, J. 1969. *Speech Acts*. London: Cambridge University Press.

Segundo, J. L. 1976. *The Liberation of Theology.* Maryknoll, N.Y.: Orbis Books.

———. 1985. *Theology and The Church.* London: Winston.

Service, E. R. 1962. *Primitive Social Organization.* New York: Random House.

Shannon, C., and W. Weaver. 1949. *Mathematical Theory of Communication.* Urbana: University of Illinois Press.

Shaw, R. D. 1981. "Every Person a Shaman." *Missiology* 9: 159–165.

———. 1986. "The Good, The Bad, and The Human." In *World View: A Reader,* I. Grant, ed. Classroom reader. Pasadena, Calif: Fuller Theological Seminary.

———. 1988. *Transculturation: The Cultural Factor in Translation and Other Communication Tasks.* Pasadena, Calif.: William Carey Library.

———. 1989. "The Context of Text." In *The Word Among Us.* D. S. Gilliland, ed. Pp. 141–150. Dallas, Tex.: Word.

———. 1990a. "Culture and Evangelism: A Model for Missiological Strategy." *Missiology* 18: 292–304.

———. 1990b. *Kandila: Samo Ceremonialism and Interpersonal Relationships.* Ann Arbor: University of Michigan Press.

———. 1994. "Transculturation: Perspective, Process, and Prospect. *Notes On Translation* 8: 44–50.

———. 1996. *From Longhouse to Village: Samo Social Change.* Dallas, Tex.: Harcourt Brace.

Shenk, W. R. 1999. *Changing Frontiers of Mission.* Maryknoll, N.Y.: Orbis Books.

Shorter, A. 1989. *Toward a Theology of Inculturation.* Maryknoll, N.Y.: Orbis Books.

Slack, Jim. 1990. *Evangelism among People who Learn Best by Oral Tradition: The Storying or Chronological Bible Communication Method.* Foreign Mission Board, Southern Baptist Convention.

Smith, E. 1930. *In the Mother Tongue.* London: British and Foreign Bible Society.

Sobrino, Jon. 1984. *The True Church and the Poor.* Maryknoll, N.Y.: Orbis Books.

Sperber, D., and D. Wilson. 1986. *Relevance: Communication and Cognition.* Cambridge, Mass.: Harvard University Press. 2nd edition. Oxford, Eng.: Blackwell, 1995.

Spykman, Gordon, et al.1988. *Let My People Live: Faith and Struggle in Central America.* Grand Rapids, Mich.: Eerdmans.

Stott, J. R. 1996. *Guard the Truth: The Message of I Timothy and Titus.* Downers Grove, Ill.: InterVarsity Press.

Stralen, J. 1977. *Search For Salvation.* Adelaide, So. Australia: Lutheran House.

Stubbs, M. 1983. *Discourse Analysis: The Sociolinguistic Analysis of Natural Language.* Oxford, Eng.: Basil Blackwell.

Sweet, L. 2000. *Post-Modern Pilgrims: First Century Passion for the Twenty-First Century World.* Nashville, Tenn.: Broadman and Homan Publishers.

Taber, C. R., ed. 1978. "Is There More than One Way to Do Theology?" *Gospel in Context* 1: 4–10.

Thiselton, A. C. 1980. *The Two Horizons: New Testament Hermeneutics and Philosophical Description with Special Reference to Heidegger, Bultmann, Gadamer, and Wittgenstein.* Grand Rapids, Mich.: Eerdmans.

———. 1992. *New Horizons in Hermeneutics: The Theory and Practice of Transforming Biblical Readings.* Grand Rapids, Mich.: Zondervan.

Tink, F. L. 1994. From Order to Harmony: Toward a New Hermeneutic for Urban Mission. Ph.D. Dissertation. Fuller Theological Seminary.

Tippett, A. R. 1971. *People Movements in Southern Polynesia.* Chicago: Moody Press.

———. 1975. *Solomon Islands Christianity.* Pasadena, Calif.: William Carey Library. (Originally published in 1967, London: Lutterworth Press.)

Tuggy, J. C. 1992. "Semantic Paragraph Patterns. A Fundamental Communication Concept and Interpretive Tool." In D. A. Black, ed. *Linguistics and New Testament Interpretation.* Nashville, Tenn.: Broadman. Pp. 45–67.

Tyler, S. A. 1978. *The Said and the Unsaid: Mind, Meaning, and Culture.* New York: Academic Press.

Tuggy, J. C. and E. W. Deibler. 2003. "Theoretical Basis of SSAs." Unpublished ms.

Turner, H. W. 1989. *Religious Movements in Primal Societies.* Elkhart, Ind.: Mission Focus Publications.

Van Engen, C. 1989. "The New Covenant: Knowing God in Context." In *The Word Among Us.* D. S. Gilliland, ed. Dallas, Tex.: Word. Pp.74–100.

———. 1991. *God's Missionary People: Rethinking the Purpose of the Local Church.* Grand Rapids, Mich.: Baker Book House.

———. 1994. "Constructing a Theology of Mission for the City." In *God So Loved the City.* C. Van Engen and J. Tiersma, eds. Monrovia, Calif.: MARC. Pp. 241–270.

———. 1996a. "The Gospel Story: Mission of, in, and on the Way." Installation address. Arthur F. Glasser Chair of Biblical Theology of Mission. Fuller Theological Seminary.

———. 1996b. *Mission On The Way: Issues in Mission Theology.* Grand Rapids, Mich.: Baker Book House.

———. 1996c. "The New Covenant: Mission Theology in Context" In *Mission On The Way: Issues in Mission Theology.* Grand Rapids, Mich.: Baker Book House. Pp.71–89.

Van Engen, C., and J. Tiersma, eds. 1994. *God So Loves the City: Seeking a Theology for Urban Mission.* Monrovia, Calif.: MARC.

van Grootheest, D. 1996. Relevance Theory and Bible Translation: An Exploratory Study. M.A. Thesis. Free University of Amsterdam.

Vanhoozer, K. J. 1986. "The Semantics of Biblical Literature: Truth and Scripture's Diverse Literary Forms." In *Hermeneutics, Authority, and Canon.* D. A. Carson and J. D. Woodbridge, eds. Grand Rapids, Mich.: Academie Books. Pp. 53–103.

Vidales, Raul. 1979. "Methodological Issues in Liberation Theology." In *Frontiers of Theology in Latin America.* Rosino Gibellini, ed. Maryknoll, N.Y.: Orbis Books. Pp. 34–57.

Waard, J. de, and E. A. Nida. 1986. *From One Language to Another: Functional Equivalence in Bible Translating.* Nashville, Tenn.: Thomas Nelson.

Wagner, C. P. 1983. *On the Crest of the Wave.* Glendale, Calif.: Regal Books.

Walls, A. F. 1996. *The Missionary Movement in Christian History: Studies in the Transmission of Faith.* Maryknoll, N.Y.: Orbis Books.

Walsh, B. J., and J. R. Middleton. 1984. *The Transforming Vision: Shaping a Christian World View.* Downers Grove, Ill.: InterVarsity Press.

Weber, O. 1981. *Foundations of Dogmatics.* D. L. Guder, trans. Grand Rapids, Mich.: Eerdmans.

Westermann, Claus, ed. 1960. *Essays on Old Testament Hermeneutics.* Richmond, Va.: John Knox Press.

Wilson, D., and T. Matsui. 1998. "Recent Approaches to Bridging: Truth, Coherence, Relevance." *UCL Working Papers in Linguistics* 10: 1–28.

Winter, R. 1974. "The Highest Priority: Cross-Cultural Evangelism." *Let the Earth Hear His Voice.* J. D. Douglas, ed. Minneapolis: World Wide. Pp. 213–225.

———. 1984. "Unreached Peoples: The Development of the Concept." In *Reaching the Unreached: The Old-New Challenge.* H. M. Conn, ed. Phillipburg, N.J.: Presbyterian and Reformed Publishing. Pp. 17–44.

Wittgenstein, L. 1953. *Philosophical Investigations.* Oxford, Eng.: Blackwell.

Author Index

Subject Index

253

About the Authors

R. Daniel Shaw is the son of missionary parents, Stan and Laurel Shaw. He grew up in South India and, subsequently, in the southern Philippines. This heritage had a dynamic effect on his interests in native peoples and eventually led to an M.A. and Ph.D. in anthropology. This interest was matched by a passion that people "hear the word of the Lord," leading him and his wife, Karen, to train at the Summer Institute of Linguistics (SIL) and join Wycliffe Bible Translators in 1967. After seminary studies at Western Seminary in Portland, Oregon, the Shaws went to Papua, New Guinea, and served among the Samo from 1969 to 1981. There they learned the language and culture in order to provide the Samo with portions of God's Word. During that time Shaw also served as an international anthropology consultant for SIL, holding anthropology workshops and assisting translators throughout Australasia. In 1981 Dr. Shaw was invited to join the faculty of the School of World Mission at Fuller Theological Seminary for the purpose of developing a translation program. He has authored, coauthored, or edited ten books, numerous articles, and many chapters in books. He regularly attends anthropological association meetings and presents professional papers.

Charles Van Engen was born and raised in Chiapas, Mexico. His parents, Rev. Garold and Ruth Van Engen, were Reformed Church in America (RCA) missionaries in Mexico from 1943 to 1978. Upon graduation from Fuller Theological Seminary in 1973, Van Engen was ordained in the RCA and he and his wife Jean were sent by the RCA to serve with the National Presbyterian Church of Mexico as missionaries from 1973 to 1985. While in Chiapas, he was involved in theological education, evangelism, youth ministry, camping ministries, and refugee relief. He completed his Ph.D. in missiology under Johannes Verkuyl at the Free University of Amsterdam in 1981. After teaching missiology at Western Theological Seminary in Holland, Michigan from 1985 to 1988, the Van Engens were invited to Pasadena, where they joined the School of World Mission faculty. In 1997 he was installed as the Arthur F. Glasser Professor of Biblical Theology of Mission. He is the author or editor of more than a dozen books and numerous book chapters and journal articles.